CHRONIC FATIGUE

GONE

A RECOVERY PLAN FOR

COVID LONG HAUL,

ME/CFS,

LYME &

FIBROMYALGIA

(And for Anyone Who Wants More Energy)

JASON BOYCE

DISCLAIMER

The information in this book is true and complete to the best of our knowledge. This book is intended to be an information resource only. There is no intent that this book be used for any diagnostic or treatment purposes. A specific physician-patient relationship is necessary before any therapies discussed in this book are adopted. In no manner should this book or any of the information in this book be used as a substitute for diagnosis and treatment by a qualified medical healthcare professional. Always consult your doctor when it comes to your personal health or before you start any treatment.The author and publisher disclaim all liability in connection with the use of this book.

Any jokes in this book are intentional, although not necessarily often thought of as funny. Whilst the primary intention *is* to be funny, I cannot guarantee laughter or even mild chuckles. Please consult with a professional comedian if you are deficient in humor and require therapy in this area. If you do fall over and hurt yourself whilst laughing to mildly amusing anecdotes or wit included herein, then blame yourself for finding unfunny things funny.

Thank you for reading.

"I would like to dedicate this book to my 2 wonderful daughters, Amelia Boyce and Arabella Boyce. They are my inspiration. I love you both very much."

Table of Contents

Acknowledgments

I would like to thank my wonderful, supportive wife, Sarah, for putting up with me for all these years. She supported me throughout the long duration of my illness and suffered a lack of attention as I concentrated on writing this book. Apart from being one of the most successful female biotech executives in America and the smartest person I know, she has been and always will be my absolute rock. I love you.

Thanks to my two wonderful children, Amelia and Arabella—always loving, always understanding. Amelia has shown me firsthand how to persevere through difficult times and how to turn a negative situation into a positive one. Amelia's in-depth knowledge and love of neurology and psychology is amazing for a 16-year-old; they will no doubt change the world with their knowledge. Arabella has taught me the extraordinary power of being positive. To be able to smile every minute of every day is a superpower and she is a true inspiration. They have taught me how to persevere and smile through adversity. I love you both. Now get to bed and stop arguing.

I would like to thank my parents, Jo and Nigel. Thanks for raising me, putting up with me through my difficult teenage years, supporting me through college and putting up with my questionable hairstyle choices. I am extremely grateful. I love you both very much.

Thanks to all my friends who helped me write this book.

Preface

There are many excellent books that detail the causes and triggers of chronic fatigue. Many are extremely well written by scholars and physicians, and I recommend you read as many of them as you can. However, not all the books written on the subject are simple to understand or particularly enjoyable to read. Many are quite scientific in nature and academic in tone. More importantly, very few offer tangible remedies or therapies that get at the heart of what sufferers of chronic fatigue are desperately seeking: a real-life CURE! Learning about COVID and chronic fatigue is all well and good, but if you can't do anything about it, then what's the point in the end? That's why the majority of this book concentrates and discusses many remedies and methods to cure your chronic fatigue no matter whether the cause is COVID, Lyme, or Epstein-Barr or any of the other causes cited in this book. This book aims to provide clear, simple information that is enjoyable and—dare I say—fun to read. You may disagree with this last assertion, but you can't say I didn't try.

If you are desperate for immediate solutions, then feel free to go right to the last chapter and skip the detailed stuff in between. The last chapter summarizes the solutions for chronic fatigue caused by COVID, retroviruses, Lyme, trauma, chronic pathogen colonization, spinal issues, and many other causes. In fact, whatever the source or trigger of your fatigue, the remedies laid out in this book will help. If you do decide to read the last chapter first, then please go back and read the entire book to learn more about the remedies. I do not go into great detail regarding COVID, as a lot has already been written and reported in the media. In this book I concentrate on potential remedies for long COVID symptoms.

I understand that undertaking all the remedies put forward in this book may be a financial drain for many people, but the good news is that the most important remedies and therapies are, generally speaking, the lowest-cost options. As you are aware, having a chronic illness is extremely expensive, with limited or nonexistent work options coupled with a constant stream of costly healthcare expenses. This book aims to help you break this negative cycle and get you back to work and enjoying life once again. The costs spent on remedies and therapies must be looked at as vital investments in your future, not unlike educational expenses. You will need to have some faith that they will work, with courage and motivation to stick at it, even if you don't see immediate results. However, I am confident that all money spent on the therapies put forward in this book will be repaid many times over in the long run.

The book is split into two parts. The first part is about the causes and triggers of chronic fatigue and the reasons why it is so persistent and disabling. This part is short and to the point, as there are many other books that detail how chronic fatigue manifests in great detail. I wanted to make sure that I didn't regurgitate other information that is already available, but provide a short and updated perspective. I have included what I believe to be almost all the potential causes of chronic fatigue, and I wager there are some causes that you do not know about, so please read this section. In particular, problems with the upper spine are becoming prevalent and are causing or contributing to fatigue in many cases.

I have spent hundreds of hours researching and reading everything I could get my hands on and have used my own body as an experimental laboratory for a range of supplements, foods, medications and electronic devices. I have gleaned excellent snippets of advice on how to beat the insidious condition of long-term fatigue. This book is the distillation and collation of all those fun hours. The result is a detailed protocol providing a cure for COVID long haulers, Lyme, fibromyalgia, and ME/CFS patients.

So please keep the faith and smile to yourself in the knowledge this book is about to change your life forever. Be warned, it won't be a cakewalk, walk in the park, a piece of cake, or anything to do with walks or cakes in particular (though walking is good for you, unless you get mugged, and cakes generally bad for you, unless made of vegetables, though I'm told that carrot cake is still not a healthy alternative).

Here is a brief instruction to help you get the most out of this book. I encourage you to keep a notebook and pen close at hand as you read through each chapter. You will want to write down certain medications, therapies, and protocols that I discuss, and there are topics that you might want to research in order to familiarize yourself with how fatigue manifests and how we can cure it. I will include keywords for you to use in Google (or Bing search, I'm not judging). I did not refer to clinical or research studies by linking citation numbers to a list at the end of the book, as I find this approach not very practical. I have read many books that have used superscript numbers and referred to studies in the references or bibliography, and I don't think I have ever used one citation to look up a study. Instead, I have provided keywords to use in a web search that will take you straight to the study referenced right in the text. I believe this is a more practical, smarter way to look up research papers and studies.

The more you know and understand, the more motivated you will become to help yourself and perhaps others like you. It is very important that you do your own research. Make the effort. I promise it will be worth your while as knowledge leads to motivation and motivation leads to more knowledge, a positive feedback loop that is vital for a faster recovery.

If you are reading this, Sarah Boyce (this bit is written directly for my wife), then congratulations on reading this far into the book. By the way I love you and can I have a cup of tea please?

I apologize for digressing so early on in this book, but as they say: a happy wife, happy life. However, I am making an important point here. The divorce rate among chronically ill people is a staggering 75% (and long COVID is not going to help this statistic). So it is vital to try to keep your spouse informed and involved as much as practically possible. Remember COVID, Lyme and chronic fatigue takes its toll on both people in a relationship and unless you look like Brad Pitt or Angelina Jolie, you're going to have work at it (just realized, they got divorced a long time ago; bad example). Make sure you fully explain your symptoms, why you can't take the kids to the park or soccer match (football in UK) and that you definitely can't go to your mother-in-law's house for Sunday dinner (maybe never?). You can ask your better half to watch a YouTube video or read a book about long COVID and chronic fatigue, sharing how you feel is very important if your relationship is to survive long term. In fact, why don't you ask them to read this book? It's really good, honest!

Going through hard times with your spouse is going to slow down your recovery time. Divorce is one of the most stressful things a person can go through (almost as stressful as dinner with your in-laws) and it is imperative that chronic fatigue sufferers stay away from stress and stressful situations as much as possible. Of course, if you're in an abusive, hateful or unloving relationship then you need to dump their ass double quick time. A poor relationship will not help you get better, so rip off the band aid (plaster in UK) and move on.

For COVID recovery patients, we are unsure how long chronic fatigue will last; for Lyme, fibromyalgia, and post virus patients who have had chronic fatigue for many years, I have formulated a theory based on everything I have read and digested over the years. The results will almost certainly work for COVID long haulers. I must stress here that I am not a doctor and I've had no medical training. **It goes without saying: Please see your doctor before acting upon any of the information put forward in this book. Please read the disclaimer at the beginning of this book, if you haven't already.**

As stated earlier, I have purposely stayed away from being overly technical or from using too much scientific terminology because quite frankly it can get a little dry and boring; however, some scientific explanation is required at times. Before any explanation that is scientific in nature, I have added the fair warning "*science bit alert*." You can skip through the science bits if you desire, though I encourage you to stick with it. As I have already said, greater understanding leads to greater motivation, and you will need motivation to beat this affliction. I have found that you will need a decent understanding of the therapies, diet changes, and supplements discussed in this book in order to have the faith to try them. If you are particularly unmotivated due to the way you feel (and this is completely understandable), I have included a chapter on positive thinking and motivation to assist in this regard. If you are having difficulty getting motivated or are self-sabotaging due to depression, I have also included a chapter on how to beat depression. As sleep issues are very common for those with chronic fatigue, I have included a chapter on how to get back to sleep, which I am confident will help you immensely. As an addendum, I have included additional resources to help you explore and research the topics discussed in further detail. I have included relevant books, helpful websites, and some movies that will help enlighten you further.

At the end of each chapter I have included a brief chapter summary, which provides short bullet points of all the salient details expounded. If you really find the barrage of information overwhelming, you can simply run through each chapter summary, but I do recommend you go back and read the entire text.

For brevity's sake I will refer to all diseases pertaining to chronic fatigue as ME (except COVID 19 and post-acute COVID syndrome – PACS, which I will simply call COVID for brevity's sake) including all the following: fibromyalgia, systemic exertion intolerance disease (SEID), postural orthostatic tachycardia syndrome (POTS), multiple chemical sensitivity (MCS), post viral fatigue syndrome (PVFS), Gulf War syndrome (GWS), complex regional pain syndrome (CRPS), electromagnetic hypersensitivity syndrome (EHS), chronically repeated ailment problems (CRAP).

You may notice (or not, I won't be offended) that I have written this book with humorous intent in order to keep the slightly morbid subject matter from becoming too depressing. The humor is intentional because I believe that humor is vital in the toolbox of recovery; it lightens the mood, creates positivity, and increases the happy brain neurotransmitter serotonin naturally. It may even help keep you alert and interested in the subject matter. In fact the first recommendation of this book is to immerse yourself in humor. Watch funny movies and TV shows and read comedy books.

Do not watch the news. Or if you feel utterly compelled to know what's going on the world, limit yourself to 15 minutes' exposure. The news media knowingly or unknowingly targets the part of the brain called the amygdala, the brain's fear center. We are hardwired to notice negativity over positivity, that's why the news networks concentrate on negative news items; negativity increases viewer numbers, which increases advertising and profits. Having your amygdala constantly stimulated uses energy you don't need to expend.

Get off social media, as watching curated snippets of other people's lives just won't help you and your recovery (or limit yourself to cat and dog videos). Stay away from discussing politics and religion with friends and family, and never, ever watch a horror movie (this genre is sure to fire up the amygdala). Stay away from news-based apps, as their algorithms can lead you down a dark path of negativity based on your political or social views. Both news networks and social media apps use your confirmation bias, which is where you unwittingly seek views and opinions that reinforce your world view over and over again, which eliminates critical thinking and forces you further down a dark path of negativity. This will needlessly sap your energy.

The goal is to create a field of positivity around you, no matter what your illness or how sick you are, there are no negative side effects to laughing more, unless you have a lot of stitches in your abdomen, then only mild chuckles for you, my friend.

The recovery information is based on a series of innovative therapies, diet changes, and supplements, the majority of which I have personally tried. You may find that some therapies may not be for you, and that's okay, everybody is an individual, so you will have to assess what you might think will work for you and try that. After all what have you got to lose? Please read through this part of the book at least twice. Oh, and to use the greatest motivation quote of all time from my favorite Greek philosopher,

"Do or do not. There is no try."

Master Minch Yoda

(From Greece or the fictional planet Dagobah, I forget which, and yes that really is his middle name.)

PART ONE

UNDERSTANDING CHRONIC FATIGUE

C hapter 1

Introduction

"The pessimist sees difficulty in every opportunity. The optimist sees the opportunity in every difficulty."

Sir Winston Churchill

This book is the culmination of all my research on how to completely cure long COVID and chronic fatigue syndrome, also known as myalgic encephalomyelitis (ME). There is some logic behind this difficult-to-pronounce word. The word *myalgic* means muscle pain. *Encephalo-* means brain. *Myelitis* means inflammation of the spinal cord. So *myalgic encephalomyelitis* means pain in the muscles, and inflammation in the brain and spinal cord.

I guess I am one of the lucky ones. I am a functioning long-term ME patient and COVID long hauler (I guess not that lucky). However, I'm not bedridden full-time like so many others out there. My symptoms included frequent headaches, brain fog, joint pain, insomnia, unrefreshing sleep, brain fog, weakened immune system, extreme post-exertional malaise, restless leg syndrome, brain fog, raging thirst, allergies to pollen, gluten, lactose and alcohol intolerance (a real bummer), brain fog, extensive grumpiness, and short-term memory loss. Did I mention the brain fog?

The road to good health has been a long and rocky one, having chronic fatigue lasting 15 years prior to getting COVID. The constant stream of challenges is exhausting, especially having to let friends and family down repeatedly. Perhaps the most frustrating part of the affliction was not being able to exercise. Ten minutes of intense aerobic exercise would leave me flat on my back for a couple of days. Anaerobic exercise such as lifting heavy weights could leave me totally exhausted for a week or so. Social interactions were challenging, especially at parties, where I didn't have the energy or the impetus to socialize. However, I have been extremely lucky to have such a wonderfully supportive family around me, never questioning when I had my bouts of exhaustion, just a lot of love and care. I am fortunate enough to be able to play golf at my local club fairly regularly nowadays, which has increased my social circle, and I have many great, supportive friends around me. If you can muster the energy to have some kind of social life, then I implore you to do so, as friends can provide a real boost to your mood and morale. Unless, of course, their name is Roger. I understand many people are not so lucky, and this is where the added stress of others' lack of empathy adds a further stressful burden. In the United States in particular, lack of empathy for others is endemic, so keep a wide berth from those who are least likely to understand or care for your condition.

It is important to educate your immediate family as to your ongoing symptoms. It is also helpful to educate as many as your closest friends as possible. I'm sure you have been in this situation: you have been invited to a wedding, baby shower, bar mitzvah, cult sacrifice, birthday party, or just a small social gathering and you've had to let down your friends many times over. The guilt of doing this is just awful, especially if they have a poor understanding of your affliction; it adds unnecessary stress to your already stressful situation. In order to assist I have written a short email that you are free to copy verbatim directed at family and friends to explicitly inform them of your symptoms and how they can help you by not adding to your burden through lack of empathy or ignorance or a combination of both. Go ahead, copy the letter, add your own personal touch, and email it out. It might even feel a little cathartic.

To (enter name here),

I wanted to let you know the current state of my health and its impact on my life and interactions with friends and family. I have been suffering with (long COVID, Lyme, myalgic encephalomyelitis; use as appropriate), a debilitating condition that leaves me completely and utterly exhausted for indefinite periods. The exhaustion is not related to normal day to day tiredness you may feel from going about daily activities. The exhaustion is hard to describe but it is complete and absolute. I have times when I can enjoy everybody's company and times when I just have to rest. I want you to know that I cannot always make any prior agreed or impromptu meetings and you must know that I am NOT trying to avoid you or anybody; it is simply a result of my fluctuating fatigue. I am working getting back to 100% health and in the not-too-distant future I'm looking forward to getting back to normal life! I love you and care about you and I wanted to let you know exactly what my condition is and how it affects me. Contact me if you have any questions. Let's speak soon. Take care.

Hopefully that should quench the inquisitive thirst that any of your friends or family hopefully have.

If you are a COVID long hauler or are new to chronic fatigue syndrome, you are now part of a club of several million folks in the United States (and potentially hundreds of millions worldwide). But the good news is that you are reading this book. I really wish somebody had written a book like this for me early on; it would've saved many years of heartache.

You have probably found out by now that primary care doctors are about as useful as an ashtray on a motorcycle. If you haven't experienced this yet, then the first conversation generally goes like this:

"Hi, Doc; thanks for seeing me."

"Of course, Patient X. How can I help you today?"

"Just call me X, or sexy X, as my wife calls me."

"Too much information."

"OK, well, I'm suffering from extreme fatigue. Some days I can barely get out of bed."

"Oh dear, how many days have you been feeling this way?"

"Oh, about 3,273 days."

"Oh, that's awful. Any other symptoms?"

"Yes, terrible joint pain, migraine headaches, brain fog, frequent upper respiratory tract infections, insomnia, unquenchable thirst, alcohol intolerance, lactose intolerance, gluten intolerance, and doctor intolerance."

"Yes, I understand. Have you tried exercise?"

"Yes, and I simply cannot do it. It makes all my symptoms ten times worse."

"Well, then, I think gradual exercise therapy would be perfect!"

"You're not listening, are you?"

"By the way, how is your mood?"

"Now that I'm talking with you, it's awful."

"Ha, ha, ha, but seriously, how are you feeling mentally?"

"Well, my wife has left me because I'm not pulling my weight. None of my friends call me anymore, and worst of all, both of my dogs stare at me with disapproving eyes because I can't take them for walks."

"Have you thought about getting a cat?"

"I'm allergic."

"Great. Obviously, you're suffering from depression leading to some lethargy. Here's a large bottle of Zoloft. I'll see you in six weeks. Take care now, and don't forget to exercise!"

It's not worth getting angry or frustrated over primary care doctors; they usually have a lot on their plate and they're simply not trained to deal with very complicated illnesses that have no associated recognized prescription drug. Long COVID is slowly changing this dynamic, and I'm hoping this book will find its way into many general practitioners' hands. When you do see your primary care doctor, be polite and kindly ask them for recommendations for ME/CFS specialists or a functional physician.

Remember, it's only in the last few years that the extent of chronic fatigue has really come to light; prior to that, the medical community believed it was an entirely psychosomatic affliction.

Currently, however, doctors in Western societies are far more likely to treat symptoms rather than the causes of ailments, especially if there is no immediate clear-cut cause. This is a disastrous problem, as the root causes of diseases are often overlooked.

Perhaps the greatest issue I found with primary care physicians was their lack of knowledge and lack of will to discuss diet and dietary needs. When was the last time a doctor asked you about your diet?

It is no secret that you can either use food as poison or use food as medicine. It is by far the most important aspect of maintaining good health. So why is it almost taboo to discuss diet? Is there some unspoken rule not to discuss diet? Or is it something that just isn't taught in medical school?

Most doctors do not want to discuss diet because they either don't want to preach or don't think patients would listen or want to listen. Furthermore, many doctors are just not qualified enough to discuss diet. To become a fully licensed doctor you need to do a four-year undergraduate program at medical school and then three to seven years in a residency program to learn the specialty you choose to pursue. How many weeks of nutritional training do you think doctors go through to become certified? Six weeks, eight weeks? That would be a small proportion of the four-year course, you would think. Considering that type 2 diabetes is one of the greatest medical disasters in the United States, with about 80,000 deaths per year and 35 million suffering from this diet-based disease, you would think that doctors are taught all about how our cells use energy from food to fuel our bodies and brain. But don't worry! It's not six- or eight-weeks of training, it's twenty-five hours or less. In fact, Dr. David Eisenberg, director of culinary nutrition at the Harvard T.H. Chan School of Public Health, said that there is a total lack of requirement in most medical schools to understand the practical skills necessary to advise patients struggling with their weight, blood sugar, blood pressure, or heart disease. Hey but no biggie! Heart disease is a minor ailment that barely affects anyone, right? Wait, my 11-year-old daughter just shouted and told me it's the biggest killer in the Western world. Good job, our medical profession is on top of it then.

Find a functional medicine or an integrative medicine doctor that specializes in chronic diseases. Integrative medicine is a holistic approach which takes into account your lifestyle and habits, including the very important aspect of your diet. Integrative medicine doctors aim to treat every aspect of your mind and body and not just treat the symptoms you're suffering from. Treatments are more likely to include encouraging lifestyle changes and to try meditation or yoga as well as effective medications.

Like integrative medicine, functional medicine takes into account the whole body and all of its interconnected functions and also focuses on individualized therapies tailored to treat underlying causes of illness (more on this in chapter 5, "Find the Right Doctor, Get the Right Blood Tests"). For now, I'm going to briefly take a look at what causes chronic fatigue in the first place.

A NOTE ABOUT THE YOUNG

Young people suffering from ME/CFS (and potentially long COVID) are at particular risk for extreme anxiety (Google: "Why do young people with CFS/ME feel anxious? A qualitative study"). This study showed that young people are especially sensitive to the perceived illegitimacy of this condition, anxious about being unable to explain their illness to others, fear of bullying from peers, and distrust from adults around them.

If you have a child suffering from this hideous condition, be sure to put your arm around them and reassure them you understand what they're going through.

CHAPTER SUMMARY

- Educate your friends and family about your condition; it may make life a little easier. Communicate clearly and directly with your spouse about how you're feeling from day to day; it might just save your relationship. Try to socialize as much as you practically can; it will help to make you feel better.
- Don't let yourself get frustrated by the medical profession. Things are changing rapidly, and the medical community is fast becoming aware of ME and long COVID symptoms and how to treat them.
- With that said, make sure you see a functional or integrative physician.

Chapter 2

The Real Triggers of Chronic Fatigue

"Whether you think you can, or think you can't, you're right."

Henry Ford

The first step in trying to find a cure was to find out by dogged research, unwavering enthusiasm, and mild stupidity, the most likely cause of my symptoms. I had ME 13 years before I got COVID, though I was negative for several tests for Lyme. I was positive for Epstein-Barr virus (the virus responsible for glandular fever or mononucleosis, also known as human herpesvirus 4), the retrovirus that was originally thought to be the cause of CFS.

Like many people before me, I thought I had found the real cause of my fatigue; however, EBV is not rare. In fact, almost the entire world's population has been infected with EBV, a human herpesvirus. Prior to COVID, chronic fatigue affected only 0.3% of the world's population. The math didn't add up for me. Why should my immune response to EBV be greater than 99.7% of those who had contracted EBV? I needed to research further. The logic behind EBV being the chief cause of ME is that the virus, like all herpesviruses, stays in the system forever, though usually remains dormant and is held in check by the immune system. However, when some people experience a period of high stress caused by psychological issues or stress on the immune system, the virus causes mayhem and reactivation occurs because of impaired cellular memory.

Okay, so many people experience nasty EBV reactivation, but it still doesn't explain why such a small percentage of the population gets

ME/CFS compared with the EBV population or why chronic fatigue lasts for years.

The blood tests also showed that I expressed antibodies for cytomegalovirus and human herpesvirus 6. Again, both are extremely common viruses. My doctor might have well stated that because I breathe oxygen, I'm more likely to get ME; there is no statistical causal relationship. So I postulated that there might be a rarer virus that is more common to the general ME population that makes more statistical sense than extremely common retroviruses.

A fanciful (but logical) idea perhaps, until I read the book *Plague: One Intrepid Search for the Truth about Human Retroviruses and Chronic Fatigue Syndrome (ME/CFS), Autism and Other Diseases* by Kent Heckenlively and Judy Mikovits. The book chronicles the extraordinary journey of Dr. Mikovits, who was exiled from her research institution and actually imprisoned for her controversial hypotheses (or at least taking her research outside of the lab without permission).

However, the crux of the story as it pertains to ME sufferers is the discovery in 2006 by scientists from the Cleveland Clinic and the University of California, San Francisco, of the novel human retrovirus xenotropic murine leukemia virus-related virus (XMRV). Although initially discovered in prostate cancer patients, it was subsequently (and contentiously) discovered in ME patients. The original study showed very striking statistics, according to Mikovits, in a controlled test (performed in 2009 and published by the National Cancer Institute jointly with the Cleveland Clinic) it was found that XMRV was found in 67% of ME patients compared with just 3.7% in the healthy control group. Unfortunately, the study was reviewed and deemed flawed due to improper procedures in the trial design.

Other studies were undertaken at a later date, and it appears that in some of the studies the original results did not hold; however, all of those studies used a different method of screening for the disease (polymerase chain reaction, or PCR). One study did uphold the results shown in the original study, an NIH study led by Dr. Harvey Alter, in which he stated, "We have to emphasize as we did in the paper that we have not proven causality for this agent. However, these findings do support the earlier study's results at the same time. Other laboratories have not found this, including the CDC, so a dilemma at present is how to reconcile that some labs find this association and others do not. At this point, we just don't know. We haven't studied enough people."

The further problem with all the studies was that there is no specific test to prove someone has ME, as the symptoms are so wide and varied.

However, the XMRV virus is real and entered the human population through zoonotic transfer from mouse to human. Though Mikovits contends that it may have transferred to humans through mouse-related murine derived vaccines, she has been derided for her contentions but has not been disproved.

The mere existence of the XMRV virus (irrespective of how it occurred) and its quiet and unknown spread throughout the population necessarily creates the proposition that an unknown virus other than COVID is prevalent among the population and causing ME symptoms. COVID was also a zoonotic virus (zoonotic meaning caused by germs that spread from animal to human) allegedly spread from bat to human in a wet market in Wuhan, China (we shall ignore that fact that one of China's largest virology labs in which they were experimenting on coronaviruses extracted from bats was only a few miles from the market and the whistleblower scientist died awfully sudden). So is it possible that there is a variety of zoonotic viruses spreading quietly around the world that we simply have no knowledge of because they may present few to no symptoms, save for chronic fatigue months or years after the initial infection? I don't know, and I suspect we will never know the answer to this question but it is very possible and dare I say probable. Did you know you may have been infected with XMRV at some point in the past? Probably not.

Fun fact: humans have learnt more about the human body since the year 2000 than all of human history before the year 2000. Our knowledge of the human body and medical advancement is constantly accelerating, compounding continuously. My children are likely to witness the first drug that will reverse aging, which may lead to them living for hundreds of years. The good news is that an effective pharmaceutical product may be available far sooner than you may think. The National Institutes of Health (NIH) in the United States is planning on using over $1billion on long COVID research, an increase on the paltry and quite frankly shameful $5 million per annum for ME. The increased funding will inevitably benefit the ME community.

Before COVID most people didn't even know that a virus could spread atypically without presenting symptoms. The first I knew that I had contracted COVID was several months after the event when I was tested for antibodies, which came back positive.

Incidentally, while COVID did nothing to help my symptoms, it appeared it did little to make them worse, either. I believe my response to COVID may be due to the fact that my immunoglobulin G (IgG) was extremely elevated, which I believe is a common factor in many ME patients, as it indicates a latent response to a prior, chronic infection. IgG is a type of antibody representing approximately 75% of serum antibodies in humans. However, a very low IgG level may also be an indicator for chronic fatigue and may mean you might be more susceptible to other infections, including COVID. I recommend that you get all your immunoglobulins checked via blood test by your doctor. If you do have low IgG, you should speak to your doctor about having an intravenous administration of IgG once every 3 to 4 weeks. You may find you have low levels of immunoglobulin A (IgA), known as selective IgA deficiency, especially if you find you contract upper respiratory tract infections on a regular basis. IgA is the body's first line of defense, inhibiting both viral and bacterial infections. While there is no booster shot for IgA, cleaning up your diet may boost your IgA levels. Selective immunoglobulin M deficiency is much rarer, but worth getting checked, as the deficiency can lead to very serious infections.

COVID 19 AND LONG COVID or LONG HAULER'S SYNDROME

As of the writing of this book over 250 million people have had COVID 19. Over 5.4 million people have died of COVID 19 globally and over 800,000 have died in the United States. No doubt many more will have suffered and perished by the time this book is published. This disaster appears to also lead to ME and chronic fatigue in many unlucky patients.

According to Penn State College of Medicine researchers, potentially OVER HALF of all COVID patients are suffering from or will suffer from some form long COVID.

While this is a dire situation, if you have had COVID and are suffering from fatigue, then the protocols laid out in this book will be of enormous help to you and may even resolve your long COVID symptoms.

The NIH has decided to call long COVID "Post-Acute Sequelae of SARS-COV-2," or PASC-CoV-2 for short. Thanks NIH, what genius came up with that nugget? You can always count on government officials to come up with a mind numbingly stupid name that nobody can pronounce or understand. To many in the United States, long haulers syndrome has become popular, but that sounds like a trucker who has fallen in love with his truck, so I'm going to use the term *long COVID*. By the way, if you're unsure as to what the NIH (National Institutes of Health) does, they are the government department responsible for biomedical and public health research.

Unfortunately, COVID is not going away anytime soon. The virus is good at mutating, with a new strain being discovered somewhere in the world regularly. It is highly likely that COVID will be with us for several more years and probably our entire lifetimes, the difference being that people may just care less and less over time and the media will shift its attention elsewhere.

There are multiple long-term effects of COVID, which include the following: tachycardia (increased heart rhythm), brain fog, extreme fatigue, hyper coagulopathy (blood clotting problems), skin rashes, hallucinations, kidney and bladder problems, persistent cough, sleep disorders, headaches, hair loss, loss of smell and taste, Sjögren's syndrome (dry eye syndrome), intermittent fever, hearing loss, burning sensation in the trachea, leg pain, chest pain, liver dysfunction issues, vertigo, diarrhea, tinnitus (ringing in the ears), excess sputum production, sore throat, decreased appetite, balance problems, foot pain, seizures, partial paralysis, lung scarring, gastrointestinal problems, abdominal pain, anxiety disorders, joint and muscle pain, conjunctivitis, and chills/sweats. Oh boy, that covers almost everything that can go wrong with the human body.

Also there appears to be long-term pulmonary complications in some patients, including trouble breathing and shortness of breath (known as dyspnea), with some not regaining full lung function. According to Dr. Conners of Brigham and Women's Hospital, COVID patients appear to have an increased clotting activity driven by persistent inflammation of the small vessels inside the lungs. This leads to scarring in the lungs, which impairs blood flow and reduce overall capacity. These symptoms may lead to reduced oxygen levels, which in turn may lead to chronic fatigue.

Being on a ventilator for several days or weeks is likely to increase the probability of reduced lung function. At Brigham's Division of Cardiovascular Medicine, several teams are leading trials to answer questions about the long-term effects on the heart function. About 33% of all hospitalized patients present some type of reduced heart function such as abnormal heart rhythms or heart attacks, with the virus causing chronic inflammation of the blood vessels. However, the degree and extent of chronic conditions appear to be highly variable and unpredictable. Dr. Lamas of Brigham states, "Some patients in our post-ICU clinic had been very ill, were on a ventilator for weeks and had a high risk for death. That said, we're also seeing patients coming to the clinic who weren't hospitalized or admitted to the ICU. Some of these people are young, otherwise healthy and only had a mild case of COVID and yet now they have a constellation of long-term symptoms such as fatigue, brain fog and an inability to concentrate."

It is common knowledge that those most at risk for contracting COVID are those with comorbidities (simultaneous presence of two or more diseases or medical conditions); however, that does not necessarily extend to those with long COVID, many of whom had mild symptoms or were even asymptomatic. With long COVID, even after the virus has left the body, inflammation (or re-inflammation) occurs creating all the nasty ongoing symptoms discussed. With long COVID (as with all types of post viral issues) calming inflammation is of extreme importance. Reinfection is a concern especially as more and more variants appear and vaccinations will eventually be rendered less effective, thus making booster shots extremely important as time goes on.

If you have long COVID, then LISTEN TO YOUR HEARTBEAT regularly and watch out for irregular patterns. Google: How to take your own pulse and listen for irregular patterns). If you are having an irregular heartbeat, you must see a doctor as soon as possible. A recent German study reviewed MRIs of 100 long COVID patients showed that 78% of them had myocarditis, that is persisting myocardial inflammation (Google: "Outcome of MRI Puntmann"). This may be the greatest risk to life for sufferers, as myocarditis can lead to heart failure and sudden death. Apart from irregular heartbeat, symptoms also include chest pain and shortness of breath.

If you are suffering from post-COVID symptoms, please do not freak out or despair. It appears that many of the symptoms are related to chronic inflammation and changing your diet to a complete anti-inflammatory diet will be hugely beneficial in abating these symptoms. In chapter 16 we will take a deep dive into a life transformative diet to end inflammation once and for all. The therapies discussed in this book are largely anti-inflammatory. By making a predetermined effort to take on the information provided throughout this book, long COVID can be abated!

ENTEROVIRUSES

Enteroviruses are an extremely common group of viruses that cause a host of infectious illnesses, the most common ones being echovirus and coxsackievirus. They can also cause polio and hand foot and mouth disease. Symptoms are similar to the flu or common cold with fever, muscle aches, rashes and gastrointestinal issues. More serious cases can lead to brain and heart conditions, meningitis, pneumonia and hepatitis. Most cases are not diagnosed as patients believe they have a cold or the flu when presented with common symptoms of these viruses and symptoms usually resolve on their own. However, the viruses are more likely to be severe if the patient has underlying health conditions or a weakened immune system.

Perhaps more pertinent to CFS/ME sufferers is that enteroviruses (as well as herpes virus types 1 and 2 along with varicella zoster virus) can cause **viral encephalitis**, which, as you are probably aware, is inflammation of the brain, a leading cause of chronic fatigue. *Frontiers in Medicine* has written an interesting article regarding the prevalence of enteroviruses and their relationship with Epstein-Barr (written by Adam O'Neal and Maureen R Hanson, frontiersin.org; Google: "Enterovirus frontiers in medicine"). Here is a brief extract detailing the enterovirus link to ME:

Several studies have documented that a certain percentage of people who contract mononucleosis from Epstein-Barr virus infection will still be ill 6 months or more, exhibiting symptoms diagnostic of ME/CFS. Surveys often indicate that a proportion of patients believe their ME/CFS followed an acute case of mononucleosis or other type of herpesvirus infection. However, given that enteroviruses are known often to cause mild or asymptomatic infections, it is possible that individuals who report ME/CFS after mononucleosis or other herpesviral infections may have also had an inciting enterovirus infection before or after the herpesvirus infection. In fact, one may speculate that an undetected enteroviral infection could make an individual more susceptible to symptomatic cases of EBV infection, for example, most individuals are infected with EBV as children, yet a number of patients have reported an adult-onset EBV infection as triggering their ME/CFS. Perhaps these adult cases are actually mis-diagnosed reactivated infections. Indeed, there are several reports of reactivated herpesvirus infections in ME/CFS patients. Furthermore, a few studies have discovered impaired immunological response to EBV in ME/CFS patients. Is this impaired response due to a prior or ongoing enteroviral infection? Whether or not herpesviruses may incite ME/CFS or merely take advantage of immune disruptions caused by enteroviral infections, they may contribute to the symptoms of the illness, and may prevent recovery, as illustrated by a subset that improves upon anti-herpesvirus drug treatment.

VACCINATION RESPONSE

While vaccinations are safe and vital for the healthy progression of the human race, there is no greater medical contribution to human health than vaccinations. There are a few anecdotal stories of individuals suffering from ME very shortly after receiving a vaccination. Vaccinations are used to stimulate the immune system to create an ongoing immunity against targeted antigens. It appears that in some individuals the immune system persistently overreacts even though there have been no studies that have confirmed this. COVID vaccinations do not cause chronic fatigue, but COVID certainly does.

LYME DISEASE

If only it were an allergy to limes! But alas no. We know for sure that Lyme disease (first discovered in 1975 in the town of Old Lyme, Connecticut) leads to ME in a substantial number of instances. Lyme disease is an insidious affliction that can affect some people for many years. It is transmitted via a tick bite from infected blacklegged ticks that transmit the bacterium *Borrelia burgdorferi*. Lyme is best treated as quickly as possible with antibiotics; the longer a person goes undiagnosed, the greater the risk for getting Post Treatment Lyme Disease Syndrome (PTLDS), the main long-term symptoms being chronic fatigue, brain fog, and arthritis. The problem with Lyme is that many people simply don't know they have the disease until they get to the latter stages and adopt the symptoms of PTLDS. The initial symptoms are joint pain, headaches, and dizziness, all extremely common symptoms that could be caused by a wide variety of ailments.

Even if your general practitioner doctor tests for Lyme the only FDA approved lab test relies on detecting antibodies, which are not necessarily detectable early on in the disease. The test therefore, only detects 29%-40% of people with the disease. Shocking right? So, it is more than likely you will get a false negative test than a positive one and you could go about your life for months or even years without ever knowing you have Lyme. The key is to go back to your doctor and get tested again a few weeks later if the first test was negative and you suspect that you do indeed have Lyme. Important! A functional medicine doctor will be more likely to offer a much wider blood panel to help detect Lyme antibodies. If you are finally diagnosed with Lyme, your doctor will prescribe long-term antibiotics. Sometimes the treatment works and sometimes it doesn't, as antibiotics may not kill all targeted bacteria, leaving any remaining to spread and cause havoc with the immune system. If you have long-term Lyme and have tried every remedy both pharmaceutical and natural without any results, there is a medical center that claims that they may be able to restore patients to full health by following their protocols and treatments. Please ensure you undertake your own due diligence in researching this particular clinic, I have not visited their clinic and do not endorse their claims. The Biologix Center based in Nashville, Tennessee makes the following claim:

While the prevailing medical thought is to first and foremost, kill any and all harmful bacteria regardless of how a treatment method makes a patient feel, the Biologix Center believes in treating the body in its entirety, and training the body to control its response to these infections naturally. Therefore, we have determined that it is not the absence or annihilation of bacteria that creates health, nor is it purely the presence of bacteria that creates disease. It is the breakdown of the body's own regulations that enable the overgrowth of various types of bacteria, and therefore disease.

Using tests such as Biospectroscopic Emission Sequence Testing (BEST), developed at the Biologix Center over 20 years ago by Dr. David A. Jernigan, D.C., we can eliminate much of the guesswork in doctoring. Our doctors focus on restoring the body's proper regulation of bacteria overgrowth through precise, real-time testing and treatments that work through natural means to optimize each patient's response to their specific bacteria. Unlike conventional blood tests that are merely a snapshot of a patient's blood on the day it was drawn, our technology provides far more insight into the root causes of a patient's symptoms as well as treatment options that are surely compatible with his or her body.

Every system of the body is interconnected and interdependent, meaning that each system must be addressed in order for the body to achieve control over the various microbes that cause its symptoms. To attend to these many issues, BRS, along with other of Dr. Jernigan's exclusive, scientifically-based technologies such as Neurophotonic Therapy, Neurocardial Synchronization, and Fractal Frequency Modulation will be used to restore the optimum functional integrity of the body.

This particular clinic claims to have a complete protocol for chronic fatigue, stating that they have a new approach that can completely eliminate infection and repair the damage that your symptoms have already caused, allowing you to finally take your life back from chronic fatigue once and for all. They claim to have the several innovative treatment methods including Induced Native Phage Therapy (INPT), which is slated to identify bacteriophages that can selectively get rid of their unique bacteria even more efficiently than antibiotics can. Biospectroscopic Emission Sequence Testing (BEST), which they state is used to dynamically diagnose and treat patients in real time. It identifies specific frequencies of coherence from any source of tissue to identify the correct remedy of treatment that will ultimately restore balance to the body.

If you are interested in further researching the Biologix Center, their website is biologixcenter.com. I reiterate, I have not attended their clinic, nor do I know of anybody who has, and therefore I cannot recommend nor comment on their procedures or effectiveness, so please do you own research.

Notwithstanding all of the above, if you follow the protocols laid out in this book, the long-term symptoms of Lyme can and will be beaten! In fact, if you have Lyme, please read the chapter on hyperbaric oxygen chamber therapy, which can abate Lyme symptoms.

MOLD INHALATION

Mold inhalation may cause a host of chronic fatigue like symptoms. Mold (spelled mould in UK) can cause the production of microbes and bacteria, including aspergillus, stenotrophomonas and myobacterium from water damaged buildings. The water damage may not be obvious, often hiding within the walls of buildings that may have been water damaged years ago. I'm not going into a deep dive regarding how it manifests, suffice to say it is certainly worth getting a mold test, even if you believe your property is mold free. If the mold test is positive, you have two choices. First, get the mold remediated or second, move away. If you believe you have been infected by chronic mold exposure in your existing property, then the best policy is to get it remediated and move anyway! You can never be sure whether the mold has gone for good, and gambling with your health is just not worth it. If you do decide to move, then make sure you move to a modern home built recently. Whilst this does not guarantee that the new home is mold free, it does reduce the risk.

Be aware that mold can grow on many different surfaces including on plants, inside spice and peanut butter jars (throw away old jars) and on rotting vegetables (stay away from compost heaps).

If you believe that you have been subject to mold inhalation, then there are several tests that you can try to help confirm diagnosis. A chest X-ray or CT scan may reveal a fungal mass (aspergilloma). A sputum test may reveal the presence of aspergillus filaments. Skin testing and blood tests may reveal allergic broncho-pulmonary aspergillosis. A blood test may indicate antibodies to the mold and a skin test may reveal an allergic reaction at the skin test site. A last resort test includes a biopsy of the tissue taken from the lungs or sinuses to confirm a diagnosis of invasive aspergillosis.

Treatments include oral corticosteroids for treating allergic broncho-aspergillosis, antifungal medications for invasive pulmonary aspergillosis, embolization to stop lungs from bleeding (temporarily), and potential surgery to remove fungal mass.

CHRONIC PATHOGEN COLONIZATION

Is it possible that all chronic fatigue starts not with a virus but by a bacterial microbial infection that never resolves? Pathogens generally colonize host tissues that are in contact with the external environment to some extent, such as nasal cavities, mouth, throat, gums, lungs and esophagus. Everybody has unwittingly succumbed to pathogens at some point in the past, with or without symptoms. The most insidious nature of pathogen colonization is the creation of protective biofilms that cover the pathogen allowing it to grow while protecting it from the immune system. Biofilms are an organized coat of extracellular polysaccharides that also block the access to all known antibiotics. All CPCs are metabolically active and thus release toxic byproducts, which inevitably get chronically ingested into the gastrointestinal tract causing many systemic problems and potentially chronic fatigue. As the microbiome gets overwhelmed with bad bacteria and the gut lining becomes leaky and leaky gut syndrome occurs, thus allowing more toxins to leach into the vascular system exacerbating all and any negative symptoms.

The most common places for CPC to gather are within the periodontal tissue, the mucosal cavities, and the epithelial cells lining the airway to the lungs. Perhaps the most common CPC is periodontitis, a potentially serious and very common form of gum disease caused primarily by poor dental hygiene. Left untreated, it can lead to tooth loss, jaw bone degradation, and increases risk of both heart and lung disease. Symptoms include red, swollen gums, bad breath, and bleeding while brushing. However, minor, consistent periodontitis can be a source of persistent ingestion of toxins into the gastrointestinal tract, leading to leaky gut and chronic fatigue symptoms.

While you may believe that various types of gum disease are relatively harmless, don't be fooled; they can be extremely damaging to your health and almost everyone has had one at some point in their lives. Areas of CPCs and their biofilms can assist in developing esophageal cancer, gastric cancer, colorectal cancer, pancreatic cancer, lung cancer and tongue cancer. Furthermore, physicians and even dentists generally do not recognize or treat CPCs primarily because biofilms make them stealthy, very long lasting and hard to detect. First, how do you get rid of CPCs in your mouth? The first step is excellent dental hygiene, sonic toothbrush followed by flossing with a waterpik. Although flossing with traditional floss is better than doing nothing, the floss can actually push food particles up into the gum if not executed correctly. A waterpik is an electronic device that has a small water tank and sprays a pressurized, focused stream of water into your mouth, which you direct with a nozzle. This forces the crud and debris to be ejected from the crevices between the teeth and potentially reduces the occurrence of CPCs. If you have ME, this protocol is a must, though it will not destroy an existing biofilm. Biofilms that have formed in and around teeth and cavities must be removed manually by a dentist or dental nurse using professional equipment. All solid plaque buildup must be completely removed, and then you must increase you home dental hygiene and have your teeth professionally cleaned at least twice as much as a non-ME sufferers. If you decide to use a waterpik (and please do, this is a must), then you can add food grade hydrogen peroxide to the tank in a 1% to 2% dilution to help keep pathogens at bay. If you don't like the taste of HP, then add some mouthwash. Incidentally, hydrogen peroxide is one of the key substances used to help reverse chronic fatigue (more on this in later chapters).

DEREGULATION OF SPECIFIC NEURAL RECEPTORS

Along my journey for seeking a cure to chronic fatigue led me to a small biotech company called Cortene Inc. that is developing a drug called CT38. I have discussed this later in the chapter on supplements and pharmaceuticals; however, their research is extremely interesting and may turn out to be a real breakthrough for ME/CFS patients. I have had a very interesting meeting with the CEO, Gerard Pereira, and he has helped explain the mechanism of this potential medication. They have formulated a hypothesis that 2 neural receptors, CRFR1 and CRFR2 (Corticotropin-Releasing Factor Receptor) in the limbic system have switched places in the brain leading to dyshomeostasis (imbalance of physical functioning).

To elaborate a little, their hypothesis is that ME patients' brains respond differently to stress triggers, in that once a stressful event occurs, the neurons remain in an alert state leading to CFS symptoms. They believe that a neuronal switch exists in the limbic system, which turns the threat response on and off. Under minor stress CRFR1 dominates triggering the release of GABA, which inhibits serotonin production. Under high stress, including exercise, the two receptors switch places and the CRFR2 takes over and releases serotonin, but after the stress event has passed the CRFR2 receptors stays activated in ME patients. This constant activation has dire consequences on the immune, endocrine and metabolic systems and especially the autonomic nervous system. They believe that all the symptoms including, brain fog, exhaustion, stimuli sensitivities are caused by the up regulation of this receptor. The differences in symptoms from one patient to the other is due to the varying numbers of neurons affected.

The CRFR1 and CRFR2 functions cannot be measured through blood tests, only through use of drugs targeting to hit these receptors. By overstimulating the CRFR2 pathway the neurons switch themselves off, rather than exciting them further. By overstimulating rather than blocking, may allow the pathway to down regulate permanently, resetting to a healthy state. Simply blocking the pathway may require taking drugs for life, as blocking is a temporary measure. The company state that overstimulating the pathway relieves all or most of the symptoms of ME/CFS sufferers.

They are in the process fundraising for a larger trial to confirm the initial positive results. In the long run, this drug may have the potential to treat a wide range of chronic diseases including long COVID and fibromyalgia.

Couple of things to note here. First their assertion about the switching of these receptors is a theory based on their own research. I cannot find independent research that confirms this hypothesis, which may make their potential drug a long shot, based on a specific assertion. However, if this drug genuinely reduces or eliminates fatigue, then the mechanisms or targets may be academic if the drug actually works and helps patients recover.

I have discussed their drug further in the supplement and medication chapter later in this book. In the meantime, you might want to Google "Cortene Inc" to get an update with regard to the development of this drug.

CHRONIC CARBON MONOXIDE POISONING (CCMP)

Chronic carbon monoxide poisoning is almost always misdiagnosed, often mistaken for CFS, viral, bacterial, or GI issues. The greatest indication that you might have CCMP is that more than one person in your household has the same symptoms. CCMP occurs from poorly installed or maintained household appliances such as cookers, water heating boilers, and heaters. Also, if you have been involved in a house fire, or are a fire fighter, then this may be the source of your CO ingestion. Faulty or nonexistent CO monitors will potentially cause you to miss this important (and potentially fatal) issue. Unusually high mortality (short life span) of pets may also be an indication.

There is a fine line between acute and chronic poisoning. Exposure to a few hours to a day or so may be deemed acute exposure, and several days or more, chronic exposure.

Symptoms of chronic and acute exposure include fatigue, visual disturbances, headache, nausea, weakness, sleepiness, and dizziness. Polycythemia may occur, which is a disease in which there are too many red blood cells in the bone marrow and blood, causing the blood to thicken, slowing blood flow throughout the body.

One of the obvious ways to see if you're breathing in CO is to get several CO monitors and put them around your house, especially close to gas-fired appliances. The other way is to see if your symptoms improve if you change your environment over several days. If you noticed that your fatigue symptoms subside while on vacation, then it will certainly be worth checking your home for CO emissions.

If you find that you have CO poisoning, then find your nearest Hyperbaric Oxygen treatment facility, this therapy speeds up the replacement of CO with oxygen. Please read the chapter on HBOT later in this book. It is an excellent treatment for chronic fatigue.

ABSCESSES

Abscesses occur in small pockets throughout the body, but most common in the gums. A gum abscess (aka periodontal abscess) is a pocket of pus inside the gum or around the tooth that gradually becomes increasingly painful and can leak pus into the mouth and thus the gastrointestinal system. Abscesses are caused by unchecked periodontitis (an inflammatory condition of the gums when plaque builds up in and around the gums) and a combination of poor dental hygiene, stress or trauma. Having a compromised immune system can contribute to the likelihood of having a gum abscess, so ME sufferers may be at a higher risk. Symptoms of a mouth abscess include sensitivity to hot and cold, localized tenderness and pain, pus discharge leading to disgusting taste, and potentially a fever. If you think you might have an abscess, see your dentist immediately, they will drain out the infection and probably prescribe antibiotics. A completely unchecked abscess can lead to the infection entering the bloodstream and cause sepsis, a potentially life-threatening complication. While abscesses are generally acute in nature, a slow leaking abscess may not be too obvious but could cause chronic fatigue if left unchecked.

CRANIAL CERVICAL SYNDROME AND SPINE INSTABILITY

This is becoming an increasingly important topic and a potential game changer in the diagnosis and treatment of ME/CFS.

A recent research paper has linked ME/CFS to cervical spine instability and evidence that pressure exerted by loose or floating vertebrae pinching nerves and compressing arteries may be the cause or a contributing factor (study information below).

I honestly didn't think this would apply to me as I never had any real, consistent pain in my neck or back. Nevertheless, due to the staggering results of the study discussed below, I thought I would get tested. To my surprise I have **cranio-cervical obstruction**. My chiropractor undertook X-rays and found that my spine was curved and that the top vertebrae (C1) was out of line with the rest of my spine. The loose vertebrae was potentially pressing on the nerves, including the vagus nerve, which runs through the top three vertebrae. A pinched vagus nerve can affect the sympathetic nervous system, the system responsible for the flight-or-fight response leading to prolonged anxious awareness and lack of sleep. I have written extensively later in this book about the importance of stimulating the vagus nerve to calm down the sympathetic nervous system and to activate its polar opposite cousin, the parasympathetic nervous system. An under stimulated vagus nerve has become extremely evident throughout my research on this topic, coming up as a contributing factor over and over again.

So how prevalent could this condition be in the ME patient population? In a study published in August 2020 in the *Frontiers in Neurology* Journal the authors tested for intracranial hypertension (pressure around the brain) and craniocervical obstructions (disc bulges and hernias) and whether they are prominent in ME patients. (Google: "Frontiers in Neurology intracranial hypertension" for the full report.)

229 patients with ME were included and they found that 50% had hyper mobility (joints moving beyond expected range), 55% had intracranial pressure, a shocking 83% had signs of intracranial hypertension. MRI of the cervical spine was performed on 125 participants and a staggering 80% had craniocervical obstructions.

If you undertake a lot of CFS research, you may have come across a gentleman called Jeff Wood, who had a very severe case of CFS at a young age. He was so debilitated with fatigue that he couldn't talk or even chew his food, reverting to drinking shakes through a straw. He went through the usual routine with physicians ("there's nothing wrong with you," "you're depressed," etc.) until he found a CFS specialist named Dr. David Kaufman. He was diagnosed with post orthostatic tachycardia syndrome (POTS) and mast cell activation syndrome (see below for more information). He found that he had neck pain at the base of his skull and his head wobbled when he walked. He found that turning head to the right could make him lose consciousness and his heart rate would drop to as low as 30 bpm at night. Fortunately, he was smart enough to figure out that he had cranial cervical syndrome (aka cranial-cervical instability), loose ligaments at the junction between his skull and spine (the atlantoaxial junction, which is the most mobile joint in the body). The weight of his skull was compressing his brainstem crushing his vagus nerve and making his autonomic nervous system become erratic. While he struggled to find the right professionals to help fix his issues, Jeff wore a cervical collar that helped relieve his symptoms, which gave him the time to find the right help. However, after switching out his collar for a less ridged one, he collapsed, leading to partial paralysis, racing heart, and dizziness. During an extremely arduous hospital stay he was eventually seen by a spine specialist who ordered the correct tests including a dynamic CT scan with flexion and extension views. He was then fitted with a halo, a metal cage device attached directly into his skull to keep his head upright. Jeff states that the halo device cured most of his symptoms. He then had spine surgery to fuse his top vertebrae, which gave him permanent relief from all of his symptoms, and now Jeff leads a perfectly normal life. Jeff's story is an important one. You may not notice any neck or back pain; you may be unaware of any pinched nerves in your neck or that you may have IIH (see below). However, you do not need to be completely incapacitated like Jeff to be suffering from these chronic issues. IIH and cranial cervical instability may occur in various degrees of severity; a relatively minor pinch of your vagus nerve may lead to life-changing levels of chronic fatigue.

IDIOPATHIC INTRACRANIAL HYPERTENSION (IIH)

As previously stated, IIH (aka pseudotumor cerebri) is pressure around the brain of unknown cause, that lingers (idiopathic means the cause isn't known). Symptoms can mimic a brain tumor, without a tumor present. Most common symptom is headache, particularly behind the eyes. **As commented above, a staggering 83% of the 229 ME patients were diagnosed with IIH. Could relieving the pressure also resolve ME?**

According to the me-pedia.org (an excellent online resource), a case study of a woman with intracranial hypertension found that her ME/CFS symptoms resolved with the placement of a transverse sinus stent. A transverse sinus stent is a stent (metallic fine mesh in tubular form) inserted into a narrowed vein to open it up and allow for greater blood flow. It is a relatively minimally invasive procedure with mild pain or discomfort for several days after the procedure. Another way to relieve the pressure is with a cerebrospinal fluid drainage via a lumbar puncture.

According to a cross-sectional study of twenty patients presenting at a headache clinic found that a large proportion of patients had borderline intracranial hypertension, with four meeting the diagnostic criteria for IIH (mean cerebrospinal fluid pressure was 19 cm H_2O (range, 12–41 cm H_2O); however, none had clinical signs of IIH. Cerebrospinal fluid drainage via lumbar puncture improved symptoms in 17 of 20 patients. Researchers speculate that a subset of CFS patients may have borderline cases of idiopathic intracranial hypertension without papilledema, that is, swelling of the optic nerve.

Go and find an orthopedic doctor and ask if they can check your cerebrospinal fluid pressure. You may also benefit from an X-ray, MRI or CT scan to check the distance between your vertebrae. If you have little space between your top three vertebrae or they are misaligned, it may be that some nerves are compressed. Find out whether your orthopedic specialist or a chiropractor can work on you to release the nerves; it may have an impact on your fatigue issues. If your doctor finds that adjusting you manually does not work or is ineffective, then inquire about a transverse sinus stent or a lumbar puncture. Remember, BE YOUR OWN HEALTH ADVOCATE, never let a doctor dictate to you, especially if you have a gut feeling that something isn't quite right. Always get a second opinion if you believe your doctor has missed something. Doctors are humans, they make mistakes and they cannot feel what your body is telling you. Your ability to communicate effectively with a doctor may also dictate the quality of care you ultimately receive, so always do your own research before you see a particular specialist and go in armed to the teeth with knowledge.

Is it possible that those with severe long COVID symptoms also have some form of craniocervical instability or intracranial hypertension that massively exacerbates symptoms? I believe this may be a very real possibility and would urge everybody dealing with fatigue to get an X-ray of the upper spine. Remember this is new ground that we are breaking here, and many doctors will not see a relationship or will be unaware of the latest developments in this area. Nevertheless, you know better now.

OTHER SPINAL ISSUES THAT MAY EXACERBATE FATIGUE

SPINAL STENOSIS

This is a narrowing of the spinal canal leading to high pressure put upon the spinal cord and the nerves therein. Common symptoms include pain (including pins and needles tingling sensation), numbness in the limbs and weakness or reduced strength in different parts of the body. The condition tends to occur later in life due to wear and tear over time, but can lead to chronic fatigue if not treated. The increased pressure can pinch the nerves in the top three vertebrae leading to similar chronic fatigue effects as intracranial hypertension. A cognizant attempt to change sleeping position can help relieve symptoms. Sleeping on your back to allow for normal curvature of the spine to help relieve pressure is the best sleeping position to find relief. Whereas sleeping while lying on your stomach can exacerbate symptoms. Remedies include various medications including anti-inflammatories and steroidal injections, physical therapy and decompression. However, if all else fails, then spinal surgery is the last resort.

CEREBRAL SPINAL FLUID LEAK

Cerebral spinal fluid surrounds the brain and spinal cord and acts as a buffer between the brain, the spinal cord, and the outside world. CSF leak occurs when there is a tear in the connective tissue (the dura mater) and the fluid leaks out, causing **intracranial hypotension** (low pressure, not to be confused with intracranial hypertension, which is high pressure). This means the loss of fluid allows the brain to sink slightly inside the skull, which can result in severe headaches. Other symptoms include vision problems, sensitivity to light and sound, balance issues, neck pain, nausea, watery leakage from one side of nose or ear when tilting head, metallic taste in mouth, and loss of smell.

A CSF leak can be caused by a variety of events including head trauma, spine injury, past surgeries, past epidurals, and spinal catheters. A potentially more common cause could be undiagnosed and untreated intracranial hypertension as discussed above.

CSF leaks are diagnosed through either a CT (computerized tomography) scan, MRI (magnetic resonance imaging), lumbar puncture (to assess fluid pressure), myelography, or cisternography.

If you are diagnosed with a CSF leak, then first you must avoid doing anything that can increase pressure in and around the skull. Therefore, do not lift heavy items, avoid bending over, take stool softeners to avoid straining, and no sneezing or blowing your nose. Initial treatments will include bed rest, caffeine and/or saline infusions. There is a medication called Fludrocortisone that may help treat neural hypotension (speak to your doctor). If further treatment is required, then surgery may be needed based upon where the leak is detected. Surgery may be performed by using a graft of tissue from a similar area as the leak, that could include fat, muscle or from the mucosal lining. Surgical adhesives may also be used.

TETHERED CORD SYNDROME

This is a relatively rare condition where the spinal cord is attached or tethered to the surrounding tissue of the spine. This prevents the spinal cord from moving freely within the spinal column, which causes several problems including spinal cord hypo-perfusion, electro-physical issues and impaired glucose metabolism. This syndrome can change the way weight is distributed throughout the body. Symptoms include back pain and/or pain in the back of the legs, spasms in the leg muscles, changes in foot shape, such as higher arches and curling toes, bladder infections, and loss of bladder control. There are increasing links to ME patients who have also been diagnosed with tethered cord syndrome as well as cranial cervical instability.

FILUM TERMINALE DISEASE

Another spinal column disease and hereditary (tethered cord) condition (that includes or is similar to Arnold-Chiari Syndrome Type 1, Idiopathic Syringomyelia, Idiopathic Scoliosis, Platybasia, Basilar Invagination, Odontoid Retroflexion, Brainstem Kinking) that affects both spine and nervous system causing instability, vomiting, dizziness, brain fog, insomnia, sensitivity to touch and temperature and chronic fatigue.

The filum terminal is a fibrous band that goes between the conus medullaris (very end of the spinal cord) to the periosteum of the coccyx (connective tissue covering the tailbone) and I'm sure you will never forget this.

The good news is that this condition can be reversed with minimally invasive surgery with few or no complications.

If you have had ME/CFS since birth (or know someone who has), then make sure you are checked for tethered cord issues and spina bifida and Google all the above conditions to see if one fits. Make sure to see an osteopath for a diagnosis.

EHLERS DANLOS SYNDROME

This syndrome is a genetic disease that affects the connective tissues (through a defect in the production of collagen), including the joints, skin, and blood vessels, which creates overly flexible joints that can easily dislocate. The symptoms include joint pain, skin that bruises easily, digestive problems including acid reflux and constipation, dizziness and chronic fatigue. People can suffer from this to varying degrees dependent upon faults in certain genes that make connective tissues weaker. There are 13 types of EDS that include hyper mobile EDS (most common type), vascular EDS, kyphoscoliotic EDS and classical EDS. If you think this may be a syndrome that you might be suffering from, then see an orthopedic specialist and don't be shy in asking to be tested.

Remedies include anti-inflammatories, physical therapy and potentially surgery to repair joints damaged by dislocations or to repair ruptured blood vessels and organs. While fatigue may linger, some of the remedies laid out in this book will help manage the symptoms.

INFECTIONS OF THE SPINAL CORD

You are no doubt aware by now that the family of herpes viruses are high on the list of suspects for triggering ME. Viruses including Epstein Barr, cytomegalovirus (CMV), herpes simplex virus and varicella zoster (VZV) can all seriously infect the spinal cord and potentially lead to some of the issues already highlighted. VZV causes chickenpox and the nasty adult version of chickenpox, known as shingles, which is a reactivated virus near the spinal cord and brain. A flare up of CMV in the spinal cord can cause transverse myelitis (inflammation of the spinal cord) as can most forms of herpes viruses. Other types of viruses that infect the spinal cord include West Nile Virus (mosquito borne), enteroviruses such as polio (virtually eradicated nowadays thanks to vaccines, save for a few rare cases in Africa), amyotrophic lateral sclerosis (ALS), and syphilis.

Syphilis is a sexually transmitted bacterial infection and is relatively common. If unchecked it can cause a common spinal cord disorder known as tabes dorsalis, which develops 10 to 15 years after the initial infection. It also causes meningomyelitis, which is inflammation of the tissue surrounding the spinal cord leading to vasculitis that can cut off the blood flow to the spinal cord and can compress it due to abnormal growths called gummas. This compression can affect the nerves and, potentially, the vagus nerve leading to chronic fatigue and major sleep disturbances.

Other infections of the spinal cord include bacterial abscesses, fungal infections and parasitic infections. Bacterial abscesses are acute in nature and unlikely to cause chronic fatigue unless the abscess bursts and leaches into the blood. Fungal infections of the spinal cord are rare, but can lead to growths called granulomas that may compress the spinal cord leading to vagus nerve compression. Parasitic infections are also rare (usually found in South America, Africa, and eastern Asia) and tapeworms can cause cysts that can compress the spinal cord. If you travel extensively or have travelled a lot in the past, then it might be worth discussing these types of infections with your doctor.

It should be very apparent to you that spinal or cranial issues are either THE major cause of ME/CFS or a very serious contributing factor. These issues may make long COVID far worse. If the fatigue is absolutely debilitating, then one of these spinal issues is more than likely the cause. It is absolutely imperative to get yourself checked out as soon as possible by an osteopath, spine specialist or at least a chiropractor even if you feel no pain or discomfort. Write the following down and take it with you. I'm serious, no skipping this bit!

Say to your doctor that you want to be examined to eliminate the following:

- **Cranial Cervical Syndrome**
- **Spine instability (hernias and disc bulges)**
- **Intracranial hypertension (pseudotumor cerebri)**
- **Spinal stenosis**
- **Cerebral spinal fluid leak (and intracranial hypotension)**
- **Tethered cord syndrome and its associated disorders (filum terminale disease, Arnold-Chiari syndrome type 1, idiopathic syringomyelia, idiopathic scoliosis, platybasia, basilar invagination, odontoid retroflexion, brainstem kinking).**
- **Ehlers-Danlos syndrome**

Write down this list or print or photograph this page and take it with you to see the specialist. I would be grateful if you could email me at <u>chronicfatiguegone@gmail.com</u> if you have one of these issues, so I can compile a list of more common occurrences that I can share with the ME community.

MAST CELL ACTIVATION SYNDROME

Mast cells are allergy cells that cause immediate allergic reactions by releasing so-called mediators that are stored inside the cell. This occurs when the antibody immunoglobulin E (IgE) binds to the proteins on the mast cell surface that creates allergens, such as from food or pollen.

They can also be activated by medications, infections, and insect or snake venom.

MCAS is where the patient suffers instances of anaphylaxis, that is, acute hives, swelling, low blood pressure, and breathing problems not caused by a reaction to an allergen. In this instance, some of the mast cells become defective due to certain mutations that create clone mast cells that can grow uncontrollably and are sensitive to activation.

The treatments for MCAS include antihistamines, aspirin, mast cell stabilizers (Omalizub), corticosteroids (probably a last resort treatment), antileukotrienes (zafirlukast and montelukast).

OTHER TRIGGERS

If you're a woman who has had silicone breast implants (or a man for that matter, I'm not judging), there is some evidence that the implants can stimulate an immune response that may lead to ME. MD Anderson Cancer Center released the results to a study they did in 2018 regarding the long-term safety outcomes for patients with breast implants (Google: "breast implants MD Anderson," for the full report). They found that there was an association with some autoimmune diseases and cancers including scleroderma and melanoma. However, the study did not report a direct link or causative effect between implants and these diseases. If you do have silicone implants and are suffering from ME, then speak to your doctor about switching them out for saline based implants (that advice goes out to the ladies too!). If the implants are indeed causing ME you will need to take action as further degradation of the implants is likely to exacerbate your symptoms. If you can emotionally deal with having them removed completely, then more the better, as implants may affect the validity of mammogram tests, that may provide false negatives if the implant gets in the way.

DENTAL AMALGAMS

If you have old style dental amalgams with any type of base metals, then go to your dentist immediately and have them switched out for a composite mixture of glass and plastic (porcelain). Believe it or not (and I had to read this twice) the FDA continues to approve of mercury to be used as a base for fillings based on scientific evidence and, I quote, "The best available scientific evidence supports the conclusion that patients with dental amalgam fillings are not at risk for mercury-associated adverse health effects." Susan Runner, FDA spokesperson.

There's a lot wrong with this statement. They are stating that if you have mercury in your teeth, you are not at risk for mercury associated health effects. A nonsensical thing to say, as you are obviously at risk. That's like saying jumping out of a fifth-floor window won't lead to death; maybe not, but would you try it to find out? Furthermore, they added a label warning against the use of mercury for those people known to have a mercury allergy. Again, a silly statement to come from the FDA, as who on earth gets tested for a mercury allergy? Even if you did have a mercury allergy test and it came back negative, how would that be of use?

"Can I have a side of mercury dipping sauce with my fries? I'm not allergic."

Even if you were not allergic to inorganic mercury, digesting it would not be a good idea. Mercury poisoning can lead to the following symptoms: depression, anxiety, insomnia, chronic fatigue, fibromyalgia-type symptoms, brain fog, skin issues (burning, itching, rashes), IBS, weak digestion or other leaky gut issues, food sensitivities, Candida overgrowth, dysbiosis, weak appetite, alcohol intolerance, frequent urination, bladder irritation or interstitial cystitis, susceptibility to developing infections (bladder, prostate, vaginal, lung, sinus, throat, flu), substantial nutritional deficiencies, poor assimilation and methylation, hypothyroid condition. Err, no thanks. Come on, FDA, you can do better.

The list is obviously similar to ME symptoms, so if you have any metal fillings, make sure you get them out immediately.

Fortunately, most, if not all, dentists completely ignore the FDA and don't use mercury anymore in their amalgams. But double check with your dentist the next time you need a filling!

HORMONAL IMBALANCES

Science bit alert!

The most common hormone deficiency that may lead to CFS is low thyroid hormone levels known as hypothyroidism. A study by a Dutch university (University Medical Center Groningen, 2018; source: sciencedaily.com) compared thyroid function among 98 ME/CFS patients and 99 healthy controls, which showed that the ME/CFS patients had lower serum levels of certain key thyroid hormones such as triiodothyronine (T3) and thyroxine (T4), but normal levels of thyroid-stimulating hormones. Additional analysis indicated that ME/CFS patients had a lower urinary iodine status and low-grade inflammation, which possibly mirrored symptoms of patients with hypothyroidism. These ME/CFS patients had relatively higher levels of another thyroid hormone called reverse T3 (rT3). This appeared to be due to a shift in hormone production where the body preferred to convert T4 to rT3 instead of producing T3. The low T3 levels found in ME/CFS patients coupled with the switchover to rT3 could mean that T3 levels are severely reduced in tissue. The lead doctor, Dr. Ruiz-Nunez, said, "One of the key elements of our study is that our observations persisted in the face of two sensitivity analyses to check the strength of the association between CFS and thyroid parameters and low grade inflammation."

It is possible that low T3 levels may be a result of the autoimmune response that creates the inflammation, which is more likely to be the original cause of the fatigue in the first place, so while seeking a solution for low T3 may be beneficial, calming the autoimmune response is paramount.

Low cortisol levels, known as hypocortisolism, is very common in ME/CFS patients. Cortisol is produced by the adrenal glands and is the major stress hormone that fluctuates relative to stress/calm cycles. Therefore, cortisol helps to regulate your circadian rhythm and is one of the reasons that

CFS patients suffer from insomnia. Furthermore, cortisol levels spike upon wakening and help make you active first thing in the morning. Low cortisol levels make it difficult wake up and make mornings rather lethargic for CFS patients. Cortisol also helps to reduce inflammation, which may be another reason why CFS patients suffer from chronic inflammation. OKAY, so let's boost cortisol levels, I hear you say, problem solved! In a 1998 double-blind, randomized, placebo-controlled trial, it was found that low-dose hydrocortisone led to a statistical improvement, but only in one subjective score. No statistical evidence of improvement was seen with the other self-rating scales. If you test for cortisol and find you have low levels, you might ask your doctor for hydrocortisone or find a cream you can purchase over the counter. I have not tried this personally so cannot attest to its efficacy, and there might be side effects including burning of the skin, redness, dryness, acne and other types of skin irritation (or buy one with aloe that is kinder to skin). A better way to change cortisol levels is to repair a potential nervous system dysfunction. More on this later. Nevertheless, it is worth having all of your hormone levels checked as part of your blood tests.

GENETICS

First, genetics is not a trigger for CFS/ME but perhaps a precursor. It appears that based on one's genetic makeup, a likely increase in the probability of succumbing to CFS/ME is increased based upon whether certain genes are turned on or off. Several studies have found that genes that are important in activating the immune system are more likely to be turned on. Bummer. So, while genes are not a trigger per se, the expression of a gene can determine how likely you might react to environmental triggers, such as bacteria, toxins, diet, stress and viruses (including your reaction to COVID). So, if you don't like your parents that much, here's another excuse to skip Thanksgiving, Christmas or Hanukah!

TRAUMA

Trauma, and in particular, childhood trauma are serious risk factors for developing chronic fatigue. A 2009 study by Emory University

(Christine Heim et al.) revealed that childhood trauma including sexual, physical and emotional abuse along with emotional and physical neglect and depression, anxiety and PTSD, caused a 6-fold increase risk for CFS later in life. The study included 113 people diagnosed with CFS and a control group of 124 people, which confirmed the results of a 2006 study. The participants completed questionnaires and had their saliva samples taken 1 hour after waking up, typically when cortisol levels are at their peak. Low cortisol levels are common with CFS sufferers, assisting in the dysfunction of the autonomic nervous system and serious issues with sleep disturbance. The experience of the adolescent brain makes a difference in the psychological development and the way the body reacts to stress in later life. Interestingly, those with CFS but without any childhood trauma had regular levels of cortisol in their saliva. (Google: "Christine Heim CFS" for the full study.)

In a study regarding adult trauma and post-traumatic stress disorder (PTSD), it was found that those with a history of PTSD were 8 times more likely to have CFS than those who had not had a PTSD event. (Google: "Elizabeth Dansie PTSD" for the full study.)

If you have suffered or still suffering from any kind of trauma, then do not despair. There are ways to put trauma firmly in the rear-view mirror and get on with life. In chapter 4, I explain EMDR therapy (Eye Movement Desensitization and Reprocessing), a therapy guided by a therapist that has been shown to effectively deal with processing trauma and resolving its related issues. This is an area where you will need to be strong and force yourself to get through the therapy. The results will be worth the effort. In addition, calming the sympathetic nervous system by stimulating the vagus nerve will help immeasurably. Please read the chapters on both later in this book.

GULF WAR SYNDROME (AKA DESERT STORM DISEASES)

A condition affecting Gulf War veterans with a host of chronic symptoms including fatigue, headaches, joint pain, indigestion, insomnia, dizziness, respiratory disorders and brain fog issues. Possible causes are exposure to chemical warfare agents and pyridostigmine bromide (brand names Mestinon, Regonol and Gravitor), which was given to soldiers likely to be exposed to chemical warfare agents. PTSD may also play a role in the condition.

If you or someone you know has been diagnosed with this syndrome, then please follow the protocols laid out in this book (especially EMDR therapy), they will help enormously.

CHAPTER SUMMARY

- The initial triggers of chronic fatigue are Lyme disease, COVID, EBV, XMRV (or a different retrovirus that we may or may not know about), enteroviruses, possible reaction to a vaccination, breast implants or other invasive devices (that may induce immune response), potential hormone imbalances (probably a response rather than a trigger), possible leaching of mercury from dental amalgams, chronic pathogen colonizations, mast cell activation syndrome, childhood or adult traumatic event, Gulf War syndrome.
- Spinal cord problems that induce chronic fatigue include: cranial cervical syndrome, spine instability (hernias and disc bulges), intracranial hypertension (pseudotumor cerebri), spinal stenosis, cerebral spinal fluid leak (and intracranial hypotension), tethered cord syndrome and its associated disorders (filum terminale disease, Arnold-Chiari syndrome type 1, idiopathic syringomyelia, idiopathic scoliosis, platybasia, basilar invagination, odontoid retroflexion, brainstem kinking) and Ehlers-Danlos syndrome.
- However, what is equally as important to understand why fatigue manifests itself and reoccurs again and again ad nauseam.

Chapter 3

Why chronic fatigue lingers

"Success is the ability to go from one failure to another with no loss of enthusiasm."

Sir Winston Churchill

After you have recovered from COVID, other virus or bacterial infection, a few months later, fatigue starts to overwhelm you. You get enough energy to exercise or just go on a long hike, then BAM! You're knocked off your feet like a truck just slammed into you and you're flat on your back for a week.

Why?

This gets complicated, so please bear with me (and yes, *science bit alert*). Let's start with the most common theory and its potential to cause several knock-on effects.

Initially, inflammation is a good thing as it increases blood flow to the damaged areas by dilating blood vessels, then immune proteins are released into that blood. White blood cells flow out of the blood vessels into the areas to remove foreign invaders, then the tissue can heal. When the immune system targets cells that are similar to the original antigens (known as molecular mimicry) a vicious cycle begins and an autoimmune response is started.

In a 2012 study published by *Psychiatry Research* they found that CFS/ME patients had higher levels of two proteins in the cytokine family of proteins that create inflammation. (Google: "pubmed Michael Maes.") The two proteins are called interleukin-1 and tumor necrosis factor-alpha.

Cytokines are peptides (small chain amino acids) that are secreted by specific cells of the immune system that signal specific molecules to regulate immunity and inflammation.

You may recall that encephalomyelitis means inflammation of the brain and spinal cord, specifically called because there is a general consensus that the sustained immune response is known as neuroimmune or neuroendocrine immune disease revealed by studies that showed several biomarkers of inflammation in and/or around the brain. It is possible that these two cytokine proteins kick off the inflammation process.

Other researchers think that oxidative and nitrosative stress coupled with low antioxidant levels could point to an immune-inflammatory pathology. Oxidative stress is caused by an imbalance between the generation and detoxification of reactive oxygen and nitrogen in cells and tissues. Let's assume this a secondary factor in causing inflammation.

A 2013 study by Whittemore-Peterson Institute researched the possibility of retroviruses staying active in the gut lining (this might be the case with COVID also) transmitting through the gut-brain connection with the gut infection actually leading to inflammation of the brain. (Google: "health rising Cort Johnson 2015" for the full report.) The researchers found positive evidence for this theory, though the study was small. The Whittemore-Peterson Institute is seeking a molecular target that could potentially be used to shut off the retrovirus production and perhaps help resolve gut issues and even autoimmune tendencies and immune activation in CFS/ME. Let's assume that retroviruses staying active in the gut lining is another cause of inflammation.

Also, in 2013, another study by Dr. Michael Maes and reported in NIH (National Library of Medicine) found the possibility that there is an autoimmune reaction to serotonin, as it performs many important roles both in the gut and the brain. In the study, researchers said that 61.5% of the ME study group tested positive for autoimmune activity against serotonin, compared with 13.9% of the healthy control group.

(Google: "NIH Michael Maes serotonin" for further information.) Quite compelling. If you find that your antidepressant is certainly making your symptoms worse, then discuss this possibility with your doctor and perhaps switch from an SSRI to a less serotonin-targeted medication.

What if we assume that any, all or some of these theories are valid and may cause (in various combinations) chronic fatigue through multiple inflammation pathways. As everybody has differing levels of fatigue severity and symptoms then I believe this could be a plausible explanation (or set of explanations). Potentially, the more of these triggers that affect you, the more severe the fatigue and related symptoms.

Okay so we have found a sound, plausible base for defining causes of chronic inflammation/auto immune cycle. We now know what the various triggers to the inflammation are, but why does chronic inflammation lead to unrelenting exhaustion?

MITOCHONDRIA DYSFUNCTION AND THE KREBS CYCLE

Mitochondria are the energy factory of our body's cells. There are thousands of mitochondria in every cell, which are responsible for about 90% of energy that we need to function. When you burn energy, a molecule called adenosine tri-phosphate ATP is used up. The molecule adenosine is attached to three phosphate ions, hence the *tri* part. When you burn even more energy, you use one of the phosphate ions to leave the muscles with adenosine diphosphate ADP (adenosine now with two phosphate ions) and the body replenishes the molecule back to ATP, known as aerobic cell respiration using oxygen. If you lift heavy weights, run, or even walk a little too far, your muscles use up all the ATP available and lactic acid fermentation occurs, creating a sharp pain in the muscle, which slowly subsides. People with ME/CFS may suffer from lasting lactic acid buildup, which doesn't clear as fast as in healthy people (also possibly the cause of fibromyalgia symptoms). The body therefore uses up the one of the two remaining ions to turn ADP into adenosine monophosphate AMP. The problem is your body needs to convert the molecule back to ATP from scratch, which is a very long and slow process. In a Swedish study a group of healthy men exercising had a 25% drop in ATP. After three days of rest their ATP levels were still down by 19%, only a 6% recovery. In ME/CFS patients, the recovery is extremely slow, hence the complete and utter exhaustion and the reason it takes many days to get energy levels back after exercising.

(Further *science bit alert*, so hang in there.)

A research study (by Norman E Boothe et al. at Dept of physics, University of Oxford, 2012) as reported in the International Journal of Clinical and Experimental Medicine, studied 71 CFS patients and 53 healthy controls. Blood sample was taken for the "ATP profile" test, designed for CFS and other fatigue conditions. Each test produced 5 numerical factors which describe the availability of ATP in neutrophils, the fraction complexed with magnesium, the efficiency of oxidative phosphorylation, and the transfer efficiencies of ADP into the mitochondria and ATP into the cytosol where the energy is used. (Google: "Norman E Boothe CFS" for the full study.)

When the factors are combined, a remarkable correlation was observed between the degree of mitochondrial dysfunction and the severity of illness ($P<0.001$). Only 1 of the 71 patients overlaps the normal region. The "ATP profile" test is a powerful diagnostic tool and can differentiate patients who have fatigue and other symptoms as a result of energy wastage by stress and psychological factors from those who have insufficient energy due to cellular respiration dysfunction (ME and potentially COVID patients).

The study also found that there was considerable evidence that mitochondrial dysfunction is present in some ME patients. Muscle biopsies studied by electron microscopy have shown abnormal mitochondrial degeneration. Biopsies have also found severe deletions of genes in mitochondrial DNA (mtDNA), genes that are associated with bioenergy production.

(Okay, I know this bit is dull reading, but please stick with it!)

One consequence of mitochondrial dysfunction is increased production of free radicals which cause oxidative damage. (Please see chapter on glutathione to help reduce oxidative stress). Such oxidative damage and increased activity of antioxidant enzymes has been detected in muscle specimens. Some essential compounds (carnitine and N-acetyl L-carnitine) needed for some metabolic reactions in mitochondria have been measured in serum and found to be decreased in patients with CFS. Both studies found that the carnitine levels correlated with functional capacity.

Reduced oxidative metabolism and higher concentrations of xenobiotics, lactate and pyruvate have been reported. In one group of patients a decrease of intracellular pH after moderate exercise was observed and a lower rate of ATP synthesis during recovery was measured. These findings support what I stated earlier, namely that of impaired recycling of ADP to ATP in the mitochondria. Okay that's enough science thanks, I hear you say. The low down is that a viral/bacterial infection leads to a chronic autoimmune response, leads to chronic inflammation, leads to mitochondria dysfunction and autonomic nervous dysfunction.

PYRUVATE DEHYDROGENASE (PDH)

Do you feel awful after eating too much sugar? Does it lead to fatigue crashes? There have been some studies that suggest that CFS/ME patients are not able burn carbohydrate sugars in the normal way to generate cellular energy and instead use amino acids and fats. Burning these alternative, low yielding fuels produces lactate quickly when energy is expended leading to major crashes after exercising.

A group of researchers at Haukeland University Hospital in Bergan, Norway, led by Oystein Fluge, studied amino acids in 200 ME patients and found that the women in the group had abnormally low amino acid levels. However, they found that both men and women had the same obstruction in carbohydrate metabolism and both sexes had high levels of several enzymes known to suppress pyruvate dehydrogenase (PDH), which is vital for moving carbohydrates and sugars into a cell's mitochondria. (Google: "Fluge PDH CFS" for the abstract.)

So what makes the body switch from burning sugar to other sources?

"We don't think it's just PDH," says Chris Armstrong of the University of Melbourne in Australia, whose research has also uncovered anomalies in amino acid levels in patients. "Broadly, we think it's an issue with sugar metabolism in general. The result is not unlike starvation," says Armstrong. "When people are facing starvation, the body uses amino acids and fatty acids to fuel energy for most cells in the body, to keep glucose levels vital for the brain and muscles as high as possible."

"We think that no single enzyme in metabolism will be the answer to CFS, just as no single enzyme is the 'cause' of something like hibernation," says Robert Naviaux of the University of California at San Diego, who has found depletion of fatty acids in patients suggesting they were diverted as fuel.

Fluge believes that the body's immune system might be the cause of turning off the PDH enzyme initiated by a prior infection.

Okay, so what can we do about our PDH enzymes? We can take L-carnitine supplements. We already know that carnitine levels have been found to be decreased in reactions in the mitochondria, so I researched L-carnitine supplements and their effect on PDH enzymes and, YES! There was a study in 1994 by J Arenas et al. titled "Effects of L-Carnitine on the Pyruvate Dehydrogenase Complex and Carnitine Palmitoyl Transferase Activities in Muscle of Endurance Athletes." The effects of L-carnitine on the PDH complex were studied in the muscles of 16 long distance runners during a 4-week period of training. The athletes that received the L-carnitine showed dramatic increase in the PDH complex activities (compared with placebo). (Google: "PDH J Arenas" for the study abstract.) This could be an important part of the recovery puzzle for all chronic fatigue sufferers. I have discussed L-carnitine supplements in the supplements chapter later in this book.

HEART RATE AND BLOOD PRESSURE VARIABILITY

In a study in 2012 by J. Frith et al. titled "Impaired Blood Pressure Variability in Chronic Fatigue Syndrome—A Potential Biomarker" (Google: "J Frith CFS" for abstract), 68 people with CFS and 68 controls had their heart rates and blood pressure measured continuously for 24 hours. The CFS group showed that their blood pressure variability was significantly lower than control and their heart rate variability (HRV) markers were shown to be significantly higher (HRV is the variation in the time interval between heartbeats). CFS patients also had lower blood pressure overall suggesting an impaired cardiac pump causing reduced output and leading to reduced perfusion of downstream organs (blood pressure flow from the heart). The study also showed a significant increase in sympathetic autonomic nervous system activity (the fight-or-flight part of the nervous system discussed in detail later in this book and calming the sympathetic nervous system is a very important part of recovery).

The results of this study allow of doctors to use objective abnormalities of blood pressure variability as a potential diagnostic tool. If you are still unsure whether you may have ME, then ask your doctor to review this study and test you for blood pressure variability.

INFLAMMATION OF THE BRAIN

One of the more prominent researchers in the ME field is Dr. Jarred Younger of the University of Alabama at Birmingham, who has used the latest, most advanced brain imaging technology to study ME patients. The ongoing research has already produced results that have found widespread metabolic abnormalities by using whole brain magnetic resonance spectroscopy on ME patients. His research has revealed:

- ME patients had an elevation of choline in a particular part of the brain (anterior cingulate on the left side, responsible for emotions and mood regulation). Choline is an essential nutrient to help create acetylcholine, which is a neurotransmitter that regulates memory, mood and intelligence. However, an increase in choline is associated with immune cell activation that creates cytokine induced fatigue.

- Lactate was also found to be elevated in many various parts of the brain. Lactate is a byproduct of glycolysis in an oxygen limited environment and causes an energy deficit at the cellular level. Lactate in the brain causes inflammation through increased metabolism.

- Higher than average temperatures were found in several areas of the brain caused by inflammation and not differences in blood flow. The increased immune cell activation increases metabolic demand that overpower the cooling effect of circulating blood. If you find that you have a hot head most of the time and frequent headaches, then this may be why.

I have extolled the benefits of buying an ice cap to cool down your head in this book. It is simply a hat or cap that has several small ice packs that insert into little pockets inside the cap. You wear it when you feel your head is hot or you have a headache. This is a short term hack but can work for some people to relieve pain and useful for those who do not want to consume too many pain killers. They are available on Amazon.

Google: "Jarred Younger CFS" to find out more about his research.

AMYGDALA AND FEAR CONDITIONING

The amygdala is the part of the brain that controls our levels of anxiety and fear in reaction to external responses. A doctor named Ashok Gupta has devised a hypothesis based on the possibility that a traumatic event combined with a viral infection leads to the amygdala becoming chronically sensitized to negative symptoms. The symptoms then cause an unconscious negative reaction initiating auto immune reactivation and stimulation of the sympathetic nervous system.

I have written a chapter (chapter7) on the sympathetic nervous system and the vagus nerve, as they are an extremely important part of the puzzle in curing chronic fatigue. As if chronic fatigue is the main debilitating symptom of long COVID (which it appears to be), then stimulating the vagus nerve may be a very important part of long COVID recovery.

Dr. Gupta has devised a CBT (cognitive behavioral therapy) program that is devised to help calm the amygdala and reduce the symptoms of fatigue called "The Amygdala Retraining Program." He credits his own recovery from CFS to amygdala retraining which he calls mind-body medicine derived from neurolinguistic programming (NLP).

If you would like to learn more, go to guptaprogram.com.

CRFR2 (CORTICOTROPHIN RELEASING FACTOR RECEPTOR 2)

'Oh no more science stuff, please stop'. I understand, but having even some basic understanding of the science is likely to help increase your motivation to take on board the advice offered, which may lead to a faster recovery of your symptoms.

A biotech company called Cortene Inc is developing a drug called CT38 for CFS and long COVID patients and has initial success in their Phase 1/2 study. The drug targets two receptors, CRFR1 and CRFR2 neural pathways in the limbic system (part of the brain involved in behavioral and emotional responses, you know the part of the brain that makes you want to scream at academics for making things stupidly complicated).

They believe that chronic fatigue is caused by prolonged stress in which the two receptors (CRFR1 and CRFR2) switch place and cause a constant heightened stress response from the metabolic, autonomic and endocrine systems.

Couple of things to note here. First their assertion about the switching of these receptors is debatable. I cannot find independent research that this is the case, which makes their potential drug a long shot, based on a specific assertion. However, if this drug genuinely reduces or eliminates fatigue, then the mechanisms or targets may be academic if the drug actually works and help patients recover.

I have discussed their drug further in the supplement and medication chapter later in this book. In the meantime, you might want to Google "Cortene Inc" to get an update with regard to the development of this drug.

CHAPTER SUMMARY

- Chronic fatigue lingers because of a variety of factors that cause chronic inflammation. Two types of cytokines have been found to be elevated in those with CFS that cause inflammation.
- Oxidative and nitrosative stress coupled with low antioxidant levels also leads to an immune-inflammatory pathology. Coupled with the possibility of retroviruses staying active in the gut lining leading to further inflammation of the brain through the gut-brain connection.
- Another study showed that CFS patients had an autoimmune response to serotonin also increasing inflammation in the brain.
- Mitochondria dysfunction leads to disabling fatigue and post exertion malaise as patients can't make ATP fast enough coupled with lactic acid build up that clears very slowly.
- Pyruvate Dehydrogenase suppression leads to sugar been metabolized incorrectly and not allowing sugar to enter a cell's mitochondria. The body uses amino and fatty acids as energy instead of glucose, which is reserved for more vital uses, such as brain functioning. Take L Carnitine supplements to increase PDH complex activity.

PART 2

THE PLAN FOR BEATING CHRONIC FATIGUE

"One day...or day one. Decide."

Anon.

Chapter 4

Conquer Depression First

"It's never too late to be what you might've been."

George Eliot

Okay, we know doctors really love to dish out antidepressants; however, depression is a consequence of chronic fatigue and not a cause. To all the primary care doctors in the world: You cannot cure chronic fatigue with antidepressants.

That said, it is extremely difficult to cure chronic fatigue while depressed. At least, not without an iron will and the patience of a saint. Therefore, if you are depressed, the first stage of recovery is to take your doctor's advice on the best antidepressant for you. If your depression is mild and don't want to take on the risk of pharmaceuticals, there are natural ways to beat depression as described in this chapter. An increased uptake in serotonin is vital if you are to start to get better as you will need both positivity and motivation before you even start. Untreated depression leads to alcohol abuse, drug abuse, poor eating habits, and poor dress sense, making recovery from any ailment almost impossible. If you are not depressed, then woo-hoo! Feel free to skip this chapter.

SUICIDE

If you are suicidal do this right now. Call the National Suicide Prevention Lifeline at 800-273-8255 and just talk to someone. If you do not live in the United States, please search the web for "suicide hotline" to get the number. It may not feel like it now, but life is worth living no matter how desperate your situation may feel. Remember, your feelings always change over time periods. Today's absolute despair is tomorrow's average day, which is next week's awesome day.

Just go outside and look at the sky. Feel the sun on your skin or the breeze on your face. Take a deep breath and KNOW that tomorrow is a new day and you WILL feel different. Make sure you find a therapist, psychiatrist or both. You may find that they can help you immeasurably.

So take a deep breath and read on, this book may change your life forever. Even if it doesn't, you will have increased your knowledge and hopefully have a few laughs along the way.

If you are not a sufferer of long COVID or other fatigue afflictions and you know someone who may be suicidal, then please take action. Do something, anything. Check on them several times a day, get them outside, make them do things! And ensure they get proper treatment. Sit with them and watch the movie *Airplane*, its' difficult not to laugh at that one! Or *Spaceballs*—err, actually no, that one was awful.

Many studies have shown that people who hint at suicide are not seeking attention and should be taken very seriously. *The Lancet* publication reported on a study on suicide in ME/CFS patients:

The findings for suicide deaths were striking—five people died during the 7-year period. Based on the suicide rate in the general population of England and Wales, the expected number would have been less than one death by suicide. In other words, suicide risk was increased 7-fold.

That's a 700% increase in suicide for those who suffer from chronic fatigue. While this was a small study, other studies reflect that the 700% number is repeated.

GO AHEAD, CHOOSE YOUR ANTIDEPRESSANT (Doctor assisted)

There are several types of antidepressants: The ever-popular selective serotonin reuptake inhibitors (SSRIs) such as Zoloft, Prozac, Lexapro and Celexa. The almost as popular serotonin-noradrenaline re-uptake inhibitors (SNRI's) such as Cymbalta, Pristiq and Effexor, noradrenaline and specific serotonergic antidepressants (NASSAs), such as Aptazapine and Mirtazapine. The good ole original tricyclic antidepressants (TCAs) such as Elavil and Norpramin (which have more side effects and largely superseded by SSRIs, but may be quite useful for sleep), and not forgetting the often forgotten but spunky Monoamine oxidase inhibitors (MAOIs) such as Nardil and Emsam (careful, they can interact with some foods).

Don't forget the rowdy, stand out from the crowd antidepressants called atypical antidepressants, which do not fit neatly into the above classifications and can affect three neurotransmitters at once, serotonin, dopamine and norepinephrine such as Wellbutrin, Remeron and Serzone.

Don't let your doctor just hand you Prozac and walk out. Discuss the type of depression you're feeling (anxious, sad, high/low, angry, irritable, suicidal, or any combination thereof) and maybe you can get an antidepressant that may be more tailored for you. Incidentally, if you are suffering from anxiety only, antidepressants may not work for you as they don't target the neurotransmitter gamma aminobutyric acid (GABA), which is an inhibitory neurotransmitter because it blocks or inhibits certain brain signals and decreases activity in the nervous system and thus regulates anxiety. Part of the problem with the rise in anxiety in society is that we don't get naturally occurring GABA from our food, which is generally only available in kimchi, tempeh, and miso. You may have to take GABA supplements for this.

Make sure you discuss with your doctor when you can stop taking antidepressants and always taper off! Never stop cold turkey; it will make you feel just awful and may compound mental health problems.

SUPPLEMENTS FOR DEPRESSION

St. John's wort. No, it's not giant zit on a posh Brit, it's a flowering plant in the Hypericaceae family and the type of species of the genus *Hypericum,* and I'm sure you've always wanted to know that. There is some anecdotal evidence that it relieves depression in some people. According to the National Center for Complementary and Integrative Health,

St. John's wort appears to be more effective than a placebo (an inactive substance) and as effective as standard antidepressant medications for mild and moderate depression. It's uncertain whether this is true for severe depression and for time periods longer than 12 weeks.

There's not enough reliable evidence to know whether St. John's wort might be beneficial for quitting smoking or improving memory or for many conditions, including anxiety, ADHD, and seasonal affective disorder. However, it has been clearly shown that St. John's wort can interact in dangerous, sometimes life-threatening ways with a variety of medicines.

If you do your own research and decide to take this supplement, do not under any circumstances take it with an antidepressant. The combination can lead to dangerous levels of serotonin, known as a serotonin syndrome. In fact, if you do decide to take it, make sure you are not already on any prescribed medication and talk to your doctor first.

SAM-e (S-ADENOSYL-METHIONINE)

Like most other supplements, evidence of efficacy is anecdotal. It appears to work very well in some people and not at all in others. It does appear to have other positive effects, such as a pain killer that is kinder on the body than ibuprofen and NSAIDS, though it does not work quite as quickly. Side effects are not as potentially as serious as St John's wort, but include gastrointestinal issues, dry mouth, headache, and in high doses may cause anxiousness.

5-HTP (HYDROXYTRYPTOPHAN)

5-HTP is produced in the body from the amino acid tryptophan and is a precursor to serotonin and melatonin (the sleep hormone). The supplement 5-HTP is made from the seeds of a plant. In a few small clinical trials, 5-HTP was found to be as effective as prescription antidepressants with the benefit of having fewer side effects. As it also creates an uptick in melatonin production and may assist in abating insomnia. There is some evidence that it reduces the frequency and intensity of migraines and headaches as well. Furthermore, in a double-blind study reported in Journal of International Medical Research, 5-HTP can help reduce the symptoms of fibromyalgia.

If you have mild depression and do not want to take prescription antidepressants, then 5-HTP may be an interesting place to start. Side effects are reported to be minimal, with some people complaining of nausea, dizziness, and diarrhea.

GABA

Gamma-aminobutyric acid (GABA) is an amino acid in the body that acts as a neurotransmitter in the central nervous system. GABA limits nerve transmission, which inhibits nervous activity and is the neurotransmitter responsible for calming your nerves.

With low levels of GABA, nerve cells are activated more frequently, making mental illnesses worse, such as social anxiety disorder (SAD) and depression. Low GABA activity has been shown to cause more severe symptoms, while normal levels of GABA may help calm symptoms and make them more manageable for you in your everyday life. GABA supplements are widely available, but again, quality is important.

MAGNESIUM

The potential of magnesium to reduce depression has been confirmed by the results of numerous clinical studies. It would appear that magnesium supplementation works well in addition to and supporting conventional antidepressant treatments. It is quite clear that magnesium is an underrated mineral that, in addition to helping reduce depression and anxiety, is vital to help keep inflammation in check. It also helps keep bones strong, the heart in a regular rhythm, and blood pressure within normal range. Need any more reasons to take this supplement? (Yes? Then please see chapter 17 regarding supplements for further information on magnesium.)

FOLIC ACID AND VITAMIN B12

Folic acid is a synthesized form of vitamin B9. Low folate levels (folate is naturally occurring B9) have been found in studies of people suffering with depression. Low folate levels are furthermore linked to a poor response to antidepressants, and increased consumption with folic acid supplements has shown to improve response.

A recent study also suggests that high vitamin B12 levels may be associated with better antidepressant treatment outcome. Folate and vitamin B12 are major determinants of one-carbon metabolism, in which S-adenosyl-methionine (SAM-e) is formed (as discussed above), which is crucial for neurological function. High levels of homocysteine (amino acid found in plasma) is a marker of both folate and vitamin B12 deficiency. Increased homocysteine levels are found in depressive patients. In a large population study from Norway, increased plasma homocysteine was associated with increased risk of depression but not anxiety.

Some doctors are not keen on recommending different types of supplements for a wide variety of reasons. Some are not trained in how supplements work, they are reticent to recommend a substance that has not gone through the pharmaceutical FDA channels and it's just not the doctor thing to do. There is also the litigation issue that is unique to doctors in the United States, which forces them to err on the side of caution. It is true that not all supplements are created equal. Some can have major side effects, and the quality between brands varies wildly. It is very important to do your own research on the best brands with the purest ingredients and naturally, the more expensive, the better the quality, generally speaking.

If you tell a doctor that you're taking ten or more supplements every day, this is a probable exchange:

"Did you say you take ten different supplements every day?"

"Yes, Doc, that's what I said!"

"Honestly, Patient X, I don't think that is entirely safe, and I can't recommend you keep taking that many."

"It's sexy X if you please, Doc."

"I do not."

"The supplements are vital to my recovery and are much safer than the hardcore antidepressants, acid reducers and sleeping tablets you've prescribed to me over the last two months."

"But the cross indications of that many supplements must be causing you some gastrointestinal problems?"

"Not really, no. Actually, I was going to ask you about a new workout energy booster with a mass combination of chemicals I was going to take when I get home today. The ingredients are: reduced iron, niacin, thiamine mononitrate, riboflavin, folic acid, corn syrup, sugar, high fructose corn syrup, animal shortening, soybean oil, cottonseed oil, canola oil, beef fat, whole eggs, dextrose, modified corn starch, glucose, sodium acid pyrophosphate, baking soda, monocalcium phosphate, sweet dairy whey, soy protein isolate, calcium and sodium caseinate, salt, mono and diglycerides, polysorbate 60, soy lecithin, soy flour, cornstarch, cellulose gum, sodium stearoyl lactylate, sorbic acid, yellow 5, red 40. I hear good things about this combination of chemicals, and I need a short-term energy booster occasionally. What do you think, Doc?"

"You probably shouldn't take all that stuff in one go; that's 35 or more ingredients in one supplement, and I've never even heard of polysorbate 60 or sodium acid pyrophosphate. It sounds dangerous."

"But you've already consumed these chemicals yourself earlier today."

"No, I haven't! That's ridiculous!"

"They're the ingredients of a Twinkie. I see the empty wrapper sitting on top of your trash bin. So, before you lecture me about consuming a variety vital body- and brain-nourishing nutrients that I can't get from our wonderful food supply, you should take a long hard look at what you're putting in your own body, Doc!"

"Mmm. I see you're making quite a good point here. Now get lost and never darken my door stoop again, Patient X."

"It's sexy X."

"GO!"

PSYCHEDELIC DRUGS

LSD (lysergic acid diethylamide) and magic mushrooms have been a main staple of the hippy drug culture for decades and have been outlawed as class A narcotics, illegal in all states (with the exception of Oakland, California, and Denver, Colorado) and in most countries around the world.

Recently, there have been a number of clinical studies showing potential of hallucinogenic drugs rapidly reversing depression and resetting the misfiring brain.

In 2019, the FDA approved the very first mind-altering drug called esketamine (brand name Spravato from Johnson and Johnson subsidiary Janssen) after the studies demonstrated that it could completely abate severe depression even in people resilient to traditional antidepressant treatments. This medication is a form of ketamine, which is currently available in many clinics throughout the country (see below). In trials, treatment-resistant depression was diagnosed in adults who were struggling with major depressive disorder and had not responded adequately to at least two different antidepressants of adequate dose and duration in the current episode. The drug is administered by a nasal spray along with an oral antidepressant under the supervision of a healthcare provider at a certified treatment center. The drug is self-administered twice a week for 4 weeks, then taken once a week for a month. After this, it is then taken either once a week or once every 2 weeks. You can find your nearest treatment center by visiting www.spravato.com. A very interesting and promising treatment.

The psychoactive drug found in magic mushrooms is called psilocybin and is now in multiple clinical trials by several biotech companies throughout the world. Both Compass Pathways (based in London) and nonprofit Usona Institute (based in Wisconsin) are in late-stage trials. Compass has just released the results of their phase IIb trial with 233 patients taking COMP360 psilocybin therapy. The study group was split into three, and given 1 mg, 10 mg, and 25 mg. The 25 mg showed statistical significance in response and remission of treatment-resistant depression. The purpose of the study was to identify which dose was most appropriate for their phase III study. This was the largest study of its kind and provides hope for those with treatment resistant depression. Usona should be providing trial study results imminently.

Imperial College, London, has a Center for Psychedelic Research and is currently examining how psilocybin's effectiveness for treating depression compares with that of Lexapro. In 2017 the researchers at the college found that half the patients with severe treatment-resistant depression who were given psilocybin showed improvement after only three weeks and for many the effects lasted up to a full year. Psilocybin appears to affect the amygdala (the part of the brain regulates fear and anxiousness) by reducing electrical activity while increasing interaction between neural circuits that had been slowed by depression. By the time you read this book, the results should have been made public, so go ahead and look these companies up on the web.

Other biotech companies developing psilocybin for depression but in early stages include Cybin Inc (cybin.com) and Atai Life Sciences (atai.life).

KETAMINE TREATMENT

Ketamine is a tried and tested anesthetic that has psychoactive properties and induces a trancelike state in lower doses. There are many clinics throughout the United States that provide ketamine treatment under controlled conditions for treatment-resistant depression. Also, there is a chain of clinics in the United States (and Europe) run by Field Trip Health (fieldtriphealth.com) that offer ketamine psychedelic-assisted therapy for depression.

I have discussed ketamine as a potential remedy for fatigue in chapter 15, "Other Innovative Remedies." I have undergone this therapy myself and found it to be an incredible medication to help reset the brain. (Google: "Ketamine treatment near me" if you would like to find out more.)

Other types of psychedelic drugs, including MDMA (ecstasy), DMT, and its chemically different sibling 5-MeO-DMT (found in the venom of Sonoran Desert toads), are being studied by different research institutions.

You may have heard of the curious case of the 49-year-old woman who massively overdosed on LSD, believing it to be cocaine. In September 2015 she took 55 milligrams (the typical dose is around 0.1 mg) 550 times the standard dosage. Instead of dying of an overdose, the woman blacked out and vomited frequently but reported to have felt pleasantly high over the next 24 hours. She had previously suffered from Lyme disease, which had left her ankles and feet in significant pain. After the overdose she said that the pain had gone the next day. The pain did come back, but she controlled it with micro-doses of LSD.

Driving, operating machinery, or walking on balcony ledges has inevitably led to some deaths under the influence of hallucinating after taking LSD. However, while LSD has been somewhat feared as dangerous drug by governments around the world, there has never been a single death attributed to an overdose, making it by far the least deadly illegal drug in the world and far safer than alcohol from a mortality standpoint!

There is a biotech company called MindMed Inc that is developing drugs based on LSD (mindmed.co), check their website for development updates.

Needless to say, research into the medical uses of psychedelic drugs is very exciting and hopefully will offer significant increase in the options for treating depression in the near future.

DIET, DEPRESSION AND INFLAMMATION

It's no secret that diets high in processed foods, sugar, trans fats, and carbohydrates can increase anxiety and depression. That's unfortunate because the Western diet is based on these substances.

A number of related studies as reported by the *International Journal of Environmental Research and Public Health* published in March 2020 revealed that high adherence by study subjects to healthy dietary recommendations showed a significant protective effect against depression, depressive symptoms and inflammation. The extract below is enlightening:

In one study high adherence to healthy dietary advice was associated with a significantly reduced risk of developing depressive symptoms in first-time mothers in Australia and in a similar study, a lower risk of depressive symptoms in adults in France. High intake of fruits, vegetables, fiber, and low intake of trans fats were in the same study associated with a lower risk of recurrence in depression.

An analysis of dietary points based on AHEI (alternative healthy eating index - created by Harvard professor in response to the governments HEI - healthy eating index, which turns out wasn't particularly healthy) revealed a dose-response relationship that was significant for women. The women who improved their AHEI scores over 10 years had a 65% lower risk of recurrent depressive symptoms compared to the women who continued to have low AHEI scores.

Chronic Fatigue Gone!

In a study from Finland, a healthy diet with a higher proportion of vegetables, fruit, chicken, fish, whole grain products, legumes, berries, and low-fat cheese was compared to a typical Western diet. A significant protective effect was found with a higher degree of adherence to a healthy dietary pattern. The protective effect was measured at a 25% reduced risk of suffering from depressive symptoms.

Several studies showed an association between dietary intake with inflammatory potential and risk of depression in different populations. Products associated with less of an impact on systemic inflammation have been found to be vegetables, whole grains, olive oil, and fish. Products such as sweets, refined flour, high-fat products, red and processed meat were associated with a greater impact on systemic inflammation.

The results showed that a pro-inflammatory diet was associated with a significant increased risk of depression in the subgroup of women, middle-aged adults and overweight and obese people.

In another study, the inflammatory potential of the diet was investigated in teenage girls, and the results showed a significant increase in stress levels in teenage girls when the diet consisted of a high proportion of pro-inflammatory food, namely overloading on glucose-based foods, including sweets, soda and candy. Meta-analysis demonstrated that avoiding a pro-inflammatory diet was associated with a lower risk of depression, supporting the results of the present study.

The available research on the relationship between inflammation, intestinal flora, and mental illness showed that probiotics (intake of good bacteria) and prebiotics (food for the good bacteria) lead to improved intestinal health, which can reduce inflammation and thus result in fewer symptoms of mental illness. Foods with a pro-inflammatory effect should be avoided for preventive purposes before and in case of mental illness.

The intake of micronutrients showed a protective effect against depressive symptoms. Higher intake of magnesium, folic acid, B6, and

B12 through the diet had protective effects against mental symptoms in different populations. The diet's content of fatty acids was important for mental illnesses due to increased inflammation, different fatty acids increased, or decreased the risk of depression. These findings in our study are supported by studies in older people where significant associations were found between low levels of folate and B12 in serum and increased risk of depression in both sexes and a high dietary intake of B6 and B12 showed significant protective effect for the development of depression. Furthermore, a low intake of magnesium in the diet has also been associated with increased risk of depression in populations of younger and older persons in other studies.

The evidence is absolutely overwhelming: eat healthy to reduce inflammation and depression. Recovering from chronic fatigue is almost impossible without a major dietary change away from the sugar, *trans* fat and processed foods that we have all become accustomed to. Later in this book, I discuss exactly how you can achieve a long-lasting dietary change that will transform your life. First, however, you should try to incorporate some feel good foods into your diet immediately.

FEEL GOOD FOODS

There are a variety of foods that are purported to reduce depression. As most healthy foods have no side effects (apart from potential allergens in some people), then you might want to try these first, especially if your depression is relatively mild. Of course, see your doctor first. According to *Medical News Today*, a UK-based health news media outlet and an excellent online resource (medicalnewstoday.com) there are nine foods you may want to consider to help reduce anxiety and depression.

BRAZIL NUTS

Brazil nuts are high in selenium. Selenium may improve mood by reducing inflammation. Selenium is also an antioxidant, which helps prevent cell damage. It is also anti-carcinogenic, which helps to prevent cancer from developing. Other nuts, animal products, and vegetables, such as mushrooms and soybeans, are an excellent source of selenium.

It is important not to consume too much selenium as it can cause side effects. The recommended upper limit for selenium for an adult is 400 micrograms (mcg) per day. So be careful not to take supplements with high doses or eat more than a three to four Brazil nuts a day.

Brazil nuts and other nuts are also a good source of vitamin E. Vitamin E is an antioxidant. Antioxidants can be beneficial for treating anxiety, while some research has shown that low levels of vitamin E may lead to depression in some people.

However, I understand that Brazil nuts can be an acquired taste for some people, so chop them finely (in a blender) and add to a salad, smoothie, granola, oatmeal etc, you won't notice you're eating them and you'll still enjoy the benefits.

FATTY FISH

Fatty fish, such as salmon, mackerel, sardines, trout, and herring, are high in omega-3. Omega-3 is a fatty acid that has a strong relationship with cognitive function as well as mental health. I would caution against eating too much ocean caught fish as the levels of mercury poisoning and other toxins are rising, this is a rare instance where the supplement might be better than eating the actual food. If you love fish, however, Dr. Tim Harlan, internist and editor of "Dr. Gourmet," says this:

The rule of thumb for seafood is to mix it up. Eat it 2 to 3 times per week, but don't eat the same type more than 2 to 3 times per month. With the wide variety of choices, you could eat a different type of seafood—shrimp, crab, salmon, scallops, cod, trout, mussels, catfish, tuna, halibut—and not have to repeat the same seafood choice twice in a month.

However, recent research has shown that if a person eats too much of another fatty acid, called omega-6, and not enough omega-3, they may increase their risk of developing mood disorders, such as anxiety. Everybody, regardless of age or health status, should take omega-3 fish oil supplements not just to balance out your omega-6 intake, but to enjoy the following benefits: lower blood pressure, reduced triglycerides, reduced likelihood of heart attack or stroke, slow the development of plaque in the arteries and reduce the likelihood of heart disease, the number one killer in the Western world. Seriously, you should be taking this supplement. Make sure to buy a high-quality clean omega-3 fish oil that is unlikely to have significant levels of mercury.

Science bit alert!

Omega-3-rich foods that contain alpha-linolenic acid (ALA) provides two essential fatty acids: eicosapentaenoic acid (EPA), and docosahexaenoic acid (DHA). EPA and DHA regulate neurotransmitters, reduce inflammation, and promote healthy brain function.

A small study on 24 people with substance abuse problems found that EPA and DHA supplementation resulted in reduced levels of anxiety. However, more research is required. Current recommendations suggest eating at least two servings of fatty fish a week. A study conducted on men found eating salmon three times a week reduced self-reported anxiety. Salmon and sardines are also among the few foods that contain vitamin D.

Researchers are increasingly linking vitamin D deficiency to mood disorders, such as depression and anxiety. A report in the *Journal of Affective Disorders* states that there is enough evidence to prove that vitamin D positively helps depression. Other studies on pregnant women and older adults have also highlighted how vitamin D might improve mood. Vitamin D may also improve seasonal disaffected disorder (SAD) during winter. Vitamin D is the most important of all vitamins (it's actually a hormone) and I have written an entire chapter later in this book, which you must not skip!

EGGS (and why the internet can be quite useless)

If you do a web search "Are eggs good for you?" You will find thousands of positive articles, blogs, books and videos all extolling the virtues of eggs. if you do a web search "Are eggs bad for you?" You will find thousands of the polar opposite opinions. That's why the internet is can be a confusing nightmare of misinformation.

You have probably heard that eggs are bad for you because they raise LDL cholesterol levels, but the truth is more complex. Cholesterol is present in all of our cells and is a vital building block in creating healthy cell membranes. Cholesterol moves around the body via lipoprotein molecules in the blood. Lipoproteins come in a variety type that are different in every person and determine the actual level in risk for developing heart disease. While it was previously agreed that cholesterol could build-up over time in the blood vessels and increase the risk of cardiovascular disease, studies have not shown a definitive link. Unlike saturated fats, which many studies have shown a definitive link. Eggs (along with prawns) are the only food that is high in cholesterol but low in saturated fats and its actually saturated fats that increase blood cholesterol.

"This has been demonstrated by lots of studies for many years," says Maria Luz Fernandez, professor of nutritional sciences at the University of Connecticut, whose latest research found no relationship between eating eggs and an increased risk of cardiovascular disease.

The discussion on the effects of eggs has changed because we now know that our bodies can compensate for the cholesterol we consume.

"There are systems in place so that, for most people, dietary cholesterol isn't a problem," says Elizabeth Johnson, research associate professor of nutritional sciences at Tufts University in Boston.

In a 2015 review of 40 studies, Johnson and a team of researchers couldn't find any conclusive evidence on the relationship between dietary cholesterol and heart disease.

"Humans have good regulation when consuming dietary cholesterol, and will make less cholesterol themselves,"

Furthermore, eggs can help the body absorb nutrients from other foods more easily and help make testosterone, estrogen and vitamin D.

With regards to depression, eggs also contain tryptophan, which is an amino acid that helps create serotonin. As you are aware, serotonin is a chemical neurotransmitter that helps to regulate mood, sleep, memory, and behavior. Serotonin is also thought to improve brain function and relieve anxiety. If I say so myself, that was an eggsellent explanation (but a terrible yolk).

PUMPKIN SEEDS

Pumpkin Seeds are an excellent source of potassium, which helps regulate electrolyte balance and manage blood pressure. Eating potassium-rich foods such, as pumpkin seeds, may help reduce symptoms of stress and anxiety.

Pumpkin seeds are also a good source of the mineral zinc. One study carried out on 100 female high school students found that zinc deficiency may negatively affect mood.

Zinc is essential for brain and nerve development. The largest storage sites of zinc in the body are in the brain regions involved with emotions.

DARK CHOCOLATE

Experts have long suspected that dark chocolate might help reduce stress and anxiety. A 2014 study found that 40g of dark chocolate helped reduce perceived stress in female students. Other studies have generally found that dark chocolate or cocoa may improve mood. However, many of these studies are observational, so the results need to be interpreted with caution.

Although it is still unclear how dark chocolate reduces stress, it is a rich source of polyphenols, especially flavonoids. One study suggested that flavonoids might reduce neuro-inflammation and cell death in the brain as well as improve blood flow. Chocolate has a high tryptophan content, which the body uses to turn into mood-enhancing neurotransmitters, such as serotonin in the brain.

Dark chocolate is also a good source of magnesium. Eating a diet with enough magnesium in it or taking supplements may reduce symptoms of depression. When choosing dark chocolate, aim for 70% or more. Dark chocolate still contains added sugars and fats, so a small serving of 1 to 3 grams (g) is appropriate.

TURMERIC

Turmeric is a spice commonly used in Indian and South-East Asian cooking. The active ingredient in turmeric is called curcumin. Curcumin may help lower anxiety by reducing inflammation and oxidative stress that often increase in people experiencing mood disorders, such as anxiety and depression. A 2015 study found that curcumin reduced anxiety in obese adults.

Another study found that an increase of curcumin in the diet also increased DHA and reduced anxiety. Turmeric is easy to add to meals. It has minimal flavor, so goes well in smoothies, curries, and casserole dishes. However, don't do what I did (true story). I bought a large bag of turmeric on Amazon, as it was a cheap way to purchase it. I put two tablespoons in warm water and knocked it back, convinced it would cure some mild arthritis in my hand. Big mistake! Two hours of vomiting later, I had learnt my lesson. Less is more when adding turmeric to anything.

CHAMOMILE TEA

Many people around the world use chamomile tea as an herbal remedy because of its anti-inflammatory, antibacterial, antioxidant, and relaxant properties. Some people believe that the relaxant and anti-anxiety properties come from the flavonoids present in chamomile. A recent study found that chamomile did reduce anxiety symptoms. However, it did not prevent new episodes of anxiety. Chamomile tea may be useful in managing anxiety and is an excellent before bedtime drink.

YOGURT

Yogurt contains healthful bacteria, Lactobaccilus and Bifidobacteria. There is emerging evidence that these bacteria and fermented products have positive effects on brain health.

A 2015 study found fermented foods reduced social anxiety in some young people, while multiple studies found consuming healthful bacteria increased happiness in some people.

Including yogurt and other fermented foods in the diet can benefit the natural gut bacteria and may reduce anxiety and stress. So, eat plain natural yogurt and add sliced banana and your favorite berries. Stay away from granolas, as they are usually loaded with sugar.

Of course, avoid yogurts with sugar, artificial flavorings and color as these will have the exact opposite effect.

Other fermented foods include cheese, sauerkraut, kimchi, kefir and fermented soy products. Furthermore, I drink a bottle of Kombucha every day and I believe it has helped reduce the number of colds I get.

GREEN TEA

Green tea contains an amino acid called theanine, which is receiving increasing scrutiny due to its potential effects on mood disorders. Theanine has anti-anxiety and calming effects and may increase the production of serotonin and dopamine.

A 2017 review found that 200 mg of theanine improved self-reported relaxation and calmness while reducing tension in human trials. Green tea is easy to add to the day-to-day diet. It is an excellent replacement for soft drinks, coffee, and alcoholic beverages.

OTHER WAYS TO REDUCE DEPRESSION

Immerse yourself in humor. Watch funny movies and TV shows and read comedy books. Do not watch the news! I stopped watching all news sources recently and it has helped me become a happier, more balanced person. If something is really important, it will reach my ears somehow. News is almost always negative; the networks know that negativity hits the amygdala part of the brain that controls fear and they know fear trumps other emotions and is instantly reactive. This automatic response from the amygdala keeps viewers tuned in and the ratings high, which keeps their sponsors happy. Don't be an unwitting pawn in the media's fear mongering game, you're smarter than that!

Fear and anger use a lot more energy than calm and happiness, so why waste precious energy this way? Stay away from discussing politics and religion with friends and family and never, ever watch a horror movie. The jump scares alone can fire up the sympathetic nervous system and increase anxiety and depression. It sounds obvious, but don't watch depressing or sad movies, they're not going to help you.

Yeah, Yeah, I hear you say. Laughing doesn't do much for me! Oh really? The following is an abstract from a controlled study undertaken in Korea by The Korean Oncology Nursing Society on Breast Cancer patients.

The purpose of this study was to investigate laughter therapy on depression, anxiety, and stress among patients who underwent radiotherapy. Methods: Participants in the study were comprised of 60 breast cancer outpatients who received radiotherapy. Thirty-one of the patients were assigned in the experimental group and the other 29 patients made up the control group. Laughter therapy was consisted of the delivery of information and active motion resulting in laughter. We provided laughter therapy 4 times for 2 weeks. Each session lasted 60 min. Results: There was significant decrease in the degrees of depression, anxiety, and stress in the experimental group compared to those in the control group ($p<.01$, $p=.04$, and $p<.01$, respectively).

Conclusion: This study provides evidence that laughter therapy is an effective intervention in improving depression, anxiety, and stress in breast cancer patients.

(Any number below $p < .05$ reflects a statistical significance). So whose laughing now?

THERAPY OR COUNSELING

If you are depressed, go see a therapist. Not only will discussing your issues and problems with someone not involved in your life can be extremely cathartic, their knowledge and advice could help you immeasurably.

If you are depressed due to a singular or multiple traumatic events, then there are therapies that can really help. Post-traumatic stress disorder (PTSD) may be a trigger for chronic fatigue and apart from the potential remedies discussed above, a therapist is vital for recovery. If you have suffered a trauma, then ask your therapist if they (or a colleague) can perform eye movement desensitization and reprocessing therapy (EMDR) on you.

EMDR THERAPY

EMDR therapy is a therapy used to help beat the negative effects of a traumatic episode (or episodes) and PTSD (post-traumatic stress disorder).

EMDR therapy starts by using eye movements to track a therapist's hand as it moves back and forth while simultaneously thinking about the memory. It is thought that the eye movement replicates the rapid eye movement found in REM sleep, which allows transformation of the painful event to be digested and processed on an emotional level, thus releasing the pain and anxiety related to the memory. The result is that the patient feels empowered by the event rather than traumatized by it. There are eight phases of the therapy.

Phase 1 - The therapist helps find specific memories to target and assesses if the patient is ready for the therapy. The therapist will help develop specific behaviors that might be needed in future situations. The therapist will assess the possible duration of treatment based on the number of traumas experienced. A single trauma can be successfully treated in under 5 hours.

Phase 2 - The therapist will teach the patient how to effective handle emotional distress, including imagery and stress reduction techniques.

Phase 3 to 6 - The client is asked to identify visual images related to the memory, a negative belief about themselves and related emotions and body sensations. Then the client identifies a positive belief as well as the intensity of the negative emotions, while the therapist simultaneously starts the EMDR therapy, which may include eye movement tracking, taps or sounds. After each type of stimulation, the therapist tells the client to notice whatever sensation comes to mind. If the client feels too much distress, the therapist follows protocol and restarts the EMDR until the client is calm and is ready to proceed to the next step. The client is then asked to think of a positive belief and then focus on that during the next session if he or she feels distressed.

Phase 7 - Between sessions, the therapist requests that the patient write down their emotions and feelings related to the trauma to help track efficacy of the treatment. The patient is encouraged to use the calming techniques learnt in response to their emotional responses.

Phase 8 - To ensure closure of the trauma, the therapist assesses progress and provides a plan for reacting to future events that may trigger regressive thoughts, emotions or behavior.

Reliving traumatic events can be exhausting and will contribute significantly to ME/CFS. Be brave, get help and work through your emotional problems. It may be painful or difficult at first but getting these issues out of the way and into the rear view mirror will help you on your road to recovery.

REMOVE NEGATIVE RELATIONSHIPS FROM YOUR LIFE

If you have friends or family members in your life that drain your energy for one reason or another, then you have two choices. If you genuinely care for that person and want to keep them in your life, then you need to sit down with them and have an honest discussion. You need to tell them that you are starting down the road of recovery and genuinely need their help. Tell them that you don't have the energy to spare to deal with their dramas or traumas. Tell them that if they cannot give you the space that you require, you will take a break from the relationship and revisit them at later time when you are healed. If you live with that person and you feel that they won't comply with your requests, you can either try to avoid them or possibly move out temporarily until you heal. The second choice is to split with them on a permanent basis if you honestly believe that the negativity in the relationship cannot be mended. This is a very tough personal decision, but your health must come first. After all, you cannot give the best of yourself to a relationship if you have no energy to spend.

It is, of course, easier to split with friends or acquaintances. We all know them. That person that makes jokes at others' expense, usually as a defense mechanism or just because they think they can get away with it. If you have people like that in your life, then make the split. If they're good people, they will understand. If they don't, then they're probably not good friends anyhow.

FORGIVENESS IS THE KEY

If you are holding on to a traumatic event or episode that was caused by another person, such as physical or verbal abuse, being consumed with anger and revenge is disastrous for your health. Your only option is to simply let it go and forgive them. Is this too hard for you to do? Think about it for a moment, being angry and revengeful will keep you in a heightened state of stress, which will exacerbate your chronic fatigue. In order to forgive somebody, you must look at the situation from a completely different angle. Whatever somebody did to you or a loved one, they did that thing because they are broken in some way or form. Maybe they were beaten, abused or abandoned as children, maybe they had a severe trauma you do not know about. Most people who behave badly, do so because the world has not been kind to them. Sympathize with them, understand their pain and let them be, just forgive them. As Paul McCartney wrote, "Speaking words of wisdom, Let it Be."

Ask yourself this question, what would Ted Lasso do? If you have not seen it yet, Ted Lasso is a TV show about an American football coach who goes to England to coach a soccer/football team, a sport he knows little about. What appears to be incompetence on the surface, turns out to be brilliant coaching skills as he imparts his kindness and wisdom on a bunch of troubled athletes. Ted only sees the good in people, he is completely unflappable in the light of criticism and tries to do the right thing, no matter what the circumstances. I would wager that Ted will probably never suffer from a chronic condition. We could all do well to be a little more like Ted.

CHAPTER SUMMARY - CONQUER DEPRESSION FIRST

- Get antidepressants from your doctor if you need them.
- Supplements to consider are St. John's wort, SAM-e (S-adenosyl-methionine), 5-HTP (hydroxytryptophan), gamma-aminobutyric acid (GABA), magnesium, folic acid, and B_{12}.
- Do some research on the progress of psychedelic drugs for depression. By the time you read this, there may be some exciting new drugs on the market.
- If your depression is mild, introduce the happy foods to replace the high sugar and carbs you may have in your diet, which include Brazil nuts, fatty fish, eggs, pumpkin seeds, dark chocolate, turmeric, chamomile tea, quality plain yogurt, green tea, and kombucha.

- Try to watch comedy on TV instead of the news, news apps, social media, horror movies or anything else that might increase stress. The same applies to all web-based browsing and reading materials.
- Take a break or split if you have negative relationships.
- Forgive those who have hurt you. It's the only way to move on.

This is step one in the recovery phase.

Chapter 5

Get the Right Doctor, Get the Right Blood Tests.

"Don't give up. don't give up. don't give up. When you feel like giving up, don't give up."

Jason Boyce

CONVENTIONAL MEDICINE

Conventional medicine categorizes problems by diagnosis reflecting the symptoms you show or reveal and then uses pharmaceuticals or surgery to alleviate those symptoms. Conventional doctors are great if you have a heart attack, physical trauma, or any disorder that requires symptoms that need treating. Conventional medicine treats your body by splitting it up into categories and depending upon your primary symptom you are referred to a doctor that specializes in that particular body system. Often conventional medicine struggles when there are several body systems presenting symptoms simultaneously and you have to see several specialists in different fields that may prescribe several medications that may or may not interfere or interact with one another. The body's organs are not segregated islands; the body is a complex series of interconnected systems that complement one another. Conventional medicine fails spectacularly when presented with complex disorders, especially complex fatigue disorders. If you have dizziness, nausea, headache and a shooting pain in your leg simultaneously, who should your primary care doctor refer you to if she fails to diagnose you? One of the following? Immunologist, endocrinologist, gastroenterologist, allergist, hematologist, infectious disease specialist, nephrologist, neurologist, pathologist, physiatrist, psychiatrist, pulmonologist, rheumatologist, urologist, cardiologist, or some other type of doctor? It's a crapshoot and you have to get lucky to get to see the right person. So let's leave conventional medicine for now and look for alternatives.

INTEGRATIVE MEDICINE

This approach to healthcare combines part conventional medicine with part alternative medicine (homeopathy, herbs, acupuncture etc). It still assesses symptoms and diagnoses accordingly, but has a wider range of therapies available. It takes into account the whole person and all aspects of their lifestyle including diet, exercise and stress levels. However, getting to the root cause of an illness is not necessarily the main goal of its approach.

FUNCTIONAL MEDICINE

Functional medicine is a newer approach on how to treat human beings where suppressing symptoms is a temporary measure while the root cause of the illness is found. It is an integrative approach whereby the doctor seeks to understand the prevention, management and root causes of complex chronic diseases. Functional medicine doctors tend to cross over from conventional medicine to functional medicine when they come up against a series of patients that they know they cannot really help, but desire to do so. Functional doctors use genetics, environmental factors coupled with lifestyle factors and use them in a holistic way to treat patterns of dysfunction and imbalance throughout the body. Functional medicine treats the person and not the disease. It is a logical, intellectual approach that yields greater results and undoubtedly the future of healthcare and medicine.

Find a functional medicine doctor also known as holistic physician or naturopath that has had considerable experience with chronic fatigue. Do some research, narrow down your choices, then call them and ask if they have had experience with chronic fatigue patients. If you sense that they have not, then move on, life is too short to educate your own doctors on your own ailments, been there, done that.

HOLISTIC v NATUROPATH

Is there a difference between a holistic doctor or naturopath? All really good practitioners could be labelled as holistic if they take interest in the whole body as a large interconnected system. However, specifically, holistic doctors generally use only natural remedies to help the body heal itself. Naturopaths focus on diet, lifestyle modifications, detoxification and other natural interventions and other non-conventional modalities such as acupuncture or homeopathy. However, naturopathic physicians will use mainstream pharmaceuticals with nutraceuticals and botanicals in combination with one another. This, in my opinion, is the best approach to treating chronic diseases, so seek out a naturopath or functional physician.

If you are still unsure as to whether you should move on from your conventional doctor then read the following probable exchange regarding a simple, common problem, acid reflux:

"Hi, Doc. How are you today?"

"Ahh, Patient X, I'm fine. Now tell me what ails you today?"

"Sexy X, please. I seem to have recurring heartburn. Every time I have a large meal and when I lie in bed, I get a terrible pain in my upper chest. And a terrible taste in my mouth first thing in the morning."

"Sounds like acid reflux. You need a proton pump inhibitor. I'll prescribe you Prilosec; take one a day and you'll be just fine."

"Ok, but how long will I have to take them for?"

"Well, for as long as you have acid reflux."

"So weeks, months, or years?"

"Yes."

"Well that's not an answer, but okay, thanks. Any side effects of taking these?"

"No not really except, headaches, diarrhea, constipation, abdominal pain, flatulence, fever, and sometimes nausea. You'll probably be fine."

"Oh great, thanks."

As you can see, probably not an uncommon response from a primary care doctor. Again treating the symptoms without a single care for the cause. This is how a naturopath or functional medicine doctor might treat you:

"Hi, Doc. How are you today?"

"Ahh, Patient X, I'm fine. Now tell me what ails you today?"

"Sexy X, please. I seem to have recurring heartburn. Every time I have a large meal and when I lie in bed, I get a terrible pain in my upper chest. And a terrible taste in my mouth first thing in the morning."

"Oh dear, may I ask what your usual weekly diet consists of?"

"Sure. On Sunday night I eat stir fry white rice with steak and veggies. Monday night I'm tired from work so we usually order a large BBQ pizza from Domino's or Pizza Hut. On Tuesday we have spicy chicken tacos with fries, Wednesday we have our special weekly treat from Carl's Jr and eat large cheeseburger and fries, Thursday we like to experiment with Chinese food, and Friday is game night! So obviously we have hotdogs, jalapeño poppers, and chips. Saturday night we usually go out for dinner to our favorite Italian restaurant and I have chicken alfredo followed by tiramisu."

"Yum! What do you have for breakfast and lunch?"

"Well sometimes I have pancakes or toaster waffles for breakfast, I sometimes get an Arby's giant meat sandwich for lunch, because they're so healthy, but often I only have time for McDonald's. I usually get hungry before bed and I love sour cream Pringles! Sometimes I eat the whole tube."

"OK, here is a little tough love. Don't eat huge meals! Slowly reduce the size of the portions you eat, cut out 50% of the junk food if you can and never eat before bedtime. In fact don't eat after 6 pm. Eat some whole foods, you know, stuff that grows in the ground on a bush or a tree. Put a couple of books under the legs of your headboard to tilt your bed. Quit smoking and don't drink alcohol too close to bedtime. If you do as I say you probably won't need medication."

"Aww, Doc, can't you just prescribe me Prilosec."

"Well the downsides are just too great. Reducing your stomach acid can lead to serious gut infections as microbes that would normally be destroyed by the acid can pass into the small and large intestines. Small intestinal bacterial overgrowth (SIBO) is exacerbated by lack of acid, which actually leads to further heartburn. More PP inhibitors lead to worsening of SIBO leading to more heartburn. It's a vicious cycle I don't want you getting in to. PPIs also increases risk of stroke, risk of impaired liver function and can lead to an iron deficiency. So best to cut out the Pringles. Oh, don't eat tomatoes, citrus fruits, or fruit juices or anything spicy or fatty. You might want to switch to cauliflower, green beans, asparagus and non-fried potatoes for a few weeks, that will reduce acid. Take a ginger shot every day and eat oatmeal for breakfast. Also chew some non-minty gum before bed as it increases saliva in your mouth and helps keep acid out of the esophagus. If you do this you won't need PPI's and won't have to risk all the side effects."

"Got it, Doc. You're the best. Thanks."

Get a functional medicine doctor.

GIGANTIC BLOOD TEST

Ask your functional physician to undertake the largest, widest blood test available, even if it is outside of your healthcare network coverage. If you have a limited budget, then this is where you should concentrate your spending. What we don't know can kill us, gaining knowledge is the best defense against something serious and urgent threatening our lives. Even if your doctor believes it is unnecessary, urge them to do it anyway, a wide blood test may show up the unlikeliest of scenarios that you or your doctor may never have thought of.

The results may provide the vital clues on how to treat your chronic fatigue. Make sure it is your functional physician that asks for and analyses your blood test results, they will look far wider and broader than your GP.

These are blood panels I have had: complete blood count, prostate panel, thyroid panel, diabetes panel, liver and kidney function panel, anemia and nutrition, cardiac health panel.

The more complex panels for assessing micronutrients are vital. The blood sample is spun so serum is taken from the top and red blood cells from the bottom and peripheral blood mononuclear cells from the remainder. All three subsets are processed to isolate appropriate macronutrients, which include the following: glutamine levels, vitamin C, E, K, A, B_1, B_2, B_3, B_5, B_6 levels, choline, iron, coenzyme Q10, cysteine, inositol, glutathione, EPA, DPA, DHA, 25-OH, copper, magnesium, asparagine, folate, omega-3, omega-6, serine, arginine, citrulline, isoleucine, valine, leucine, selenium, calcium, manganese, zinc, chromium, carnitine, MMA, LA, MA, AA/EPA ratio, sodium, potassium.

Several of these vitamins and minerals were way out of range including B_{12} and vitamin K. Correct supplementation has helped me balance out the problems.

GIGANTIC POOP TEST

Yes, you read that right. Get a gigantic poop test that covers as much of your microbiome as possible. Gut health is hugely underrated part of health and wellbeing and largely ignored by conventional medicine, which I find incomprehensible.

You will be surprised how many different types bacteria you have in your gut both good and bad types. The balance of your microbiome is extremely important for your overall health and a stool test can show major deficiencies that affect how leaky your gut is (nutrient absorption rate), can show whether you have certain cancers, viruses, irritable bowel syndrome (IBS), pancreatic issues, bacterial infections, or parasites.

If you know that you have blood or mucus in your feces or you have persistent diarrhea, excessive gas, constipation, or cramping, you should have a stool test immediately. The test can show whether your pancreas produces enough enzymes for proper digestion. Low levels of elastase may signal a condition called pancreatic insufficiency.

If you have high level of fats in your feces, it may signal that you have impaired digestion and fat malabsorption. Blood in your stool may be a signal of colon cancer or low iron levels. You should ensure your doctor orders an ova and parasites exam, as that test screens for a variety of microscopic parasites that might exacerbate fatigue symptoms. Stool test can also detect the helicobacter pylori infection, which is a spiral shaped bacteria that can lead to stomach ulcers and ultimately stomach cancer.

The test can also detect an elevated protein called fecal calprotectin, which is a marker for inflammatory bowel disease and can detect Crohn's disease and ulcerative colitis.

THE MICROBIOME PANEL

The microbiome panel includes gut commensals, which entails providing a rating on intestinal permeability (leaky gut), cardiovascular health, metabolic health, IBD (inflammatory bowel disease), hormones, SIBO (small intestinal bacterial overgrowth), autoimmune health, nutrition, liver health, IBS (irritable bowel syndrome). The panel will also provide a score on gut diversity, Phyla (types of bacteria as a % of the whole).

A detailed gut microbiome panel will list many different types of bacteria and the amount you have in relation to the whole. But why is this important? Whether you're in the optimal range or not can have extremely important ramifications for your health. This panel will find out whether you have SIBO, cardiovascular disease, digestive sufficiency, adequate butyrate production (regulates blood sugar and cholesterol levels) or are at risk for: Parkinson's disease, obesity, autism, depression, multiple sclerosis, Alzheimer's disease, Crohn's disease, fatty liver, liver cirrhosis, alcohol hepatitis. So is it important to know this stuff? Your life might depend on it, so don't take no for an answer from your doctor.

It will also provide markers of digestive insufficiency and malabsorption. These are extremely important to know as they show you whether meat or vegetable fiber is present, which indicates inadequate chewing or bile insufficiency. Fat malabsorption levels will tell you your total fecal fat, total fecal triglycerides, long chain fatty acids, total cholesterol and total phospholipids.

Another vital panel is the inflammation markers, which include your current levels of calprotectin, fecal lactoferrin, beta defense 2 (elevated levels indicate activation of the immune system in response to IBS), lysozyme, fecal S100A12 (marker for active IBD), MMP9 (marker for types of intestinal cancers), fecal eosinophil protein X (elevated levels show possible parasitic infections, IBD, or food allergies).

If your doctor thinks that you don't need a poop test, kindly disagree and find a new doctor.

CHAPTER SUMMARY

- Conventional medicine treats the symptoms of ailments, rarely the cause. Excellent for broken bones, not so good for complex chronic diseases.
- Make sure you get a functional, integrative naturopath or holistic physician.
- Get the widest blood test possible. What you don't know can kill you. The blood test will show up any deficiencies, which you may be able to bolster through supplements or medications, potentially relieving fatigue.
- Get a poop test to cover as much of the bacteria in your microbiome as possible.

C hapter 6

Let's Get Back to Sleep

"I've missed more than 9,000 shots in my career. I've lost almost 300 games. 26 times I've been trusted to take the game winning shot and missed. I've failed over and over and over again in my life and that is why I succeed."

Michael Jordan

Getting back to sleep is absolutely vital to beating long COVID and chronic fatigue. Unfortunately, one of the cruelest twists in suffering from chronic fatigue is one of the major symptoms is insomnia. Why couldn't it just be incessant laughing? But no, insomnia it is.

If you are lucky enough not to suffer from any sleep abnormality, then congratulations, feel free to skip this chapter. For everyone else, prop your eyelids open with matchsticks, stab yourself in the leg with a fork, and read on. (By the way, please don't actually stab yourself in the leg; it is not part of the recommended recovery program).

Long COVID and ME patients do not cycle through sleep cycles in the orderly manner that regular people enjoy. Both COVID and ME patients have more disruptions in both REM sleep and through both 3 and 4 stages of sleep. Our brains will skip from REM sleep straight into stage 1 sleep or being awake instead of cycling through, which does not provide the rest necessary for regular cognitive functioning or proper energy restoration.

These issues point to an endocrine dysfunction in potentially both cortisol production (as previously discussed) and serotonin production. The HPA axis (hypothalamic pituitary adrenal axis) is the central response system that combines the nervous system with the endocrine system and appears to be suppressed in almost all ME patients. This suppression is also known as adrenal fatigue.

A growing body of research supports the hypothesis of autonomic dysfunction in both long COVID and ME/CFS, which is a problem with the autonomic nervous system (ANS). The ANS is made up of the sympathetic and parasympathetic nervous systems, which work in balance with each other and maintain homeostasis (harmonious regulation of the body's functions). When the sympathetic nervous system is activated, it puts you into fight-or-flight mode. Conversely, parasympathetic activation is referred to as a rest-and-digest mode. If the sympathetic and parasympathetic systems are out of balance due to autonomic dysfunction, it could result in problems like heightened arousal and awareness when you're trying to sleep. It's a lot like how a new parent is always on alert for a crying baby: never really getting into a good, deep sleep. We look at autonomic nervous dysfunction in more detail in chapter 7 as it one of the critical areas that must be addressed to achieve recovery. We also investigate the myriad ways to calm the SNS (sympathetic nervous system) and turn on the parasympathetic nervous system. We also investigate the vagus nerve and how to stimulate it to aid sleep.

We need a healthy endocrine system that produces the right hormones at the right times in the right amounts to regulate sleep. To put it as simply as possible, we need to produce more tryptophan, which is converted to 5-HTP (5-hydroxytryptophan), which in turn is converted to serotonin, which is converted to melatonin.

Tryptophan is converted to 5-HTP with the use of vitamins including iron, magnesium, calcium, zinc, and vitamins B_6 and C. In the chapter on supplements, I recommend taking a mega multivitamin every day, which will help this process to occur.

However, an increase in tryptophan can come from foods such as turkey (think how sleepy you can get after a large turkey meal), chicken, peanuts, eggs, cheese, fish, pumpkin and sesame seeds; however, you may not want to eat half a turkey just before bed each night, so supplements are the way to go. You can find an array of tryptophan supplements on Amazon, and you might want to start with a low dose of, say, 300-400 mg and gauge your tolerance and sleep quality before increasing. Scientist do not recommend supplementing with 5-HTP supplements for sleep because it blocks other important transmitters and while it may help you sleep initially; the effects are short term and may cause side effects. Don't combine tryptophan supplements with tricyclic antidepressants (TCAs) or trazodone, as the combination may increase serotonin levels too much (please consult with your doctor).

ANTIDEPRESSENTS FOR SLEEP

As hinted above both tricyclic antidepressants and trazodone can help with sleep. TCAs can be very sedative for most people, like watching a season of *Antiques Roadshow*. In particular, nortripyline and amitriptyline can be very sedative; they can also reduce pain (as they increase epinephrine) but should be used in much lower doses than for depression and taken just before bedtime. Nortripyline comes in liquid form, which is handy, as you can start on a low dose and test to see how it affects your sleep and increase dosage gradually.

Trazadone is another antidepressant with sedative effects and has shown to help patients cycle through stages 3 and 4 deep sleep. Unlike many oral sleep aids trazodone does not lose its effectiveness over time, though may have the side effect of tachycardia (increased heart rate). It blocks the neurotransmitter acetylcholine, which helps regulate the parasympathetic nervous system that dilates blood vessels, increases bodily secretions and slows heart rate. Again, you might want to gauge your initial reactions to the drug and proceed accordingly.

Speak with your doctor about these medications specifically for sleep, as most doctors are familiar with off-label usage.

SEDATIVES

Sedatives include Ambien, Lunesta, and Sonata, and like so many prescription medications, some work well for some people and not so much on others. While sedatives can help you fall and stay asleep, they don't increase the quality of sleep and will not help you cycle through the stages in the correct sequence. Incidentally avoid Valium, the newer sedatives (listed above) may work better without being as addictive or causing daytime drowsiness. However, there are side effects to be considered such as irregular heartbeat, appetite loss, nausea, diarrhea, memory loss, anxiety, confusion, dizziness and depression. Not a whole lotta fun, so converse with your physician.

BENZODIAZEPINES

"Benzos" are a class of psychoactive drugs that lower brain activity, reduce anxiety, and come with potentially serious side effects. FDA-approved benzos include estazolam, flurazepam (Dalmane), temazepam (Restoril), quazepam (Doral), and triazolam (Halcion). Have a long, serious discussion with your doctor before considering taking these drugs. Apart from the nasty side effects, they are also addictive.

OVER THE COUNTER SLEEP AIDS

There are several over the counter medications that can help you get to sleep and stay asleep. The most common forms are diphenhydramine (brand names are ZzzQuil, Benadryl, Unisom) and doxylamine succinate (also Unisom), on alternate nights. Make sure you check the ingredients of Unisom as there are two types), but get the generic versions; they're cheaper.

Both diphenhydramine and doxylamine succinate are both antihistamines with drowsy side effects that are now commonly used as sleep aids. Doxylamine succinate is the stronger of the two and can make you drowsy the next morning. To get around this, take doxylamine succinate at least an hour before bed. They are supposed to be non-habit-forming, as they have no addictive ingredients, though if you can't sleep without them, then they may as well be. I am currently trying to phase out these antihistamine sleep aids as they may block the neurotransmitter acetylcholine, which can make you more anxious and decrease functioning of the parasympathetic nervous system. They also become less effective over time.

DELAYED MELATONIN PRODUCTION

ME/CFS patients with delayed nocturnal onset of melatonin production, found that significantly improved fatigue, concentration, motivation, and activity by taking melatonin supplements. There are many melatonin supplements on the market, most offer doses around 3-12 mg, but you might want to start with a lower dose first, to make sure you don't have any adverse reactions.

From anecdotal research, it appears to work well for some and not at all for others, so you will have to see if it works for you. Many melatonin supplements contain ashwagandha root, which some people can be allergic to.

Whatever medications you take, make sure you're getting the right nutrients in order to help the medications work more effectively, especially for hormone inducing supplements. Magnesium is the most important one, but make sure you get the more easily absorbed versions such as glycinate, malate, or l-threonate. Avoid the more common versions of magnesium such as oxide or citrates as they are poorly absorbed and may cause diarrhea.

SERMORELIN

Sermorelin is synthetic medication used for stimulating the pituitary gland, which releases growth hormone. There is a myriad of health benefits of this substance which include: Increased lean body mass, fat reduction, improved energy, increased strength, increased endurance, improved cardiovascular health, improved immune function **and improved sleep.** Please talk to you doctor about prescribing this for Long COVID and CFS, as I have found it very useful; however, it takes a few months for it to work effectively.

So how does it help me sleep exactly? Glad you asked, I was going to skip over that. It helps by up-regulating the release of orexins, a very important class of neurons that help the brains' arousal, wakefulness and appetite functions. As we age, we naturally have less and less of these important neuropeptides. If we get to the point of having too few, then narcolepsy ensues as well as memory loss and depression. DON'T FORGET, discuss sermorelin with your doctor and find out whether this may help you.

OTHER SUPPLEMENTS FOR SLEEP

VALERIAN

Valerian is a plant whose roots are processed into an oral supplement slated to be an effective sedative. There is not a huge amount of evidence proving efficacy, though some studies suggest it works efficiently as a sedative. Side effects are minimal including headaches, possible upset stomach, irregular heartbeat and mild anxiety; however, in some people it may reduce anxiety. It makes other sedatives more effective, so taking it with other sleep medications may make you drowsy the next morning. Valerian interacts with any drugs that are broken down by the liver, in that it might decrease how quickly the liver metabolizes medications, such as Mevacor (lovastatin), Nizoral (ketoconazole), Sporanox (itraconazole), Allegra (fexofenadine), and Halcion (triazolam) amongst others.

If you want to explore this product more, there are thousands of reviews on Amazon that throw up valuable nuggets of views and opinions. For some people it works extremely well; for others, not at all. It is worth a try; it might work for you.

HOPS

Hops are flowers from the hop plant that are used to make beer. That does not mean drinking copious amounts of beer makes a good sleep medicine, it does not, but the herb itself does. In a 2004 study, students who drank non-alcoholic beer found their sleep was greatly improved.

However, you do not have to guzzle nonalcoholic beer to benefit from the drowsiness effects of hops. There is a product called xanthohumol, which is a hop supplement and slated to be a far more potent antioxidant than resveratrol. It is also more convenient to take, as it is capsule form. Search for xanthohumol on Amazon. It can also be consumed in form of loose tea, pre-made iced tea and hop water.

Side effects are minimal, but can make depression worse, so if your mood take a dive, stop taking it immediately.

PASSIONFLOWER

Passionflower is another plant slated for its calming and drowsy effects and often mixed with other herbal medications. In a 2016 study (Stephanie Villet et al. in Pubmed. Google: "passiflora pubmed" for the full report) passionflower showed a marked improvement when taken for four consecutive weeks or more with the conclusion that passionflower significantly improved sleep disorders and anxiety.

It can be taken in tea or capsule form and is readily available in pharmacies and on websites. Side effects may include dizziness, inflamed blood vessels, confusion, loss of coordination, and altered consciousness.

LAVENDER

Lavender is a plant with a strong fragrance that has been used as a sleep aid for many years (ask your grandma). In a study in 2015 (by Mahnaz Keshavarz Afshar et al., as reported on Pubmed. Google: "Lavender fragrance pubmed 2015" for the full report), lavender was used as an aromatherapy to help postpartum women increase the quality of their sleep. It was a controlled trial that showed the participants' sleep improved only after 8 weeks of treatment.

There are no side effects to inhaling lavender, so put some oil on your pillow or use a diffuser by your bed at night. There appear to be little downside in trying this.

GINSENG

Ginseng is the root of a plant in the slow-growing genus *Panax* in the family Araliaceae that has 11 different varieties and is purported to be calming. In a 2013 study titled "Effects of red ginseng extract on sleeping behaviors in human volunteers," by Hyun Jeong Han et al. (Google: "red ginseng pubmed"), the results indicated that wake time was significantly reduced, and rapid eye movement (REM) was increased, thus increasing overall quality of sleep.

Ginseng is also said to have a variety of benefits, including boosts immunity, helps regulate blood sugar, improves focus, may help fight cancer and heart disease, reduces high blood pressure, and relieves menopausal symptoms.

With most supplements purported to help sleep, they work for some people and not others. It is well worth the time and effort to buy the supplements discussed above and take them in different combinations and record the results. There is likely to be a particular combination that works for you. Furthermore, there are some capsule form pills available that combine some of the supplements discussed above. For example, there is a company called Mt Angel Vitamins that produces a product called Sleepy Sleep that combines chamomile, hops, passionflower, magnesium, 5-HTP, lemon balm leaf and melatonin. This can be purchased on Amazon. Happy experimenting!

SLEEP STUDY

If you haven't already had one, it is worth undertaking a sleep study. This entails staying overnight in a sleep study clinic (think 1970s Holiday Inn), where they attach a multitude of wires to various body parts hooked up to electronic devices. Someone then monitors your brainwaves and movements all night to determine whether you have sleep apnea, restless leg syndrome or narcolepsy. Personally I found that I couldn't sleep while entrapped in a hundred wires while hooked up to machines that beeped all night. I felt like an evil Spiderman was experimenting on me, so it is certainly a challenging endeavor. Don't expect them to help diagnose ME or long COVID; they are not set up to look for symptoms outside of common sleep issues. Nevertheless, it is worth going ensure you don't have sleep apnea or narcolepsy.

SLEEP STRATEGIES

Try to go to bed about the same time every night and set your alarm to go off at the same time every single morning including weekends, regardless of how you feel when you wake up. While not guaranteed, it may help you get to sleep more easily at night. Staying in tune with your body's natural, or circadian, rhythm can help stave off insomnia.

Stop looking at blue light before bedtime. All electronic screens radiate blue light and it has been shown that blue light suppresses the body's ability to release melatonin. If you absolutely must keep up with Facebook posts your favorite Netflix show, then try wearing blue light blocking glasses. There's a company called Low Blue Lights, www. lowbluelights. com, that sell a range of glasses in different styles and reasonable prices (ironically the glasses are orange) and you can buy them on Amazon, surprise, surprise.

If you are glued to your PC or tablet in the evenings, then download an app that blocks light on the blue/green spectrum at night. You can search for the following apps: F.lux, Redshift, Sunset Screen, Iris and Twilight to name but a few.

Reading a book or a non-blue light reader for an hour or two before bed is an excellent way to get sleepy as your eyes will tire, which will help you produce melatonin. So read this book for two hours a night, it will send you straight to sleep…. Err, hang on there, I didn't mean to say that.

Wind down methodically before bedtime. First, and most obviously, make sure your bedroom is as dark as can be. If you have light pollution that you cannot control outside, then get some blackout blinds. Watch out for electronic devices that radiate light, including clock radios, wall thermostats (the new modern one I recently installed radiates too much light), even a TV's standby light can affect sleep. Always charge your phone in a different room, sometimes you will forget to turn on the do not disturb function or forget to mute it, which will lead to periodic disturbed sleep and that's just not worth it. Furthermore, your phone emits radiation which can mess with your circadian and cardiac rhythms. I repeat, charge your phone in a different room.

If there are various external noises that you have no control over, then get ear plugs. By blocking all light and noise will make it considerably easier to sleep through the night and get back to sleep quickly if you do wake up. If you don't like the feel of ear plugs, then get a white noise machine (hundreds of them available on Amazon) or buy a fan.

Make sure your bed is comfortable. Sounds obvious, but many people put up with lumpy mattresses or itchy sheets. Buy a new mattress! They have come down considerably in price over the last few years and memory foam mattresses can be bought on Amazon for under $400. Memory foam mattresses can also help to keep you cool and they are insanely comfortable.

Don't be an idiot and drink coffee, tea, or cola in the evening. Caffeine will make it difficult to sleep, so stick to warm milk or decaf tea. Chamomile tea is known for its calming effects and makes an ideal drink before bedtime.

Alcohol is not a good idea either as it is a diuretic, so your body has to work hard to metabolize it, creating large volumes of urine, leading to waking in the wee hours (pun absolutely intended, you're welcome). It also increases the short-term production of adenosine which is a sleep inducing chemical, which gets you to sleep quicker; however, it subsides quickly once it is boosted, leading to waking in the night.

In fact, it might be better to avoid drinking anything at all an hour before bed, so you don't have to get up to urinate in the middle of the night.

Don't get into an argument or a fight after 5 pm! The rise in your stress hormone, cortisol, will make it more difficult to get to sleep. If you can, it is best to keep all your violent and murderous activities to before lunch. If you're a serial killer, just stop! Thanks.

Do not take naps during the day if at all possible; for many people this disturbs their circadian rhythm. If you are a severe narcolepsy sufferer, however, you might need to nap after lunch so you can get through the evening. If you are one of the lucky ME patients who can exercise occasionally, then don't do it within 2 hours before bedtime, as you may not be able to wind down in time.

Open the blinds or curtains first thing in the morning to let as much light in as possible, that will reduce melatonin production. Go outside for extensive periods during the day and soak up as much sunlight as possible, that will increase cortisol production.

Should you get up and do something if you are having trouble getting to sleep? Many commentators believe you should get up and undertake a quiet activity such as reading or murdering. However, I find that you are much more likely to get back to sleep if you are lying in bed with your eyes closed. But each to their own. (Note to self: must stop watching documentaries about murderers.)

ELECTRONIC DEVICES FOR SLEEP

There is an interesting device on the market called Cove, www.feelcove. com. It is a device that wraps around the back of your head and loops over your ears. It delivers vibrations to the skin that activates a brain pathway that helps you sleep better and overcome stress, according to their website. Here is their advertising blurb:

Your brain has a powerful system, called the interoceptive pathway, that monitors what's happening inside your body. When functioning smoothly, this pathway promotes feelings of relaxation; and when it's compromised, you may feel tired and stressed out. New evidence from neuroscience reveals that it is possible to activate the interoceptive pathway through the skin and, in doing so, enhance well-being.

Interoception: The sixth sense you've never heard of. Just as we use our eyes and ears to detect what's happening in the outside world, we use a sense called interoception to keep tabs on what's happening inside our bodies. Awareness of hunger, your heartbeat, or breathing patterns, for instance, are examples of interoception at work.

The interoceptive pathway receives signals from the skin, lungs, stomach, and the rest of your organs and extremities. It also interacts with the brain's emotion and memory centers, combining all this information to shape how you feel and act. Indeed, your sense of interoception is deeply entangled with your sense of wellbeing.

When the interoceptive pathway runs smoothly, you experience tangible benefits like good sleep and emotional balance. Compromised interoception, by contrast, can lead to a whole host of problems, including chronic stress and exhaustion. Fortunately, researchers have discovered ways to boost your interoception and, in doing so, improve your wellbeing.

Cove improves sleep and reduces stress by enhancing interoception. These benefits have been validated by a series of clinical studies, including multiple brain imaging experiments. In a single session, Cove activates the interoceptive pathway and relaxes the brain. Using a technique called electroencephalography, scientists tracked brain activity during a 20-minute Cove session. They observed an increase in alpha waves, a type of brain activity that often appears during meditation and indicates relaxation.

EEG also revealed that Cove prompts changes in brain activity just above the insula, confirming that the device works by activating the interoceptive pathway. While users experience calming brain changes after just one session, further research showed that consistent sessions can lead to more profound changes, including improved resilience to stress. Using MRI, a type of brain scan, we showed that these benefits are the result of stronger connections between key brain regions. Over time, Cove strengthens the interoceptive pathway. MRI studies show that, with consistent daily use, Cove strengthens connections between the insula and brain regions that process emotion. These changes show that Cove's long-term benefits, including resilience to stress, are the result of a strengthened interoceptive pathway. These benefits have been validated by rigorous research, including independent studies at Brown University and the work of a leading clinical researcher from Harvard Medical School. 3500 total participants took part in several clinical studies, including exploratory research. Their stress, anxiety, and sleep quality were analyzed while using Cove for both single sessions and over 30-day periods. 90% of participants stressed less and slept better. Various clinical studies proved that Cove effectively reduces stress. A significant majority of participants experienced less stress after wearing the device, with many still feeling the effects months later.

- *94% of highly stressed individuals reported a decrease in stress symptoms.*
- *82% of participants would use the device again to regulate their stress.*
- *41% average decrease in participant stress after using Cove.*
- *53% of participants still felt positive effects of Cove 6 months after the study.*

Sleep studies conducted over 30 days reveal that consistent daily use of Cove led to improved sleep quantity and quality, as well as falling asleep faster.

- *91% participants reported improved sleep quality.*
- *56% reduction in insomnia reported by participants.*
- *77% participants reported falling asleep faster.*
- *61% participants reported increased sleep hours.*

I have not used Cove, so cannot comment on its efficacy. The company uses a monthly subscription model, which I really don't like as I find that, over time, too many subscriptions add up to a real financial liability. But if this really helps you get back to sleep, then it may be worth it. Google "Cove reviews" to help you make up your mind whether this device might help you.

On a slightly less technical note, there is a device called Restore (www.hatch.co), which the company calls a smart sleep assistant. I call it an expensive alarm clock, but it does have some cool features, such as a white noise, sunrise alarm, meditation app, and an alarm clock in one device. Their advertising blurb is as follow:

FEATURES

- *Personalize a routine to help you fall asleep, stay asleep and wake up refreshed.*
- *Create a mood any time with a selection of soothing sounds and lights.*
- *Relax with a soft-glow reading light without the eye-straining blue hues.*
- *Enjoy wind-down content that prepares your mind & body for sleep.*
- *Hatch Sleep Membership enabled — an optional in-app subscription that gives you unlimited access to an ever-growing library of sleep content.*
- *Gently wake to a custom Sunrise Alarm that supports healthy cortisol levels.*
- *Control with soft-touch buttons or use the free companion app for iOS or Android*

If you can't seem to sleep because the temperature is never quite right for you, then there is a company that produces a device that provides both heat and cooling under the sheets. The device is called Bedjet (www.bedjet.com) and there are a few different models to choose from including a couples version that allows for two different temperatures for each side of the bed. The cost ranges from around $400 to about $1,000 for the couples version. I haven't tried this personally, as I generally find the temperature okay at night as I live in San Diego and weather is usually very agreeable (British speak for awesome). BedJet was the first company to introduce dynamic temperature control biorhythm sleep technology, enabling pre-programmed personalized cooling and warming settings for every hour of the night. You can also program the climate control to change throughout the night. Their website states:

If you toss and turn all night because you're sweating one hour and freezing the next, you'll sleep better with BedJet's biorhythm feature— no more waking up to adjust a thermostat.

Biorhythm programming is available for BedJet 3 units on both the included remote and in our smartphone app (available for <u>Android</u> and <u>iOS</u> devices).

There is a wearable device that looks like a watch called DreamOn (<u>www.dreamon.co</u>) that the company says relaxes, meditates, and gently nudges you to sleep. They state that:

When a mother gently taps the back of her baby until it is relaxed - that's tactile entrainment - and this is the key to DreamOn. Since our launch earlier this year, we have recorded over 20,000 nights of sleep data. Users are not only falling asleep significantly faster, they are also sleeping longer and waking more refreshed. Over 1 month of use, we found that users are getting up to 40 minutes of extra sleep a night!

The device costs $149. I've bought a unit and it taps my wrist in a rhythmic pattern, which stops after a short period. It didn't help me get to sleep, but everybody is different, so it may help you.

STOP SNORING

Snoring is caused by partial obstruction of the airway to and from the lungs by the tongue or throat tissue. Snoring is not a welcome addition to sleep problems for long COVID or ME patients and must be dealt with.

Snoring can disrupt quality of sleep leading to fatigue and irritability. If snoring is a problem for you or your better half, then there are literally hundreds of aids available on Amazon. Some of the most effective anti-snoring aids include breathe right strips, which are similar to band aids (plasters in UK) with a small metal strip inside which aims to keep the nostrils open. Another simple aid, which appears to work well for many, is mouth tape, which is simply tape that keeps the mouth closed, forcing nasal breathing, thus arresting snoring. There are also anti-snoring head straps, nasal dilators, magnetic nose strips, nose vents, and anti-snore electronic rings.

Mandibular advancement device is an oral device that you insert just before bedtime that forces the jawbone forward to open the airway to reduce both snoring and sleep apnea. It looks like a sports mouth guard and is molded to your teeth to provide a platform and advances the jaw forward incrementally until there is balance between the back of the tongue and the soft tissue of the throat. There are basically three types of MADs (great acronym!):

- Boil and bite. You soften the resin or silicone in hot water to make it malleable in your mouth as you chomp down on it to make sure the fit is perfect.
- Semi-custom devices. You take a custom mold of your teeth, then mail the mold to a company who then send you the finished MAD.
- Custom dental MADs. This is where your doctor refers you to a dentist to get custom fit, more expensive but probably ensures a better fit.

There are some side effects to be aware of including discomfort, especially if the device doesn't fit perfectly, a stiff jaw, toothache, and teeth potentially moving out of alignment. Also dry mouth and over salivation may occur. Costs range from $50 for the basic over-the-counter models, up to $2,000 for the custom dental options.

MORE TIPS FOR SLEEP

If your partner is sleeping next to you and you are still awake, then listen to their breathing pattern and try to mimic it. By forcing yourself to breathe as if you were already asleep by taking very slow rhythmic breaths, you can trick you brain into thinking that it really should already be asleep. You can also record your own breathing pattern by using a recording app on your phone and leaving it running all night. Then you can listen to your own sleep breathing patterns for few minutes each night before you sleep and try to mimic the slow rhythm as you're lying there.

THE TAP TAP METHOD

As you may recall from the dream-on wrist device from earlier in this chapter, the device uses something called tactile entrainment (aka brain entrainment or brain synchronization) by tapping a rhythmic pattern on your skin. This works well because the brain likes to follow and synchronize with rhythm both physical (such as tapping) and auditory (such as listening to a beat). You may notice that when you listen to a song you like that has a strong beat, you tap your fingers or bob your head in time with the beat. This represents your brain becoming synchronized with the beat and it's one of the reasons people like to dance.

There is a very simple and very effective way to use this phenomenon to help you get to sleep faster and stay asleep for longer each night. Sit up in bed before you go to sleep and rest your hands on your lap. Then start gently tapping your hands against your lap at a medium speed of about once per second while taking deep breathes. Alternate the taps and make sure your eyes are closed and you feel relaxed, then very methodically start to slow the tapping down until you're tapping once every 3 seconds instead of every second. This process should take about 4 minutes, longer if you feel necessary. You should feel extremely relaxed, with heavy eyelids and maybe a yawn or two. Turn off your light and nighty night. This is an amazing, yet simple and safe way to get to sleep at night. If at first you don't succeed using this method, make sure you stick with it for several consecutive nights, as it may take longer for some people for their brains to recognize the pattern and respond accordingly.

HOW TO AVOID ANXIETY KEEPING YOU AWAKE

If one of your major hinderances to getting a good night's sleep is worry and anxiety, then there are a few ways to reduce this occurrence. Calming your autonomous nervous system is a good place to start and there is a complete chapter on this later in this book. Jump to that chapter now if this is a real problem for you. To help avoid anxiety keeping you awake, have a pad and pen by your bed. Before you go to sleep, write down all the probable thoughts that you think might keep you awake, such as "I must email so and so," "I must do such and such."

If you can think of any actions you might take in the coming days to resolve any issues or at least ameliorate some of them, then go ahead and write these down. Say to yourself that now you have written them down, you will deal with these issues tomorrow and they are as good as solved. This should help alleviate the conscious worries that you may be carrying and help you get through the night undisturbed.

CHAPTER SUMMARY

You will recover much quicker from long COVID and ME if you get a good night's sleep every night. Please reread this chapter and take on board as many of the excellent tidbits of advice thrown at you. To recap:

- Take control of your autonomous nervous system (ANS). Learn how to stimulate your vagus nerve to calm the ANS. The next chapter discusses the vagus nerve and will provide all the advice you need.
- Try natural herbal supplements before you try sleep aids, antidepressants and sedatives . The list of herbal supplements includes multivitamins, tryptophan, melatonin, valerian root,

hops, passionflower, magnesium, chamomile, and ginseng. Try different combinations that best suit you.

- If herbal supplements definitely don't work for you, then try over-the-counter sleep aids next, such as ZzzQuil, Bendryl and Unisom (but get generic versions). These are tried and tested antihistamines that will leave you drowsy and help you sleep.
- Harder hitting medications include antidepressants such as tricyclic antidepressants and trazodone (nortripyline and amitriptyline), but come with side effects.
- Sedatives include Ambian, Lunesta, Silenor, Restoril, and Rozerem and also come with some side effects.
- Take the time to get a sleep study. They can find out if you have sleep apnea or narcolepsy.
- Sleep strategies include consistent bed time and wake time. Make sure it's very dark at night so use blackout blinds or curtains and make sure there are no electronics emitting light. Use blue light-blocking glasses at night when watching TV or using a computer. Read for an hour or two before bed to tire your eyes and calm your system. Wear ear plugs if you are sensitive to sounds. Make sure bed is comfortable and room temperature is optimal before going to bed. Don't drink caffeine after midday. Don't drink a lot of fluid an hour before bedtime to save having to go to the bathroom in the night. Avoid taking naps in the daytime if at all possible.
- Check out the latest electronic devices that may help you, including Cove (feelcove.com), Bedjed (bedjet.com), Dream on (dreamon.co), and Restore (hatch.co).
- If you snore, try Breathe Right strips, mouth tape, head straps, nasal dilators, magnetic nose strips, nose vents, anti-snore electronic rings, or mandibular devices.
- Further tips include listening to your partner's breathing rhythm and trying to match it. If that doesn't work, record yourself breathing while asleep and play it back at night to help your brain get in sync with your sleep breathing pattern.

- Try the tap-tap method. Sit up in bed, close your eyes and gently tap your hands alternately on each thigh at 1-second intervals. Slow this down over 5 to 10 minutes to about 3 seconds between taps. This form of tactile entrainment can work for many.
- Avoid letting anxiety keep you awake by writing down all the issues that you think will keep you awake. This should lighten the load and help you sleep.

C hapter 7

What Happens in Vagus - A Key Piece of The Puzzle

"The place between your comfort zone and your dream is where life takes place."

Helen Keller

As touched upon in the previous chapters, the nervous system may play a huge role in the ongoing symptoms of ME.

Recent studies have reached the same conclusion: there is a dysfunction of the autonomic nervous system (ANS) in people suffering from chronic fatigue. The deeper I research, the more apparent it has become that one of the top three vertebrae may be out of alignment with the majority of people suffering from chronic fatigue. This misalignment causes kinks in the ANS nerves that run through the spinal column, putting undue pressure on these nerves and in particular, the vagus nerve.

The ANS runs throughout the human body connecting all organs, tissues with each other and the brain and is an involuntary part of the peripheral nervous system. The ANS governs all of our vital unconscious actions, including breathing, digestion, urination, saliva, perspiration, blinking, and, somewhat importantly, keeps our heart beating.

The ANS comprises of two equally important parts that should be in balance with one another in order to achieve homeostasis (to be in harmony with ones' environment, in this case, in one's own body). The two parts are the sympathetic nervous system and the parasympathetic nervous system. The sympathetic nervous system governs our fight-or-flight response mechanism and is vital in order to keep us safe from danger. It pumps us full of adrenalin, increases heart rate, increases breathing, increases blood to the muscles and slows digestion. The parasympathetic nervous system has the opposite effect; it calms us down, relaxes our minds and muscles, and tells us that everything is fine and dandy. **The sympathetic nervous system uses huge amounts of energy to be active.** As it is active almost permanently with ME sufferers, then it's understandable that someone with ME is always tired, especially when coupled with a mitochondria dysfunction. The question is: Why is it so active?

In a couple of MRI studies of ME patients carried out by Unger et al., 2012 (Google: "Unger et al. basal ganglia") and Miller et al 2014 (Google: "Miller et al. 2014 basal ganglia") found that an area of the brain called the basal ganglia were not responding in the same manner as healthy people. **Research suggests that ME sufferers have inflamed neurons around this area of the brain which inadvertently activates the sympathetic nervous system**. The MRI images showed various levels of blood flow in the brain between ME patients and healthy controls while they played a card game, which rewarded the subjects with money if they guessed the correct color of random playing cards to simulate feelings of reward. After they made their choice of red or black they were shown the card and their blood flow to the basal ganglia part of the brain was measured during both winning and losing choices. **The ME patients showed significantly less change in blood flow than healthy volunteers. The level of intensity of fatigue was closely correlated with lower blood flow. Misalignment of the cervical spine (even fractionally misaligned) can reduce blood flow to the brain. Remember you do not have to feel any pain for one of your vertebrae to be out of alignment.**

If you're curious as to what the basal ganglia areas do (and why wouldn't you be?) I shall briefly explain. The basal ganglia are a group of subcortical nuclei responsible for motor control, motor learning, emotions, and executive functions and behaviors. The basal ganglia use dopamine as their dominant neurotransmitters and Unger et al. postulated that dopamine metabolism may play a pivotal role in understanding how chronic fatigue manifests.

Scientists from Emory University think they have found evidence that chronic inflammation can adversely affect the brain's dopamine production.

"When your body is fighting an infection or healing a wound, your brain needs a mechanism to recalibrate your motivation to do other things so you don't use up too much of your energy," says corresponding author Michael Treadway, an associate professor in Emory's Department of Psychology who studies the relationship between motivation and mental illness. "We now have strong evidence suggesting that the immune system disrupts the dopamine system to help the brain perform this recalibration."

All roads lead back to chronic inflammation. **Calming the sympathetic nervous system and beating inflammation is absolutely key to beating chronic fatigue. The first step is to get an X-ray of your upper spine to see if you have craniocervical instability. If you have, you will need a chiropractor or osteopath to work on you to get your spine back in alignment.**

In the meantime, there are a couple of short-term hacks that can help you beat fatigue by relieving pressure in your upper spine.

CERVICAL COLLAR

A cervical collar or neck brace is a device that lifts and immobilizes the head and stabilizes the spine. I use an inflatable cervical collar that inflates with a small hand pump and costs $19 on Amazon. It looks like a travel pillow that wraps around your neck, but three stacked on top of each other. I use it for about 10 minutes, three times a day. It relieves the pressure caused by the weight of my head pressing on my slightly misaligned C1 (top vertebrae) as it separates and lifts my head upwards. **It has had an extraordinary effect by relieving my fatigue, especially on crash days. This gave me the proof I needed to get my neck looked at by a spine specialist, as it confirmed to me that my vagus nerve was indeed pinched in my spinal column.**

If you want to see if this might work for you and provide temporary relief of your fatigue, then search for "Inflatable Cervical Neck Traction Device" on Amazon. Of course, consult with a chiropractor before trying this, as they are not for everyone and may come with unforeseen side effects.

INVERSION TABLE

An inversion table is a stand-alone machine that pivots on its axis and tips the body upside down based on its tilt setting. You insert your ankles, which are held by clasps, lean back, put your arms up and the table does the rest. My chiropractor told me not to invert more than 45 degrees and only do it in 30-second time intervals. It relieves pressure on the spine and feels wonderful; however, the effects wear off when standing up again, so it is not as effective as the collar.

If you have an X-ray and your chiropractor confirms that you do not have any upper spine issues, then there is a myriad of other ways to calm the sympathetic nervous system by stimulating the vagus nerve.

THE VAGUS NERVE

The word vagus means wandering in Latin, and the vagus nerve wanders from the brain stem all the way to the colon, meandering to various parts on its merry way. The vagus nerve is a cranial nerve that has both sensory and motor functions. The sensory functions include providing somatic information (sensations felt on the skin and muscles) and also includes sensation information for the larynx, esophagus, lungs, trachea, heart and the digestive tract. The motor functions include stimulating muscles in the larynx, pharynx and muscles in the heart.

Yeah, yeah, but why are you telling me all this?

I'm telling you this to impress upon you that the vagus nerve is extremely important puzzle piece in beating chronic fatigue. It's the best way to calm the sympathetic nervous system and turn on the parasympathetic nervous system. It may even arrest chronic inflammation over time if stimulated enough and beating inflammation is paramount!

So can we hack the vagus nerve to reduce the effects of an overactive SNS? The good news is that you can. There are several ways to reset the SNS by stimulating the vagus nerve (medically known as increasing vagal tone). By inducing relaxation using several concurrent approaches, over time it is possible to calm the SNS and stimulate the PNS.

The following are various ways to stimulate the vagus nerve. I recommend you write down each method and try them one by one to see which methods work best for you.

DEEP BREATHING

Deep, slow breathing increases the sensitivity of the nerves that activate the PNS. Breathe deep so that your belly rises and falls. Breathe in for 6 seconds, hold for three or four seconds, then breathe out for six seconds, repeat for several minutes until you feel calm and you feel your muscles relax. Do this several times a day when you can be on your own or can find a quiet spot (even if you can only do this while sitting on the toilet!)

Research has shown that single nostril breathing can help both calm and focus the mind. Breathing in through the left nostril and breathing out through the right nostril has shown to have calming affects. Breathing in through the right nostril and breathing out through the left nostril has shown to increase attention and focus.

MEDITATION

This is an absolute must for calming the SNS. It is important that you try to meditate every single day. Even if you're not keen on the idea or you think it's a load of old codswallop (English phrase meaning nonsense), then stifle your incredulity and do it anyway. I can honestly say that it has helped equally as much as my diet change in reducing inflammation and increasing energy levels.

So how do we meditate successfully? There are hundreds of books and thousands of articles that can assist, and I urge you to seek some out and learn. However, I will explain exactly how I meditate and how I believe it to be the most simple and successful method.

Obviously, you will need a quiet space in your home where you will not be disturbed for at least an hour or so. If you have a space where you won't be disturbed but you will be able to hear people talking or hear the TV, music etc, then buy a box of earplugs. You can buy them from your local pharmacy or on Amazon. Be creative with the space, I sometimes use my closet and sit on a beanbag. If you simply have nowhere that is suitable, then sit in your car, take your earplugs and an eye mask and ask your family not to disturb you.

Find a comfortable sitting position, close your eyes, and relax. You do not have to cross your legs; I find this gets uncomfortable after 30 minutes or so. I find it best to stretch your legs out and rest your hands comfortably as possible on your lap, but make sure you are sitting up and not slouching or reclining. Now take deep breaths, as described above. Breathe in and count for 6 seconds, hold it for 3 or 4 seconds and breathe out for 6 seconds. Do this for 3 or 4 minutes until you feel calm. Keep breathing slowly while you concentrate on relaxing all your muscles one by one. If you find it hard to relax and cannot release tension in your muscles, then purposely tense each muscle as much as possible, then let go. You will find the muscles will relax more using this method. Once you find that you are relaxed, then count in your head "1" as you breathe in and "2" as you breathe out nice and slow. Concentrate only on your breathing and count up to 1,000! Yes you heard me right, count all the way up to 1,000. This should take about an hour and you will get a sense of achievement if you make it that far.

The difficulty in meditation is the mind wandering phenomenon, which happens to absolutely everybody. When the mind wanders, don't worry about it; just bring back your concentration to your breathing and counting. I found the best way to stop the mind wandering is to imagine you're in the basket of a hot air balloon and each intrusive thought gets put into a sand bag that hangs on to the side and then dropped. Once the thought has been physically dropped in your mind's eye it disappears as gravity takes it down.

It helps to visualize the numbers in your mind's eye as they tick by. I often see each number fade in as I breathe in and fade out as I breathe out. It also helps if you see each number as different in shape, form and color from the previous number. For example, if 33 comes in as a simple floating black number, then 34 might be made of a shiny metal. Then 35 might be made of balloons, 36 made of marshmallows, etc. This helps focus the mind on only the number and the breathing. If counting doesn't work for you, then say to yourself "Block all thoughts" as you breathe in and "relax" as you breathe out. I say this to myself when I'm really struggling with intrusive thoughts, and it works extremely well.

Sometimes the mind wandering completely takes over and the meditation becomes a futile exercise. If this occurs, you have two choices, give up and try later or keep on counting. There have been many times when I've counted up to 100 quite successfully, then lost my thoughts completely on a conversation I had with my wife yesterday or on a sports game I saw earlier. I try to count through these distractions and it often works.

If you simply cannot stop the mind wandering, then use this to your advantage. Get a pad and pen and leave it by your side. When an intrusive thought comes into your mind, write it down. You'll find that after you have written down your thought, it will probably not come back. You might find that you have inadvertently created a useful to-do list or invented a new gadget that will make you millions.

I have found something strange happens when you count up to the late 600s or early 700s. You enter the brainwave level known as the theta level, the brainwave level you enter just before you fall asleep. If you stay in the theta level you can almost feel your brain physically change. I sometimes experience a mild dizzy spell that lasts for only a couple of seconds and that's when I know I am about to experience a clearer mind with less anxiety, more relaxation, and more focus. It simply erases the common condition of brain fog. For example, if I meditate for an hour before I start writing, I find that I can write 3 or 4 times more than before the meditation session. Meditation is a fundamental and vital tool for beating chronic fatigue and long COVID. Do not skip this at any cost. However, if you find, after many attempts that meditation is impossible for you, then don't despair, there are devices that can help.

MUSE

Muse is an electronic device that attaches to the head in order to track your thoughts to help assist with meditation. I've tried this interesting device and it really does work. After you download the app, you have a choice of background sounds such as waves crashing, rainfall or birds tweeting. You set the duration of the meditation required, put on the headband that wraps around the forehead and loops behind the ears, sit back and meditate. Your goal is to make the relaxing sound get quieter by blanking out intrusive thoughts. The gizmo reads your brainwaves, and the more active your brainwaves the louder the sound becomes, thus prompting you to quiet your mind. The technology is impressive and I recommend you give it a try, especially if you have tried meditation and failed. Their website is www.choosemuse.com and here is their marketing blurb:

Muse is an EEG device widely used by neuroscience researchers around the world. It uses advanced signal processing to interpret your mental activity to help guide you. When your mind is calm and settled, you hear peaceful weather. Busy mind? As your focus drifts, you'll hear stormy weather that cues you to bring your attention back to your breath. Muse connects to your mobile device via Bluetooth. Once connected, simply start the Muse Meditation app, put on your headphones, and close your eyes. Once your session is complete, you can review your results and track your progress. Muse's 7 finely calibrated EEG brain sensors – 2 on the forehead, 2 behind the ears plus 3 reference sensors – detect and measure the activity of your brain. Muse 2 has added PPG and pulse oximetry breath and heart sensors that are located on the front, right-hand side of the forehead. Gyroscope and accelerometer body sensors are found behind the ears. Muse does not use electrical stimulation - it's a PASSIVE tool that gives you accurate, real-time feedback on what's happening in your brain. EEG has been used in hospitals and research institutions for nearly century to study the brain. After each session, you'll see how you did through a series of graphs and charts in the Muse meditation app. Muse will show you how your brain, heart, breath, and body did from moment to moment through simple, easy to understand graphs and charts. Use the Muse app to follow your progress over time and learn new things about your own mind, heart, breath, and body. To help keep you motivated and improving, Muse also gives you points, goals, challenges and bonuses to strive for. With every session you earn points, and can adjust your goal to fit your needs. Muse connects to your mobile device via Bluetooth. Once connected, simply start the Muse Meditation app, put on your headphones, and close your eyes. Once your session is complete, you can review your results and track your progress.

YOGA OR TAI CHI

If you have the energy for yoga, then you should do it. The health benefits are numerous, well understood and universally agreed upon. It encourages deep breathing and is excellent for calming the nervous system and increasing vagal tone. It also stimulates the lymphatic system by transporting lymph (fluid containing infection fighting white blood cells) around the body's extremities. Furthermore, it can improve balance and flexibility, ease arthritis, relieve back pain, benefit heart health and help manage stress.

If you are not able to attend a 45-minute or a 1-hour class due to fatigue, then simply do 5, 10, or however many minutes you are capable of by watching a YouTube video in the comfort of your own home or backyard.

TAI CHI

Initially developed as a martial art (presumably for defending oneself against aggressive snails and turtles), it is practiced as a form of moving meditation and is used to help promote posture, balance, flexibility, and strength. It is also a useful tool in the armor for calming the PNS and, like yoga, it also encourages deep breathing. It is also reputed to boost mood, alleviate pain, and strengthen the immune system. Furthermore, a research paper published in 2018 in the journal *Clinical Rehabilitation,* reviewing 10 previously published studies found that those who practiced tai chi significantly reduced the incident of falls in people with Parkinson's disease or had strokes.

HUMMING OR SINGING

You may have seen meditation gurus of the past sitting in the lotus position and vocalizing the sound *ohm* as a continuous drone. Well, it may look silly, but it appears that they were on to something. Humming or singing makes the vocal cords and its surrounding muscles vibrate, thus stimulating the connected vagus nerve. If you feel self-conscious about singing or have a horrible singing voice, then try humming to yourself frequently. You may be surprised how this simple act can calm you down. If you are still self-conscious, then you can try gargling with water in your bathroom as it has the same affect. Alternatively, you could get singing lessons, if you don't want to needlessly punish your better half. Furthermore, you could frequent a karaoke bar and step up to the stage, the only drawback with this is generally speaking you have to be drunk as a skunk to do it, which is a no-no for long COVID and ME patients.

INCREASE THE GOOD BACTERIA IN YOUR GUT

The gut-brain connection is becoming more understood by researchers and a clear connection between specific bacterial strains signaling to the vagus nerve have been demonstrated.

Try fermented foods and drinks such as kimchi, sauerkraut, kefir, goat's yogurt, and kombucha. Don't try these if you suffer for short intestinal bacterial overgrowth (SIBO), a condition affecting the small intestine where bacteria grow that should be regulated to other parts of the intestine. It can cause a wide range of symptoms, including loss of appetite, abdominal pain, nausea, bloating, diarrhea, weight loss, and malnutrition.

Healthy gut bacteria have been claimed to create a positive feedback loop through the vagus nerve, increasing its tone. Probiotics, animal protein and essential fats (omega-3 and -6 – found in oily fish, avocados, olive oil, nuts) have all been claimed to decrease an overactive sympathetic nervous system (SNS) and stimulate the vagus nerve. Also, ensuring your diet is sufficient in B-vitamins, calcium, magnesium and zinc, to support nerve function is said to help. Cutting down on or eliminating caffeine and alcohol is also important as they both stimulate the SNS.

RELAXING MUSCLES

Relaxed muscles stimulate the vagus nerve by telling your SNS that you are not currently under any type of threat. So, if you need an excuse to spend every Saturday at the local spa, well now you have one. Deep tissue massages, deep breathing techniques and a hot bath are the trifecta for relaxing muscles and if you can at least perform two out of three every day it will go a long way in calming the SNS.

ACUPUNCTURE

The globally exported Chinese art of acupuncture is an alternative therapy in which tiny needles are inserted into specific areas of the body depending upon the ailment that needs remedying. While not particularly well understood by the scientific community, I did find an interesting study undertaken in 2016 (Hee Dom Lim et al., *PLOS One*) that showed that acupuncture can be successful at stimulating the vagus nerve. (Google: "Hee Dom Lim et al. PLOS One Journal.")

(*Science bit alert*)

The present study provides evidence that acupuncture stimulation transmits signals into the vagus nerve and mediates anti-inflammatory responses in the spleen. Using an animal model of acute inflammation, we found that acupuncture stimulation attenuated inflammatory responses as measured by TNF-α productions in the serum and the spleen. Removal of vagal and splenic nerves significantly abrogated the anti-inflammatory effects mediated by acupuncture stimulation. Certain pressure points in the feet, neck and ears are believed to manually stimulate the vagus nerve (da Silva et al. 2014) and create a sense of relaxation.

I have not tried acupuncture to calm my SNS; however, if you are willing and able, it might be worth a try. Furthermore, acupuncture when used in conjunction with moxibustion may be a useful therapy for chronic fatigue (please see the "Exploring Other Innovative Therapies" chapter later in this book for further information).

AROMATHERAPY

The sense of smell is an incredibly important and vital tool in calming one's nerves. Do you recall any particular smells from your earlier life that instantly brings back good or bad memories? No? Well, you're not trying hard enough. The aromatic calming smell of your grandma's cookies? The smell of wet dog that reminds you of your first pooch? Olfaction is the most primal of our senses and is often provides the first signal of imminent danger to your SNS such as the smell of gas or smoke. Calming smells such as lavender are well known to help stimulate the vagus nerve.

In a Brazilian study in 2015 of 50 psychiatric patients (Domingos et al., Universidade Estadual Paulista Julio de Mesquita Filho) had six massages with aromatherapy, performed on alternate days, on the cervical and the posterior thoracic regions. Vital data (heart and respiratory rate) were collected before and after each session and an anxiety scale (Trait Anxiety Inventory-State) was applied at the beginning and end of the trial. There was a significant decrease of heart and respiratory rates in patients after treatment, providing significant stimulation of the vagus nerve. (Google: "Domingos et al. massages" for the full study.)

So, invest in a few scented candles or an aromatherapy diffuser with your favorite essential oils. This is a low effort, high reward strategy that costs little in both energy and money.

COLD THERAPY

Cold therapy works superbly for hacking the vagus nerve and providing a burst of energy even on your most lethargic days. Benefits of cold immersion include lowering body fat, increasing hormone levels, improving sexual performance and fertility, lowering blood sugar, cutting food cravings, improving adrenal function, fixing thyroid issues, enhancing immune function, Improving sleep quality, increasing pain tolerance, and most importantly, reducing inflammation. (Warning to men: it does make your man sausage shrink a lot!)

Cold water increases energy as the mild shock makes you gasp, which increases oxygen intake and heart rate. Blood circulation is also improved as the sudden cold causes the blood to move closer to the inner organs to keep them warm. The cold also increases your metabolic rate, which massively increases your white blood cell count and helps boost your immune system.

Everybody has differing levels of tolerance for being cold. Some people enjoy it, while others abhor being a tiny bit chilly. The good news is that you only need to be cold enough to create some discomfort and if this means taking a mildly cool shower, then this is a reasonable starting point. The key is to be cold enough to stimulate your vagus nerve, yet not too cold that you dread doing it. You have to find a comfort level, then slowly decrease the temperature over time as your body becomes accustomed to it.

Here is a program that will help you get the most out of cold therapy. It was designed by Joe DiStefani and extracted from his website, www.coachjoedi.com:

STEP 1: YOU CAN ALWAYS MAKE IT COLDER

Wim Hof, the leading popularizer of the cold immersion trend, has made a name for himself by climbing snow-capped mountains in his underwear and performing on keynote stages fully submerged in ice. This man is a lifelong yogi who has spent decades strengthening his nervous and immune system to do what he does. Wim was not built in a day. For most of us, the benefits of cold immersion begin at any temperature that makes us uncomfortable, and yet still empowers us to make the practice part of our regular routine. That means you also don't want it so cold that you'll struggle with consistency. You can always make it colder.

STEP 2: 30 DAYS OF COLD SHOWERS

Prior to investing in cold immersion equipment or overthinking the practice, I recommend starting with 30 days of cold showers. This will help you understand the basic physiological responses you'll experience in an ice bath and how to manage them. Based on my own anecdotal experience in coaching newbies into cold immersion, I recommend progressing through your 30 days as follows:

Phase 1 (Day 1-10): *Start or end each day with 60-seconds of cold showering. No days off. This can be accomplished in many different ways, but my two favorites are: "Tabata" cold showering: Step into the cold water for 20 seconds and step out of it for 10 seconds at least three* *times. Depending on your shower, you may also be able to change the temperature from cold to warm for these intervals. I use interval timer app for this.*

Phase 2 (Day 11-20): *Start each day with a 2.5- to 3-minute cold shower. Day 14 and 18 off. You should use the same techniques as Phase 1, or mix it up by changing your Tabata cold showering to 30 seconds full-cold followed by 30 seconds slightly warm for 5+ minutes.*

Phase 3 (Day 21-30). *Start each day with a 5-minute cold shower. Day 22 and 26 off. By now, this should be a breeze.*

STEP 3: BUYING YOUR FIRST TANK

Your first tank should be modest. You could even start with your home bathtub so long as it gets deep enough (more on this later). For most, a kiddie pool from Amazon is a great option as it's highly affordable, multi-purpose, and can easily be stored away when you're not using it. However, if you're in this for the social media fanfare and you know you're going to be using it a lot, the cattle trough is your best option.

There are other options, such as buying a large freezer, setting it at 38 degrees and climbing in and out of it each morning. This is often the most practical solution for people with a few draw backs, such as replacing the water, and potential danger for children. If you opt for the freezer, consider child-proofing it by placing something heavy, such as a 45lb, on the top of it when not in use. And always unplug it prior to climbing in and out, even if you opt to use an outlet timer to control its power.

STEP 4: USING CLEAN WATER

When I began filtering my hose water, my tank water started lasting longer. I then found it lasted even longer when I added 1/4 to 1/2 of a cup of food-grade hydrogen peroxide to the water. If you get a less potent solution, just use a bit more. Covering the tank at night is another must to ensure you aren't needing to refill more often than you need to.

Here are the exact products I use at home: Drinking water hose, water filter and food grade hydrogen peroxide.

STEP 5: FILLING THE TUB

I recommend filling your tank such that you can have your entire body submerged to your ears. Many have the inclination to just expose the lower body, or they don't get in enough for the neck to be fully exposed. Exposing your neck and therefore your thyroid, is hugely important in order to regulate your body temperature (and will actually make it easier for you to stay in).

To get the maximum benefits, I go for the total-body dip at the very start. The total-body dip exposes the whole body, thyroid and back of the neck to the cold, which elicits a more dramatic maximal hormonal response. After the initial dip, the depth of the pool will allow you to dip your face in periodically throughout the plunge, which continues to send a dramatic message into the nervous system.

When filling your tank and keeping in mind the above, you want to put the least amount of water possible so that the ice has less water to cool down. Be mindful of how much displacement will occur when you get in, so that you don't lose half of your ice in that initial plunge.

For starters, I recommend placing 60lbs of ice per 70 gallons of water when using a 100-gallon tank. This should bring the temperature to about 50 degrees and allow for a tolerable yet challenging jumpstart into the realm of cold immersion.

STEP 6: HOW LONG TO STAY IN

*The minimum time of a plunge, especially when considering all the effort you've now put in, is always **3-minutes**. This is why we build up to a 5-minute cold shower in the 30 days prior to investing in a tank. If you're going to start buying $50-$100 worth of ice every week, make sure you've matured beyond the "in-and-out in 30 seconds phase."*

3-minutes holds true to any temperature above 38 degrees Fahrenheit and is near the time most newcomers will begin to shiver in cold water. It's also long enough to begin a cascade of the most desirable cold-immersion benefits, such as improved blood sugar regulation and fat burning. That being said, if you are at 45-50-degrees or just over (based on my 70/60 protocol), the body can withstand far longer than 3-minutes. In fact, the goal after 4-6 weeks would be 10+ minutes at this protocol, which should then be reduced by 2-3 minutes with every 20lbs of ice added to your constant volume of 70 gallons of water.

The general protocol targets are as follows: 60lbs of ice: 10-minutes, 80lbs of ice: 6-minutes, 100-120lbs of ice: 3-minutes.

STEP 7: PREPARING YOUR MIND AND BODY

Prior to getting into the ice bath, you want to calm the nervous system. Realize that much of our pain is simply an incarnation of our held tension or fears: like our anticipation of pain at the dentist. As humans, we get into our heads about how bad something will or will not hurt, or hold tension or beliefs about ourselves which manifest and create exactly those outcomes.

*Prior to cold immersion, you want to engage the parasympathetic, "rest-and-digest" branch of the nervous system using deep full inhales and exhales. Humming can also help activate the parasympathetic system and boost nitric oxide production, which makes your cells more receptive to oxygen. Last, you always want to enter the tank holding your breath out on an **exhale**, the phase of breath that nearly defines relaxed or suspended consciousness.*

Step 8: Entering the Cold

*Always enter on an **exhale** and get in calmly, yet steadily. The process should take less than 3-4 seconds. Once you're in, submerge your entire body - and ideally your head. This will activate your nervous system and provide the greatest possible signal to your body to begin* *to regulate temperature quickly. The less of your body that's submerged the longer this process will take and potentially the more painful the experience will be.*

Another important note is the "Why?" behind stepping in on an exhale. The reason is that your first inhalation in the cold will dictate the rest of your experience. If you get in holding tension, as we do on an inhale, your first breath will always always be a stressed, gasping mouth-breath. Which, often leads to a very negative experience. Whereas if you control your breath, enter on an exhalation and ensure your first inhalation in the cold is through the nose and is relaxed, you are far more likely to have an enjoyable and rather painless experience.

And remember, the first minute is the most painful, so control your breathing and your thoughts. Nirvana is only 3-minutes away!

So there you have it, now there's no excuse to get your cold on! Except if you have the flu, COVID or other type of respiratory upper tract infection, then wait until you get better before you embrace the chill.

Another way to achieve similar results is to try hot/cold therapy, which I do most nights by having a very hot shower, then turning it to cold for 3 minutes, then back to hot, then back to cold for another 3 minutes just before I go to bed. The hot water relaxes the muscles and relieves stiffness and tension and increases blood flow. The steam relieves congestion and improves the respiratory system. Suddenly switching to cold stimulates the vagus nerve quickly and is a great start for a wonderful night's sleep.

SUNLIGHT

Being out in the sunlight helps to produce a hormone called melanocyte stimulating hormone (MSH), which activates the vagus nerve (Ottani et al. 2010) and the PNS. (Google: "Ottani et al. vagus nerve.") Naturally getting plenty of sunlight throughout the day will help set your circadian rhythm to aid sleep. Of course, it is important to protect the skin from harmful ultraviolet light by applying sunscreen, which necessitates the need to take vitamin D supplements (there is an entire chapter devoted to this extremely important vitamin later in this book).

LAUGHTER

As stated at the beginning of this book, humor is an important tool in beating ME primarily because laughter stimulates the vagus nerve. It is also thought to be good for cognitive function as it releases endorphins, which are the feel-good hormones. Be cognizant of the type of media you consume. The news and political shows are depressing and difficult to watch and will do nothing to lift your mood. Social media has unfortunately become incredibly divisive due to the anonymity it provides some users who use that anonymity to spew abuse, not to mention bots that aim to rile people against specific political or social movements. These types of media will certainly aggravate your SNS and stop you from achieving the calm you need to stimulate your vagus nerve.

Watching horror movies, especially ones with jump scares, will stimulate your SNS, so best avoid them or watch infrequently if you really can't live without *Poltergeist Freddie's Halloween the 13th* or whatever the latest slash fest is. Alternatively, you could watch a horror comedy such as *Scary Movie,* although the low Rotten Tomatoes score for this gem of a film is scary enough.

If you're in a particularly grumpy mood and really can't find anything to laugh about, then search the web for the world's funniest jokes. If nothing else, you can pass them on to others. Here's a couple I found that made me smile:

It's the Super Bowl, and a man makes his way to his seat right next to the pitch. He sits down, noticing that the seat next to him is empty. He leans over and asks his neighbor if someone will be sitting there. 'No,' says the neighbor. 'The seat is empty.' 'This is incredible,' says the man. 'Who in their right mind would have a seat like this for the Final and not use it?' The neighbor says, 'Well actually the seat belongs to me. I was supposed to come with my wife, but she passed away. This is the first Super Bowl we haven't been to together since we got married.' 'Oh, I'm so sorry to hear that. That's terrible. But couldn't you find someone else, a friend, relative or even a neighbor to take her seat?' The man shakes his head. 'No,' he says. 'They're all at the funeral.'

And here's another, if that didn't tickle you enough:

A guy meets a sex worker in a bar. She says, 'This is your lucky night. I've got a special game for you. I'll do absolutely anything you want for $50 as long as you can say it in three words.' He pulls his wallet out of his pocket and lays $50 on the bar, and says slowly, 'Paint...my...house.'

MUSIC

Aggressive music such as death metal or gangster rap won't do much to soothe the SNS or stimulate the vagus nerve. Classical music or chill jazz music won't do much for your street cred, but may help you relax. Any Norah Jones tracks will certainly do the trick. Apart from the obvious calming effects of slower rhythmic music, there is another type of music that can target the vagus nerve in a more direct manner.

BINAURAL BEATS

Binaural beats are when two tones are played simultaneously in either ear that have slightly different frequencies. For example, if the left ear is hearing a frequency of 140 hertz (Hz) and the right ear is hearing a frequency of 135 Hz, then your brain will modulate the frequencies and will actually interpret a tone of 5 Hz, which is essentially an auditory illusion.

Binaural beats between 1 and 30 Hz are reputedly similar to the effects of meditation in promoted calming of the SNS and stimulating the vagus nerve; however the specific range of hertz affects differing brain frequencies. The 1-4 Hz range is said to be within the delta range and associated with lulling you to sleep. The 4-8 Hz range affects theta and linked to help relaxation and create a state of meditation. 8-13 Hz affects alpha and is thought to reduce anxiety. The beta brainwave frequency is affected by tones in the 14-30 Hz range and is said to increase concentration, problem solving and memory.

You will find hundreds of binaural beats to choose from on YouTube, Apple Music, and most other music sources. Obviously you will have to use headphones or earbuds and will need to listen for a minimum of 30 minutes for the brain to register the frequencies.

If you think that this sounds like a load of new age baloney, then you might just be wrong, as there are a several studies that actually show that binaural beats really do reduce stress and anxiety. A 2018 meta study of 22 different studies (Miguel Garcia-Argibay et al. NIH, National Library of Medicine) titled "Efficacy of Binaural Beats in Cognition, Anxiety and Pain Perception: A Meta Analysis," states the following:

Binaural auditory beats are a perceptual phenomenon that occurs when presenting separately to each ear two tones that slightly differ in their frequency. It has been suggested that binaural beats can influence cognition and mental states among others. The objective of this meta-analysis was to study the effect of binaural beats on memory, attention, anxiety, and analgesia. Twenty-two studies met our inclusion criteria for this meta-analysis. The results, based on 35 effect sizes, showed an overall medium, significant, consistent effect size (g = 0.45). Meta-regression results indicated that it does not seem to be necessary to mask binaural beats with white noise or pink noise in terms of effectiveness, obtaining similar effects with unmasked binaural beats. Moreover, findings suggest that binaural-beat exposure before, and before and during the task produces superior results than exposure during the task. Time under exposure contributed significantly to the model indicating that longer periods are advisable to ensure maximum effectiveness. Our meta-analysis adds to the growing evidence that binaural-beat exposure is an effective way to affect cognition over and above reducing anxiety levels and the perception of pain without prior training, and that the direction and the magnitude of the effect depends upon the frequency used, time under exposure, and the moment in which the exposure takes place.

As this is simple, cheap, low effort, no side effects way to stimulate the vagus nerve, then you should definitely give it a try. I have started listening to the sounds while meditating and it certainly seems to help.

AURICULAR VAGUS NERVE STIMULATION

There are many devices on the market that that clip to the ears and provide a mild electrical current that is purported to stimulate the vagus nerve. These devices are TENS units (transcutaneous electronic nerve stimulators). If you do a web search, "auricular vagus nerve stimulators," you will find many units that you can compare against one another.

An affordable option can be found in a relatively new device called Xen made by a company called Neuvana. It is an electronic device that delivers small electrical signals the company calls micropulses through headphones directly to the vagus nerve located in your ear. It pairs wirelessly to their app, where you can customize your sessions. Here is their marketing blurb:

A team of physicians, expert engineers and wellness practitioners - today announced the availability of Xen, a revolutionary platform designed to deliver multiple lifestyle, balance and wellness benefits through non-invasive ear-based Vagus Nerve Stimulation (VNS). Xen by Neuvana was designed to safely and gently stimulate the vagus nerve, a communication pathway between the brain and the rest of the body. Xen can be used while going about your daily activities such as listening to music, watching TV or simply enjoying the ambient sounds of your surroundings. With regular use, individuals may experience reduced stress and better sleep, enhanced memory, and improved focus. Xen by Neuvana offers users a modern solution to realize these benefits in today's connected world where people are busy, overly stressed and digitally distracted.

I bought the Xen and I use it frequently. It's a bit of a faff to link it to my music app, so I just use it in its stand-alone function, which is called sensation rhythmic patterns. You use the app to choose a waveform from A to F and then select a sensation from cityscape, high and low, mountaintop, ocean waves, rolling hills, and vista. No matter what combination I select, I simply get the same ticklish feeling in my left ear with no sound. Apparently, you only experience a sensation from the left ear. You can control the level of intensity from the app. I turn it up until I can feel the buzzing to the point where it tickles but doesn't hurt.

ALPHA STIM

Perhaps the most highly rated one for stimulating the vagus nerve is the Alpha Stim device (www.alpha-stim.com). It is a small handheld device that delivers electronic stimulation via clips that connect to the earlobes. This is the unit that I use every day. Their website provides the following information:

Alpha-Stim is an electrotherapy device prescribed around the world by physicians and other healthcare professionals to effectively treat chronic, acute, and post-traumatic pain, and anxiety, insomnia, and depression.

Alpha-Stim is supported by over 100 completed independent research studies and published reports that utilize some of the most rigorous, controlled clinical study methods. Again and again, the Alpha-Stim electrotherapy device has proven to quickly and safely provide relief from pain, anxiety, depression, and insomnia.

Safety

The Alpha-Stim electrotherapy device delivers lasting results for pain, anxiety, depression, and anxiety without dangerous side effects, tolerance, or addiction. In 30+ years and clinical studies involving more than 8,800 people, Alpha-Stim users have reported no serious side effects. The two most common side effects were headaches (0.1%) and skin irritation at the electrode sites (0.07%, only seen in light-skinned people).

And Alpha-Stim is so easy to use, you can administer it yourself at home while relaxing, reading, using a computer or watching TV. Built-in safety features ensure that the electrotherapy device is functioning properly. Small and portable, Alpha-Stim is easy to take with you, wherever you go.

How Alpha-Stim works

Pain, mood conditions (like anxiety and depression), and insomnia are all controlled by your body's central nervous system. The billions of individual cells that comprise the nervous system communicate every sensation by conducting electrochemical signals between the cells in your body and brain.

The Alpha-Stim electrotherapy device works by transmitting a unique, patented electrical waveform to modulate the cells' signals to return to baseline, normal functioning—significantly reducing pain, anxiety, depression, or insomnia without medication. With Alpha-Stim, many people experience significant relief after a single treatment. With continued use, the effects of the Alpha-Stim electrotherapy device can be even greater, increasing cumulatively over time as cell function becomes more readily modulated.

I use the ear clips for about an hour a day. The sensation is one of feeling mild electrical pulses, sometimes they can irritate, so I readjust them or lower the intensity accordingly, but most of the time I feel no sensation. I've been using this for a few weeks now and I believe it has helped to make me generally calmer and has evened out my overall mood. I have fewer mood swings, especially to the more depressive side.

GROUNDING MATS

Grounding mats are thin mats made of polyurethane with a thin conductive material on the top surface that conduct a very small electrical charge via a wire that is plugged into the ground port of an electrical outlet (the round hole below the two rectangular holes in the United States).

They are supposed to mimic the earths' natural electrical charge that is purported to have many health benefits. The idea is that grounding (also called earthing) reconnects you to the earths' energy that has been lost over time due to barriers between us and the natural earth, such as shoes, buildings etc. For the mat to be effective you have to have naked skin touching a part of the mat.

The following is the abstract from a study in 2015 by James Oschamn et al. titled "The Effects of Grounding (Earthing) on Inflammation, the Immune Response, Wound Healing and Prevention and Treatment of Chronic Inflammatory and Autoimmune Diseases."

Multi-disciplinary research has revealed that electrically conductive contact of the human body with the surface of the Earth (grounding or earthing) produces intriguing effects on physiology and health. Such effects relate to inflammation, immune responses, wound healing, and prevention and treatment of chronic inflammatory and autoimmune diseases. The purpose of this report is two-fold: to 1) inform researchers about what appears to be a new perspective to the study of inflammation, and 2) alert researchers that the length of time and degree (resistance to ground) of grounding of experimental animals is an important but usually overlooked factor that can influence outcomes of studies of inflammation, wound healing, and tumorigenesis. Specifically, grounding an organism produces measurable differences in the concentrations of white blood cells, cytokines, and other molecules involved in the inflammatory response. We present several hypotheses to explain observed effects, based on current research results and our understanding of the electronic aspects of cell and tissue physiology, cell biology, biophysics, and biochemistry. An experimental injury to muscles, known as delayed onset muscle soreness, has been used to monitor the immune response under grounded versus ungrounded conditions. Grounding reduces pain and alters the numbers of circulating neutrophils and lymphocytes, and also affects various circulating chemical factors related to inflammation.

If you want to read the whole report, Google: "dove press Oschman."

I've tried using a grounding mat and can honestly say that I found it had little effect. However, everybody is physiologically different, so using a grounding mat might work for you. There are also grounding socks, wristbands, mouse mats, pillow cases, etc. On the plus side they are relatively inexpensive and can be found on Amazon, so what the heck.

OTHER WAYS TO STIMULATE THE VAGUS NERVE

On days when you don't have time for meditation, or it's not something you believe you can do successfully, then try this as an alternative. Take one large deep breath in, hold it for a couple of seconds, then let it all the way out, then hold your breath. As you hold it, push your hands together as hard as you can in a praying type motion for as long as you can while still holding your breath. When you simply can't hold your breath any longer, let a big gulp of air into your lungs. Try this for three repetitions, three times per day for a couple of months. Within a week or two you should see a shift in your mental state with more energy and less anxiety.

CHAPTER SUMMARY

- Chronic fatigue is exacerbated by a dysfunctional autonomic nervous system, which uses large amounts of energy to keep on alert. We need to stimulate the vagus nerve to calm down the nervous system.
- It is probable that the vagus nerve is being pinched by a slightly misaligned upper spine. Fixing the upper spine is paramount. A cervical collar or use of inversion table may be short-term fixes, but make sure you see a chiropractor or orthopedic practitioner.
- Ways to stimulate the vagus nerve and calm the sympathetic nervous system include: Deep slow breathing, meditation, yoga, tai chi, humming or singing, massages, acupuncture,

aromatherapy, cold therapy, more sunlight, more laughing and smiling, listening to calming music, and listening to binaural beats.

- Increase good bacteria in your gut by eating kimchi, natural yogurts, sauerkraut, pickled cabbage, etc. Also drink kombucha.
- Electronic devices that help stimulate the vagus nerve include Muse, Xen, Alpha Stim, and grounding mats.

Chapter 8

HYDROGEN PEROXIDE - KEY THERAPY NO. 1

"Do not go where the path may lead, go instead where there is no path and leave a trail."

Ralph Waldo Emerson

If you have not read her book, then I recommend you take a look. *The One Minute Cure, the secret to healing virtually all diseases* by Madison Cavanaugh is about extolling the virtues of hydrogen peroxide as a method to increase much needed oxygen molecules throughout the body. You could say it is potentially a much more economical version of hyperbaric oxygen therapy or exercise with oxygen therapy (EWOT), both are great therapies and discussed in this book.

The other excellent book to read is *Rapid Virus Recovery* by Dr. Thomas Levy. He believes that if everybody nebulized HP regularly COVID would have been beaten early, with virtually no deaths.

There is a tremendous amount of anecdotal evidence extolling the health benefits that have affected thousands of people with some remarking that it has completely changed their lives.

The more educated I got about HP (hydrogen peroxide, not HP sauce my British friends), the more excited I got, so I decided to buy some and give the therapy a go. Here is my take:

Hydrogen peroxide therapy may be the most important and effective way to ward off all potential pathogens and infections. It is the worst enemy of the COVID virus. It can provide you with an incomparable burst of energy.

It took about three days of nebulizing 2% to 3% food grade HP to start feeling better; within a week I was feeling 80% of my former self. Truly amazing.

90% of biological energy is derived from oxygen and not the food you eat. It is often the first and last line of therapy in saving lives. The first thing a medic will do upon finding a victim in car crash is not to lecture him on braking distance (that's what one of my friends would do, mentioning no names), but to use an oxygen mask. Have you ever thought why? It's because anybody suffering from trauma needs pure oxygen to increase cellular metabolism, which decreases risk of death. The last line of medication for COVID patients is supplied oxygen through ventilators that regulate breathing and force oxygen onto the lungs. Needless to say a healthy oxygen supply is vital for good health and a major symptom of COVID and ME sufferers is poor oxygen metabolism that inhibits energy production. Hydrogen peroxide therapy purports to release large amounts of oxygen in the blood, which provides a myriad of health benefits.

The author of *One Minute Cure* states:

The primary physical cause of all diseases is linked in one way or another to oxygen deficiency. In fact, many of the elaborate and expensive therapies offered by organized medicine take advantage of oxygen's effect on disease cells. Most conventional cancer therapies including chemotherapy and radiation therapy produce oxygen activated events that kill cancer cells. Another new cancer drug Verteporfin, increases the amount of oxygen within tumors and this kills tumors more effectively than radiation alone. Interferon drugs, which are vastly prescribed for the treatment of multiple sclerosis, owe their efficacy to the fact that they raise the body's oxygen level.

HP is already used around the globe by physicians (15,000 in Europe alone) to help eliminate pathogens growing in infected wounds. It is used orally by millions to help whiten teeth. The benefits of HP have been widely written about with many studies and I will go through some of the more pertinent ones in this chapter.

Because HP is extremely efficient at killing pathogens outside the body, many assume that it would be toxic inside the body. This assumption is not based on any scientific study, just musings because most cleaning agents are indeed poisonous to humans. This is logical, and HP is, of course, poisonous in high concentrations (like the majority of pharmaceutical medications); however, HP is an excellent pathogen killer agent at or below 3% concentration. It is incredibly cheap, widely available and nontoxic at this dose.

There are many extraordinary facts about of HP that include:

- HP is present in the exhaled breath of healthy humans and is naturally present in urine, which reduces risk and incidences of infections. HP is present both in and outside the cells in the body. (Google: "B Halliwell Clement M" for further information).
- HP is permeable to all cells including all pathogens.
- HP can set and influence critical thresholds for lymphocyte activation. (Reth M 2002, "HP as second messenger in lymphocyte activation," Google: "Reth M hydrogen peroxide" for the full study.) Lymphocytes are white blood cells in the immune system including T, B and natural killer cells that are activated by antigens.
- HP breaks down into water and oxygen once it has destroyed a pathogen.
- HP breaks down mucus and can eliminate secretions with any pulmonary infection. (Google: "Krishna Pillai science direct" for the abstract of the study.)

HP is a more natural option for the body than antibiotics, which destroys the beneficial bacteria in the intestines. HP is a more natural option because our bodies naturally produce HP as part of our metabolism. Part of our white blood cells are called peroxisomes that wrap around bacteria to destroy them and they produce HP as a byproduct.

As you are aware COVID can cause a serious drop in blood oxygen levels causing silent hypoxia that can damage internal organs if it goes undetected. If you or someone you know has active COVID, make sure they get a pulse oximeter/blood oxygen saturation monitor to constantly measure their blood oxygen. Too many people died when their blood oxygen levels dropped too low and breathing problems exacerbated their problems to the point of no return. Many lives could have been saved by using this cheap device (under $25 on Amazon), which would have warned many to get to the ER earlier when they had a much greater chance of survival.

HP improves blood oxygenation when inhaled via nebulization. HP is converted to water and singlet oxygen in the body and is a powerful oxidizing agent. The effect of singlet oxygen is that it inhibits the growth of anaerobic organisms (viruses and bacteria) and increases blood oxygen levels. You can use a blood saturation oxygen monitor and actually see the numbers change before and after nebulizing with HP. Your blood oxygen levels are measured by percentage and a range between 95% and 100% is considered normal. If a COVID patient's blood oxygen drops significantly below 95%, then they should carefully monitor their blood oxygen levels every hour. If oxygen levels drop below 88%, then this is a major cause for concern. Obviously a COVID patient should see a doctor immediately if blood oxygen levels drop.

Go on Amazon and search for food grade hydrogen peroxide (it is surprisingly cheap), then read the reviews of both the product and related books. There are literally thousands of anecdotal reviews all over the internet and they are certainly compelling; however, most doctors would probably not recommend you ingest hydrogen peroxide, as they likely know nothing about it, it's not FDA approved for ingestion, it is not patentable, and there is no profit to be made as it's an extremely cheap product. Even if your doctor is aware that the therapy exists, they will state that it is too dangerous to take, as there is no way they will want to take on the potential liability of a non-FDA-approved substance.

Even if they are knowledgeable about HP therapy (and even if they use it themselves), they fear that the patient will use the wrong dilution ratio and accidentally poison himself. This fear is probably based on the higher risk of drinking HP, whereas nebulizing is far safer due to the much, much smaller quantity involved in each treatment.

One of the greatest tragedies of the COVID disaster was the limited ability of doctors to treat patients effectively. The millions of Americans who tested positive for the virus were told to stay home and go to the emergency room when they had trouble breathing. In effect, you were only going to get treatment when you were on your death bed and in need of ventilator to help you breathe. What do you think would have happened if everybody was told to inhale HP through a nebulizer? Would over 700,000 people have died in the United States? We will never know the answer.

Ironically, there are thousands of clinics in the United States that do offer HP therapy, via IV (intravenous) infusion. Simply Google: *IV HP near me*, and you may be surprised how many clinics, both static and mobile offer this therapy. I did a Google maps search and was surprised to find several clinics north of San Diego that offer this treatment. So, should you take HP by IV? Personally, I haven't tried it, as inhaling through a nebulizer is less invasive, faster, cheaper, more convenient and you can use it every day.

If you are unsure or nervous about nebulizing HP yourself and want a professional to oversee the therapy, and don't mind needles, then IV infusion is an alternative.

There's a clinic called the Wilkinson Clinic (based in Washington State) that had quoted Dr. Frank Shallenberger, who had an interesting take on the therapy. This is what he had to say:

I can say that what I am going to tell you about has worked in every viral infection I have used it on to date. I'm talking about hydrogen peroxide therapy. But this is not your ordinary hydrogen peroxide therapy. That's what's different. As you may already know, hydrogen peroxide has been used for decades to conquer viral infections by thousands of doctors in thousands of patients all over the world. It was discovered by an old colleague of mine, Dr. Charles Farr, close to thirty years ago.

Hydrogen peroxide consists of a water molecule (H_2O) with an extra oxygen atom (H_2O_2). It is the extra oxygen atom that makes it so deadly for viruses. But in order for you to understand why hydrogen peroxide therapy works so well you have to understand what most people, including many doctors, fail to realize – viral infections are eradicated from the body not by killing the virus itself, but by killing the cells that produce them. Let me explain.

You see, viruses are not alive, so it is not possible to kill them. Viruses are just pieces of genetic code, and in and of themselves can neither survive nor reproduce. Viruses need to infect cells. It is in the interior of a cell that a virus is able to use the cell's own DNA and RNA in order to reproduce. In other words, what a virus does to an infected cell is to control it and use it to manufacture new viruses, which in turn can move out of the cell and go and infect other cells. The way to control any viral infection is not to kill the virus, it is to kill the infected cells that have been turned into viral factories. And that's just what that extra oxygen atom on hydrogen peroxide does.

Healthy cells, cells that are not infected by viruses, are equipped to handle the extra oxygen atom that comes with hydrogen peroxide because they have healthy anti-oxidant defense systems. But once they are infected with a virus, they lose much of their defensive capability, and are then easily destroyed by hydrogen peroxide.

Thanks to Charlie Farr I am not in the least concerned about the epidemic of any virus. Why should I be? Hydrogen peroxide has been shown to control every viral infection it's been tested against. In fact, hydrogen peroxide is so good it's what God designed your immune cells to use to kill and control infections of all kinds. When your immune cells are busy killing the infected cells that make viruses, they make their own hydrogen peroxide to do it. And that's basically how it works. Hydrogen peroxide therapy works by helping your immune cells do the job they were assigned.

THE MAJOR PROBLEM WITH THIS TREATMENT

There is, however, one serious flaw with using hydrogen peroxide to kill viral infections - it is inexpensive and un-patentable. That translates out to not profitable, and not profitable translates out to it won't be taught in medical schools. Nevertheless, regardless of this defect, it is a therapeutic slam dunk for viral infections of all kinds. I have never seen it fail. I have treated everything from flu to encephalitis to viral pneumonia, from influenza to hanta virus to West Nile virus all with the same result—the infection clears, and there are no side effects.

The only other problem with Dr. Farr's therapy is that it is an intravenous therapy. Drinking it not only doesn't work, it is dangerous. And as an intravenous therapy, that means that it needs to be done in a doctor's office. But as long as you get into the clinic for an IV or two, you can literally knock out any viral infection you will ever get. (FYI - at Wilkinson Wellness we don't do the H2O2 IVs but we do other effective treatments such as using ozone as UBI/major autohemotherapy and vitamin C.) And that brings me to something that I came upon a little over a year ago. A new way of administering hydrogen peroxide therapy that is almost as effective as the IV. And better than the IV method, this new treatment can be done at home, and is ridiculously cheap. It's called nebulized hydrogen peroxide. And this is how I learned about it.

About a year ago I saw a patient with asthma who was taking the asthma medication that her doctor had been giving her in a nebulizer. A nebulizer is device that is able to convert a liquid into tiny bubbles. I mean really tiny bubbles. Bubbles that are so tiny that they can only be seen under a microscope. When these bubbles come out of the nebulizer, they are so small that they look just like smoke. And that's the magic of a nebulizer.

The bubbles are so small that they can be inhaled deep down into the deepest regions of the lungs without any discomfort or irritation. It's a great way for asthmatics to get the medication they need to open up their lungs. But there is something else about nebulizers that I had never considered before until I treated this particular patient. It's an obvious thing, but then again, things are only obvious once you see them. I'm talking about the systemic effect of nebulizers. Let me explain.

When I asked the patient why she didn't use the nebulizer treatments as often as she was supposed to, she said it was because of the side effects, and then she said something that really struck me. "Dr. Shallenberger, when I take the drug in the nebulizer it makes me feel the side effects just as bad as when the doctors were giving me the same drug intravenously in the hospital. It is unbelievably strong, and it affects my whole body." You see, these tiny bubbles were not only delivering medicine to her lungs, they were also delivering the medicine to her entire body through her lungs. And they were delivering it in a way that was just as noticeable to her as when the same medication was given directly into her veins. And that's when I had the thought. Why not use the nebulizer delivery system to deliver treatments not just to the lungs but to the whole body?

DR SHALLENBERGER'S FIRST PATIENT

So I went to work, and began administering hydrogen peroxide to my patients through a nebulizer instead of intravenously. The first patient I used it on was me. I wasn't sick at the time, but I just wanted to make sure that the mixture I used was the right concentration for the lungs. I found the treatment extremely easy to do, and very comfortable. It was just like breathing the purest air you could imagine, and it was in no way irritating.

And then I found my first guinea pig – my wife Judy. Judy learned long ago that one of the "blessings" of marrying me was that she would often have the privilege of being experimented on. And so when she developed the first symptoms of a flu, instead of immediately plugging her into a hydrogen peroxide IV, I had her use the nebulizer for ten minutes every waking hour. Actually, she was happy about this, because she has very small veins, and it is hard for the nurse to start IV's on her. Using the nebulizer treatment, she was able to get rid of the flu within 72 hours. I knew I was on to something, because IV hydrogen peroxide doesn't work much better than that. So, I bought a dozen nebulizers and began offering the treatment to my patients.

Since then, I have treated hundreds of cases of colds, flus, sinusitis, and bronchitis all with the same great results. And I found that the nebulizer treatments actually have an advantage over the IV therapy that I hadn't considered at first. And that is, that not only is the hydrogen peroxide being disseminated into the entire body through the lungs, it is also going directly to the areas of the body that are most affected by viruses – the sinuses, throat, bronchial tract, and lungs. So here's how you do it.

First, buy yourself a nebulizer. I am now convinced that not only should every family have a blood pressure cuff and a thermometer, but also a nebulizer. You can buy an inexpensive one that runs off AC for as little as $29 (Remember, this was in 2009 - the prices are a bit different. Portable nebulizers might be less expensive, according to some sites). Or you can spend a little more and get a smaller, easy to carry around, battery operated nebulizer that will put you out about $60.

Next, we will supply you with the hydrogen peroxide solution. It's a special mixture of 100 cc of normal saline with 5 cc of pharmaceutical grade 3% hydrogen peroxide. Sorry, you can't make this up yourself. We do make this solution up for patients in the office. Let us know and we can provide it for you. We usually put appropriately more H2O2 in a 250cc bag of sterile water or saline.

139

When kept in the refrigerator, the formula will stay active for about 12 months. Sorry, it won't keep indefinitely. That's because the hydrogen peroxide will gradually convert into water over time. You can either just keep some on hand during the flu season, or have us send you some as soon as it appears you need it.

Just keep this in the fridge until you feel like you may be coming down with a virus. As with any viral treatment, to get the best results it is important to use the treatment as soon as possible. And that's one of the other great advantages of the nebulizer treatment. If you start coming down with something on the weekend or a holiday, it's not a problem – you can start treatment without having to wait until the clinic opens.

THE ACTUAL TREATMENT

The treatments are simple. Just attach the delivery mask to the nebulizer output. Then add 3-4cc of the hydrogen peroxide mixture to the nebulizer, place the mask over your mouth and nose, and breathe. It's as simple as that. You can literally do this as often as you feel you need to, but in most cases I recommend that patients do it for 30-60 minutes, 2-3 times a first day until the infection is completely resolved. In most cases, if you start the treatment early enough, before it has gotten a stronghold, this will be in 2-4 days. This treatment can also be used on children and infants of all ages.

I honestly believe that having a nebulizer and the hydrogen peroxide treatment at home would be the end to your family ever having to miss work or school because of a viral illness.

Summary

Dr. Shallenberger provides some great ideas. In his experience, this has always worked for viral issues. In my experience, it works certainly much of the time - can't say I've ever done careful research to find in what percentage of cases it will work. From a practical standpoint, I think he's probably right.

With this information, you have some options that you might not have had before. The Coronavirus doesn't kill people. It's the resulting inflammation down in the lungs that does the dirty deed. This treatment may be particularly helpful for treating issues way down in the lungs.

Use this information as you see fit. We provide it as an education. Don't avoid conventional treatment if you are not getting better. And what I mean by this is: if you are getting worse in spite of any treatment, such as more shortness of breath, more difficulty breathing, get to the emergency room for evaluation and treatment. Don't delay.

But using the information we've provided you over the past few weeks, we hope you'll be able to either not get sick or experience only mild symptoms.

THE RISKS

As I've already stated and will reiterate again, the greatest risk with this therapy is getting the dosage (dilution) wrong. Food grade hydrogen peroxide generally comes in form of 3%, 12%, 30%, or 35% concentration. Any concentration over 3% MUST be diluted down to 3% to be generally regarded as safe. Make sure you only buy 3% food grade hydrogen peroxide to take the risk out of diluting it incorrectly, even though this is a slightly more expensive way to buy it. You can find 3% food grade HP at the following websites:

www.healthandmed.com
www.vitacost.com
www.thrivemarket.com

(And by the time you read this, probably on Amazon). So what if you ingest the wrong concentration? The website poison.org states the following:

Hydrogen peroxide (H_2O_2) appears very similar to water (H_2O) – it's tasteless, odorless, and colorless. Unlike water, it has two oxygen atoms *instead of one and it's slightly thicker than water. Another important difference is that hydrogen peroxide is not as stable as water; it's reactive. For instance, when in the stomach, the molecule breaks apart into oxygen and water, causing bubbles to form. If there are enough of these bubbles, they stretch the stomach and the person vomits up the foam. A small amount of hydrogen peroxide is not absorbed from the stomach into the body; once the stomach settles down, no other problems are expected. Serious problems can occur when a large amount – more than the sip or two you'd expect someone to drink by accident – is swallowed, or if the percentage of hydrogen peroxide in the product is high.*

Swallowing a small amount (a taste or a sip) of household hydrogen peroxide might cause stomach upset, an episode of vomiting, or throat irritation, but it is not expected to cause any serious symptoms. It's different if someone drinks a large amount of household peroxide (this is unlikely to happen accidentally), or if it's a high-concentration product. This can be much more serious and result in severe stomach irritation and even burns that require a trip to the emergency room and possible hospital admission.

Another serious but rare complication that might occur with ingestion or wound irrigation of hydrogen peroxide is a gas embolism. A gas embolism occurs when bubbles of air or other gas travel to the blood or circulatory system. They then cause blockage of a blood vessel. For instance, if there is air in a blood vessel that supplies part of the brain, much-needed oxygen and nutrients cannot get to that part of the brain, and a stroke occurs. Most cases of air embolism caused by hydrogen peroxide have occurred after large ingestions or ingestions of higher concentration products. Some symptoms of gas embolism include difficulty breathing, chest pain, and confusion. Though very rare, it can be life threatening and emergent medical attention is required. During use for any purpose, hydrogen peroxide could splash into the eyes, or contact lens solution containing hydrogen peroxide can be mistaken for regular multipurpose cleaner and accidentally applied directly into the eye prior to neutralization. If this happens, immediately rinse with plenty of running water for 15-20 minutes. Then, copy this URL address:

https://triage.webpoisoncontrol.org/#!/exclusions online tool for guidance or call Poison Control at 1-800-222-1222.

Hydrogen peroxide splashed onto the skin could cause the skin to blanch, or whiten, for a short time. The area might feel tingly for a while, too. Again, rinse with plenty of running water. Skin burns are possible if high-concentration of hydrogen peroxide was involved.

Just to reiterate a very important point: any concentration over 3% may be dangerous to ingest, especially if you drink it. This is my protocol: buy saline solution and dilute the 3% down to 2%. This takes absolutely all the risk out of it, but leaves you with all the incredible benefits. I have found, in my experience, 2% to 2.5% HP is extremely well tolerated and safe to use. Be safe and only get the 3% food grade HP and dilute with saline to 2%, carefully measure out 2 to 3 ml and insert into your nebulizer. **Make sure to nebulize it and not drink it.** In nebulized form, you ingest a tiny fraction of those who drink it, taking out all the risk of ingestion (2 ml in nebulized form compared with 8 oz in a drink—that is only 0.034 oz in nebulized form). Even if you do use a high concentration by mistake in your nebulizer, you would know about it instantly, as your first breath in would sting your nose sufficiently to make you stop instantly.

Almost everybody is willing to use approved drugs that may pose serious side effects and health risks, based on their perceived risk/benefit. In the United States, doctors prescribe FDA-approved pharmaceuticals that cause over 100,000 deaths every year, ranking it the 4th leading cause of death (not including overdoses). So if a doctor tells you it's too dangerous to nebulize HP, gently remind them of this fact. So don't be put off by the potential for HP to do harm. Yes, it will do harm in the wrong concentration and if you drink it, but almost any substance is dangerous if you take the wrong dose. HP is safer than ibuprofen and acetaminophen, and I bet you don't think twice about giving those to your kids.

CANKER SORES/MOUTH ULCERS

Here is a super valuable tip. If you suffer from these intensely irritating mouth sores from time to time (they manifest when under times of stress and lack of sleep and common with chronic fatigue), swishing 2%-3% HP solution in your mouth will stop them almost immediately! Do this when you first feel the mouth sore coming on and swish two to three times per day and the mouth sore will not appear.

Google: "food grade hydrogen peroxide therapy" if you're interested in finding out more.

REMEMBER, THIS THERAPY MIGHT CHANGE YOUR LIFE OR SAVE YOUR LIFE AND IS THE MOST IMPORTANT DAILY THERAPY IN BEATING COVID AND CHRONIC FATIGUE!

CHAPTER SUMMARY

- Hydrogen peroxide therapy is the most important and effective way to ward off all potential pathogens. It can provide you with a burst of energy. It is the most important therapy for long COVID and ME patients.
- When your immune cells are busy killing the infected cells that make viruses, they make their own hydrogen peroxide to do it. And that's basically how it works. Hydrogen peroxide therapy works by helping your immune cells do the job they were assigned.
- Only nebulize HP for best results. Don't drink it, even though there are many people who do; nebulizing is both safer and more effective.

- Dilute food grade hydrogen peroxide from 3% to 2% using a saline solution. Use 2-3 ml HP in a nebulizer. Treatment takes about ten minutes for 2 ml and about 15 minutes for 3 ml. NEVER USE A CONCENTRATION HIGHER THAN 3%.
- HP therapy could change your life, save your life and extend your life.

C hapter 9

GLUTATHIONE - KEY THERAPY NO. 2

"Live as if you were to die tomorrow. Learn as if you were to live forever."

Mahatma Gandhi

Glutathione is an amino acid compound (tripeptide) that is present in the body's cells and is made from cysteine, glutamic acid and glycine. It is a vital antioxidant that reduces oxidative stress on the body and suppresses the production of free radicals, the molecules that damage the body's cells and a serious cause of inflammation of the brain.

Oxidative stress is defined as a disturbance in the balance between the production of reactive oxygen species (free radicals) and antioxidant defenses, which is a disaster for long COVID and CFS sufferers. Free radicals cause damage to biomolecules such as proteins and lipids and leads to a whole host of chronic diseases including arthritis, diabetes and potentially cancer. But most pertinent to long COVID and CFS sufferers is the creation of chronic inflammation, and if you're unsure by now, inflammation is enemy number and must be defeated.

Our body's supply of glutathione levels slowly reduces as we get older, which leaves us less able to detoxify the onslaught of chemicals forced upon us in this modern world. It is absolutely imperative to get glutathione levels back up so we can deal with all the toxins that tax and exhaust the system.

But why is glutathione so important for those with chronic fatigue and long COVID? Well, Dr. Dikoma Shungu of Cornell University has used advanced magnetic resonance spectroscopy (MRS) to measure brain lactic acid, glutathione, and metabolites in patients with chronic fatigue. These spectroscopies have shown that CFS patients have lower than average glutathione levels in their brains. This means that it is harder to defeat free radicals and clear toxins from the system and perhaps the key reason why so many suffer from chemical sensitivity issues.

High amount of glutathione exists in the liver and hepatocytes (chief functional cells in the liver) that can have as much as ten times the amount of glutathione than other cells in the body, highlighting how important glutathione is in detoxifying the body.

You may recall that a recurring theme in this book is that people with chronic fatigue have great difficulty making cellular energy via the Krebs cycle, generating ATP through mitochondrial function. But mitochondria are subject to damage by free radicals, causing oxidative stress inhibiting optional functioning. This is why glutathione is one of the key cures in helping you replenish your energy levels as it protects the mitochondria from this harmful damage.

Glutathione also promotes natural killer cell function, absolutely vital for a healthy immune system. A recent study demonstrated the liposomal glutathione had a major effect on the functioning of natural killer cells (Sinha et al. "Oral supplementation with liposomal glutathione elevates body stores of glutathione and markers of immune function," published in *European Journal of Clinical Nutrition*).

If you haven't taken the hint by now, GLUTATHIONE IS BLOODY IMPORTANT, AND VITAL FOR YOUR RECOVERY. (You need to imagine I said this in an English accent for it to have the resonance I was aiming for.)

Need more convincing? Glutathione is a vital antioxidant and is much reduced in people with chronic conditions. It supports mitochondrial health (needed for your energy) and vital for proper immune support (needed for you to stay healthy). Low glutathione levels are disastrous causing a mass of free radicals that run riot, causing oxidative stress, which means that exercising leads to post exertional malaise and the awful fatigue that plagues long COVID and ME patients.

GLUTATHIONE AND COVID 19

A recent study published in October 2020 explored glutathione as an adjunct therapy for COVID, undertaken by The College of Osteopathic Medicine of the Pacific, Western University of Health Sciences (Google: "glutathione COVID 19 study" for further information). The study concluded that glutathione inhibits viral replication and GSH deficiency is associated with a more severe manifestation of COVID. While this study only looked at acute COVID cases, one might predict that higher levels of GSH could reduce symptoms of long COVID.

There are two different types of glutathione; reduced glutathione, which is the active form, and oxidized glutathione, which is the inactive form. When the active form of glutathione does its magic and eradicates the free radicals it turns into the inactive form.

What form of glutathione should you take?

You can get some glutathione from foods, such as garlic, asparagus, broccoli, avocados, and spinach, but not enough to materially boost your levels; however, you should be eating these foods to boost your overall health anyway.

You can take glutathione via IV (intravenous) at a local clinic, this is useful if you need a quick pick-me-up, but this may not be the best way to take it, as it is costly, time consuming and you may find that you go back to your baseline levels a day or two after the IV.

You can take it orally; liposomal glutathione and S-Acetyl Glutathione can survive the arduous journey through the intestinal tract and can increase GSH levels. There is a form of glutathione called trizomal glutathione, which is a liposomal solution comprising S-acetyl glutathione combined with reduced glutathione and N-acetyl cysteine (NAC). The NAC allows for greater intracellular biosynthesis and provides a double layer of the glutathione molecule providing greater protection through the intestinal tract.

Transdermal glutathione, used as topical cream, can be effective; however, it has skin lightening properties, so be careful where you use it.

In my opinion, the best way to get glutathione into the body is to use reduced glutathione in a nebulizer and inhale 3 ml once per day. I also take 1,000 mg liposomal glutathione in capsule form each day.

There are few to no side effects of using glutathione. It is a natural substance found in cells in the human body. If you take very high amounts, you may get stomach upset and diarrhea.

The combination of nebulizing 3 ml glutathione once per day and nebulizing 3 ml of 2% to 2.5% food grade hydrogen peroxide once a day is a one-two knockout punch for all pathogens, while boosting the immune system and increasing mitochondria function. Make sure you clean the nebulizer between uses.

Through experimenting using this combination on myself, I can state with confidence that using both glutathione nebulization and hydrogen peroxide nebulization (separately, not together!) is the remedy for fatigue that I have been seeking for all these years. While I cannot guarantee that this will work for everyone, there is no reason why it shouldn't provide the same therapeutic advantage for those who try it. However, I was very disciplined in my approach, making sure I nebulized HP in the morning and glutathione in the evening every day of the week.

CHAPTER SUMMARY

- Glutathione is an amino acid that is present in the body's cells. It is a vital antioxidant that destroys free radicals and reduces oxidative stress. Free radicals cause inflammation in the body and brain and must be kept in check to avoid chronic fatigue.

- Natural levels of glutathione reduce slowly as we get older. We need to boost our levels in order to protect ourselves from the pollutants and chemicals that exist in our modern world. Long COVID and ME patients have lower amounts of glutathione in brain matter than healthy subjects of the same age.

- Mitochondria are subject to damage by free radicals. Glutathione is the key substance to abate this and allow mitochondria to help generate ATP.

- Glutathione also promotes natural killer cell function, absolutely vital for a healthy immune system.

- A study in 2020 concluded that glutathione inhibits viral replication and that glutathione deficiency is associated with a more severe manifestation of COVID.

- Reduced glutathione is the active form and can be taken orally (liposomal glutathione best as s-acetyl-glutathione) as a topical cream or, optimally via use of a nebulizer.

$\mathbf{C}$ hapter 10

HIGH DOSE VITAMIN D$_3$ - KEY THERAPY NO. 3

"To achieve great things, two things are needed: a plan and not quite enough time."

Leonard Bernstein

I first found out about high dose vitamin D$_3$ from a book titled *The Optimal Dose, Restore Your Health with the Power of Vitamin D* by Judson Somerville, MD. The book is fascinating and I recommend you pick up a copy. The author's story is one of tragedy and tough challenges leaving him paraplegic after a bike accident, followed by a spider bite that required part of his leg needing amputation. He suffered with a host of illnesses included various infections and sleeping problems. He persevered, carried on practicing as a doctor and found his own route to health when traditional pharmaceuticals failed him.

His research led him to find that almost all of his patients were deficient in vitamin D$_3$, which weakens the immune system, prohibits deep sleep and slows food metabolism. He purports that high dose vitamin D$_3$ reduces symptoms of chronic fatigue, autism, Lyme, influenza, cancer, multiple sclerosis, obesity, diabetes, sleep apnea and dementia. He claims the high dose (which he calls optimal dose) vitamin D$_3$ saved his life and the life of some of his patients.

Vitamin D$_3$ is not a vitamin but a hormone that is produced from direct sunlight and some foods and has a role in calcium and phosphorus metabolism. The body uses vitamin D as a hormone to perform endocrine and autocrine functions. Vitamin D is known as ergocalciferol (vitamin

D_2) and cholecalciferol (vitamin D_3). D_2 is not produced in the body, but made by plant materials in response to ultraviolet light. D_3 is produced by the body through sun exposure and foods.

Originally the suggestion of an optimal dose came from a presentation the author saw from Dr. Stasha Gominak, a Harvard-trained neurologist whose research showed a link between lack of deep restorative sleep (DRS) and low D_3 levels. She discussed the link between D_3's effect on how it governs our muscle movements at night, controls our appetite and how it affects our immune system. She recommended 20,000 IU of vitamin D_3 per day for 6 weeks and then a reduction to 10,000 IU per day to increase blood levels up to approximately 50-60 ng/ml levels. The author states:

The fact that she was comfortable recommending such a dose gave me the confidence that I too could take that dose. So I immediately upped my dose. I also recommended the same dosing to patients under my care. Very soon after I saw the beneficial effects. The first and soonest to appear for me was improved sleep, which looked to be the solution to my problems helping patients overcome their fatigue. I was sure that if I were more rested, it would also help me tremendously.

The author states that the recommended dietary allowance (RDA) as set by The Institute of Medicine (IOM) is insanely low. He explains that the dangers of D_3 toxicity only occur if extremely high doses are taken. D_3 was discovered as a substance that cured rickets in the 1930s and the dosage was set based on the required amount to be effective for rickets. It was erroneously labeled a vitamin because other fat-soluble vitamins that accumulate in the body can become toxic, the early scientists assumed it must be the same for vitamin D as well. They assumed the lowest dose that cured rickets would suffice and assumed a level above that dose might prove toxic. The conclusion was that a dose below 100 ng/ml (250 nmol/L) was the safe level. That made little sense as their own data suggested that levels might prove toxic are at around 300 ng/ml (750 nmol/L) and the difference was simply a buffer to allow for a wide safety margin. This super wide safety margin was a huge mistake, the author exclaims, as it has helped fuel the massive deficiency in the United States population exacerbated by fewer hours in direct sunlight (working indoors, using sunscreen, etc.). The author goes on to state:

Because of this arbitrary decision, I hesitated in taking higher doses of vitamin D3, afraid that I would poison myself. It's why I hesitated in recommending higher doses to my patients as well. I based my understanding of vitamin D3 toxicity on a standard that was not even based on evidence, but on someone's arbitrary decision hoping to be helpful. Not only is this arbitrary standard not helpful, but also it has not made us safer and healthier. I argue that this decision has kept people from achieving the health they deserve. The decision has hurt us.

So what exactly is D_3 toxicity? If you take too much D_3 it raises calcium in the blood that can cause a condition known as hypercalcemia, the symptoms being nausea, constipation, decreased appetite, peptic ulcer disease, abdominal pain, frequent urination, kidney stones, confusion, memory loss, aching bones. The best way to check for potential overdose is to check your calcium blood level (not vitamin D blood level). If you follow his advice and try higher doses of D_3, then make sure you have your calcium blood levels checked.

With regard to dosing, the author states:

With Dr. Gominak's recommendations serving as further validation, I increased the doses to her recommended loading dose of 20,000 IU per day. It was only when patients took 20,000 IU per day that they reported a noticeable positive effect, better sleep and overall better feeling. However, when the patients dropped down to 10,000 IU per day, without exception they reported returned sleep difficulties and loss of that state of good feeling. I continued to experiment and soon increased my dose to 30,000 IU per day. After a year of no side effects and many notable improvements, I recommended to all my patients under my care that they too take 30,000 IU per day. All my future patients started on this dose and it has been working great. Initially I was testing patients' blood levels with the aim of maintaining their vitamin D3 blood levels between 80-120 ng/ml. However, over the years I've come to the conclusion that with optimal vitamin D3 dosing at 30,000 IU per day, the optimum level of D3 in the blood should be between 100-140 ng/ml. With this conclusion I'm now calling 30,000 IU per day the 'optimum daily administration' or ODA, of vitamin D3 and 100-140 ng/ml of D3 in the blood the 'clinical optimal blood level' or COBL of vitamin D3 in the blood.

For the past 8 years my patients and I have been taking this ODA of vitamin D3 and maintained COBL as well. Other than two patients who complained of upset stomachs upon starting the optimal dosing treatments, there have been no other negative side effects. There hasn't been a single case of hypercalcemia, which shouldn't be surprising considering in chapter 3 we went into detail about how findings indicate that hypercalcemia does not start until vitamin D3 blood levels reach the 300-450 ng/ml level. For readers still worried about toxicity, recall that I also discussed how difficult it is to increase a person's vitamin D3 blood level. Thus it is extremely unlikely that anyone would accidentally overdose themselves at the 30,000 IU per day optimal dose I recommend. Of the thousands of patients whom I have recommended this dose to and who have been taking it daily over the years, the highest blood level I ever saw was 250 ng/ml. It turned out this patient had accidentally been taking double the recommended dose. Even at this blood level, her calcium levels were normal. Other than that patient, the highest level I encountered was 150 ng/ml, a level 10 ng/ml above the upper threshold of COBL, but one that I found to be safe in me and my patients. I found ingesting the ODA of vitamin D3 at 30,000 IU per day, we stayed well out of range of vitamin D3 toxicity.

VITAMIN D AND COVID 19

Vitamin D is a known immunomodulator, a substance that modifies the immune response in a beneficial way. After an initial immune response such as swelling and pain, the slower response to a pathogen is executed by the adaptive side of the immune system. This adaptive side has a long-term memory and prevents pathogens infecting us more than once. Immunomodulators, such as vitamin D can help defend against pathogens by adjusting the immune response to respond more effectively once a pathogen has been detected.

There has been a study titled, "Impact of daily high dose oral vitamin D therapy on the inflammatory markers in patients with COVID 19" published May 2021 by Maheshwar Lakkireddy et al. (Google: "high dose vitamin D and covid 19" for the full report.)

The study aimed to investigate the impact of vitamin D in reducing inflammatory markers of COVID 19 using daily supplementation of 60,000 IUs for 8 to 10 days depending on the subject's BMI (body mass index). The analysis of inflammatory markers in the dosed group before and after treatment showed highly significant reduction ($p<0.01$) in ALL measured inflammatory markers (with a significant increase in vitamin D blood levels). Inflammation in the placebo group remained unchanged.

The study is further proof that vitamin D is an extremely useful tool in reducing inflammation throughout the body and remains an incredibly important supplement for battling chronic fatigue.

The online medical news site, www.medscape.com, recently reported that **vitamin D deficiency on admission to hospital was associated with a 3.7 fold increase in the odds of dying from COVID 19.**

CONCLUSION

The Mayo clinic did a large meta-analysis of vitamin D deficiency in the United States, a short excerpt of the report as published on the website www.wholehealthchicago.com stated the following:

To give you an idea of the numbers involved, it is estimated that 60,000 Americans die prematurely of cancer every year because of vitamin

D deficiency. Add to this premature autoimmune disease (such as multiple sclerosis), heart disease, allergies (like asthma), diabetes, and Alzheimer's and the numbers become mind-boggling. Moreover, a pregnant woman's vitamin D level can imprint genetic susceptibilities onto her developing fetus. It was likely quite shocking for researchers to realize that low levels of D during pregnancy increased a newborn's later risks for autism, schizophrenia, multiple sclerosis, and a variety of chronic illnesses, any of which can shorten longevity and most of which compromise the quality of our lives.

According to another study in 2018 titled "Prevalence of Vitamin D Deficiency and Associated Risk Factors in US population," by N Parva et al. (Google: "Vitamin D deficiency N Parva" for the full report), 41.6% of adults in the United States are deficient in vitamin D, with deficiencies in 63% of Hispanic adults and 82% of African Americans.

RISKS OF OVERDOSE

So what are the actual risks of vitamin D overdose? I could not find any adult fatalities in the United States caused by vitamin D overdose; however, there was a case of a 2-year-old boy who was accidentally overdosed and admitted to the ER. Unfortunately, his mother gave him an entire ampule of vitamin D supplement per day (600,000 IUs) over 4 days instead of 2 drops from one ampule per day. The 2-year-old boy took 2,400,000 IUs over 4 days. His serum calcium level hit a very high peak of 470ng/ml and his hypercalcemia persisted for two weeks. The boy made a complete recovery and asked his mom if she wouldn't mind letting him check the dose of future medications. She said yes, but finish your fourth gallon of milk first.

The Mayo Clinic (www.mayoclinincproceedings.org) published a paper in May 2015 titled "Vitamin D is not as toxic as was once thought: A historical and up to date perspective." Google: "Mayo Clinic vitamin D toxicity" for further information.

If you doctor tells you it's too dangerous to take high dose vitamin D3, ask him to do some research and advise you after he has become educated on the subject. You might also want to remind your doctor that the risks of vitamin D deficiency are greater than the risks of taking too much. Those deficient in vitamin D are unwittingly risking their lives as they are 3.4 times more likely to die from COVID.

CHAPTER SUMMARY

- Vitamin D3 is not a vitamin, but a hormone that is produced from direct sunlight and some foods and has a role in calcium and phosphorus metabolism. The body uses vitamin D as a hormone to perform endocrine and autocrine functions.
- Vitamin D is a known immunomodulator, which is a substance that modifies the adaptive immune response. This adaptive side has a long-term memory and prevents pathogens infecting us more than once. Immunomodulators, such as vitamin D can help defend against pathogens by adjusting the immune response to respond more effectively.
- A study aimed to investigate the impact of vitamin D in reducing inflammatory markers of COVID 19 showed a significant reduction in ALL measured inflammatory markers. The study is further proof that vitamin D is an extremely useful tool in reducing inflammation and incredibly important for battling chronic fatigue.

Chapter 11

PULSATING ELECTROMAGNETIC FIELD THERAPY (PEMF)

"PEMF is a benefit for mankind and will lead to a change in the paradigm of medicine."

Dr. Linus Pauling, 2 x Nobel Prize Winner

Pulsating electromagnetic fields sounds like something you might hear on an original Star Trek episode from Scotty: "I canny get the pulsating electromagnetic fields to synchronize captain. She's gonna blow." But rather than being a far futuristic mumbo jumbo new age therapy, the technology is actually based on earth generated magnetic fields, which has been around for billions of years (allegedly). PEMF is provided in a mat (different sizes available) that you either lie down on, sit on or wrap around a particular part of the body. A PEMF mat produces electromagnetic waves that penetrate the body, and as the waves pass through the body, they increase the spin of the electrons in your cells. The technology has been around for over 50 years and there are over 7,000 studies and clinical trials, so please forgive me for not listing them all. (Google: "PEMF clinical trials.") However, the most prominent study was undertaken by NASA to test PEMF therapy on returning astronauts to help them regain bone and muscle mass. The study found that PEMF stimulated tissue growth and repair and enhanced cell function.

PEMF is also purported to do the following: increase blood circulation, reduce inflammation, reduce pain, boosts immune system and increase quality and duration of sleep.

So how does this therapy actually work? Well, it's all starts with the Schumann resonance and, no, it has nothing to do with the German composer who died in 1846. The Schumann resonances are a range of very low frequencies that can be identified in the Earth's electromagnetic field. The Schumann resonances range from 0-30 Hertz, with the predominant harmonic being 7.83 Hz, which is the magnetic frequency that also occurs in all living organisms. PEMF mats emit a magnetic frequency that mimics the Schumann resonance and electrically charges the body's cells by stimulating the electrons in the cells. These Earth-based magnetic frequencies send a small voltage across the cell membrane, exciting electrons that help to generate ATP adenosine triphosphate. You will recall the slow creation of ATP is the reason you can't exercise without crashing and any therapy that can help you generate ATP faster is extremely important to aid in your recovery.

According to Bryant A Meyer's book *PEMF: The 5th Element of Health*, there are seven cellular benefits that are derived from PEMF therapy:
- Recharges the trans-membrane potential or TMP. (TMP is the difference in electric potential between the interior and exterior of a cell).
- Increases ATP production in the mitochondria. Yes sir! Absolutely vital for chronic fatigue sufferers.
- Enhances the sodium-potassium pump. (The sodium–potassium pump is found in many cell (plasma) membranes. Powered by ATP, the pump moves sodium and potassium ions in opposite directions, each against its concentration gradient. In a single cycle of the pump, three sodium ions are extruded from and two potassium ions are imported into the cell).
- Increases cellular pH to make the cells and body more alkaline.
- Improve oxygen uptake and assimilation into the cells.
- Lowers blood viscosity and improves circulation and microcirculation.
- Creates a healthy level of electroporation (openings in the cells for improved nutrient transport and elimination).

CELLULAR VOLTAGE

The German physiologist and Nobel Laureate, Otto Warburg, stated that healthy cells have a voltage of 70-100 millivolts, with the heart cells having the highest voltage of around 90-100 millivolts). His research found that as we age our cellular voltage declines gradually and persistently depending on environmental factors. The cellular voltage levels of those with chronic fatigue had a vociferous decline in voltage (30-50 millivolts). He found that people with cancer had even lower voltage levels of around 20-30 millivolts.

The higher the voltage in your cells the healthier you are and the longer your life expectancy. PEMF is essentially a battery charger for the cells that assist in producing ATP in the mitochondria. Would you like further explanation? Okay, you asked for it (science bit alert). There are approximately 100 trillion cells in your body and between 200 to 300 mitochondria in each and every cell. Their purpose is to covert fatty acids and glucose that you ingest into an electrical charge that is stored in your ATP. Mitochondria are truly extraordinary and fascinating as they have their own DNA that is circular shaped (not double helix like the rest of your DNA) and can live independent of the cell they inhabit. 90% of all your energy comes from mitochondria, which stores electrons inside their double-walled membrane and they can reproduce and multiply like bacteria.

ATP is also extraordinary as, believe it or not, you actually expend your entire body weight of ATP each day! As there is only about 50 grams of ATP in your body, then the ATP is recycled between 1,000 and 1,500 times per day by your mitochondria. That's why the higher the voltage (or electron activity) in the mitochondria, the faster you can replace your ATP and have more energy to burn.

PEMF AND FIBROMYALGIA

In a study undertaken in 2007 titled "A Randomized, Double Blind, Placebo Controlled Clinical Trial Using a Low Frequency Magnetic

Field in the Treatment of Musculoskeletal Chronic Pain," by Alex Thomas et al. (Google: "Alex Thomas PEMF" for the full report), the study found that a PEMF device fitted to subjects' heads and used twice a day for 40-minute periods over 7 days showed statistical significance over the control group in reducing pain in fibromyalgia patients. The authors state that PEMF is a novel, safe, and effective therapeutic tool for use in patients with chronic, nonmalignant pain.

There are several other purported benefits, too:

- Decreased pain
- Increased micro-circulation within minutes
- Enhanced uptake of nutrients
- Reduction of stress in the body
- Improved sleep patterns
- Faster healing of soft tissue
- Reduced inflammation and swelling
- Acceleration of nerve regeneration
- Faster functional recovery
- Enhanced capillary formation
- Increased cellular energy levels
- Improved ability to rejuvenate cells
- Improved immune response

There are several things to be aware of before you buy a mat. Check the type of waveform the mat offers. The best waveform is a square wave, which is best for healing. If the mat offers different waveforms, then get that one, as a sawtooth wave is best for relaxation. Don't buy a mat with the highest intensity; less is more, and low field strength of 1 to 20 micro-tesla are purported to work best.

Like intensity, the frequency should be low. Research shows that the optimal frequency is between 6 and 20 Hz. You should also check the PEMF resonance effect. This means that the mat should stimulate the cells to vibrate at their optimum rate, so ask the seller if the device creates a cellular resonance effect.

The PEMF device should switch polarities by varying the signals emitted. The switching between signals keeps the cells responding over the longer term.

PEMF therapy is therefore worth the effort and expenditure as it increases the speed and rate of ATP production thus increasing energy, it appears to able to reduce chronic pain too. Like all other medical devices for the home there are many types, sizes, quality levels available to buy.

You can read reviews on these websites:
www.pemfnews.co.uk,
www.healthmatreview.com and
www.pemfadviser.com.

Here is a list of sites where you can purchase PEMF devices:

healthyline.com
oxfrodmedicals.com
biobalancepemf.com
omnipemf.com
pemfglobal.com

PEMF therapy is an excellent adjunct therapy to fire up your mitochondria. Happy shopping.

CHAPTER SUMMARY

- PEMF therapy works by emitting very low electromagnetic fields that stimulates the electrons in cells.
- It helps to increase ATP production and enhances the sodium potassium pump. It also increases cellular pH to help make the cells more alkaline and improves oxygen uptake and improves circulation.

- Other benefits include: decreased pain, increased micro-circulation within minutes, enhanced uptake of nutrients, reduction of stress in the body, improved sleep patterns, faster healing of soft tissue, reduced inflammation and swelling, acceleration of nerve regeneration, faster functional recovery, enhanced capillary formation, increased cellular energy levels, improved ability to rejuvenate cells, improved immune response.

C hapter 12

RED LIGHT THERAPY

"We are all faced with a series of great opportunities brilliantly disguised as impossible situations."

Charles R Swindoll

Red light therapy is red light and near-infrared light that delivers energy to cells by applying different ranges of visible and invisible wavelengths of light that penetrate the skin. Sounds a little scary right? Well, I can tell you that it is not at all scary.

Red light therapy is FDA approved for acne, muscle and joint pain, arthritis, blood circulation issues and most importantly, hair loss! Other purported positive effects are many, including anti-aging, pain relief, fat reduction, clearer thinking, wound healing, reducing anxiety and depression, increasing testosterone, building muscle, increasing bone density and potentially reducing addiction to substances.

Impressive as this list surely is, **red light is purported to reduce inflammation and increase mitochondria function. Exceptionally important for Long COVID and CFS/ME sufferers.**

Light therapy sounds like a new age, almost futuristic therapy, but the truth is it has been around for a long time. The technical name is photobiomodulation and was first used in the late 1800s to help treat lupus vulgaris a type of skin tuberculosis.

There are tens of thousands of scientific and clinical studies on the safety and efficacy of red-light therapy, and it's now thought to be extremely safe, with possible side effects being cell damage and skin irritation if you overdo your sessions in duration and frequency.

Until very recently, red-light therapy was only available in a therapist's office or clinic, with expensive hourly rates. But prices have dropped enormously in the last few years and now there are many home devices available.

With most at home devices, the light is provided by LED (light emitting diodes) in both red light and near-infrared light. Red light on its own is great for clearing up skin problems, healing wounds, or growing hair. Near-infrared light penetrates much deeper into the skin and provides pain relief, muscle healing, and recovery and is responsible for energizing the cells and providing anti-inflammatory benefits.

These devices come in many sizes and shapes. I have purchased two units from Hooga (www.hoogahealth.com) at cost of about $1,700 for both. They are about 3 feet long and 10 inches in width and I lay them down edgeways on the floor and lie between them on a PEMF mat. A session usually lasts for 15-20 minutes and I make sure there is an air conditioning vent above the mat, as the infrared warms the body up (only needed in the summer months). The sensation is like lying in the sun on a perfect 72 degrees day, without the risk of cancer (in fact may even help to reduce the risk of cancer). It is a very pleasant experience, especially on a winter day. The lights are very bright, so make sure you wear blackout goggles for comfort and safety. You can find a review of different manufacturers here: www.oglf.org

Here is a list of other companies that sell red light devices:

www.revivelighttherapy.com
www.joovv.com
www.platinumtherapylights.com
www.mitoredlight.com

TOP TIPS FOR USING RED LIGHT

Don't wear clothes or sunscreen. Fabric and the chemicals in sunscreen will block the light from reaching your skin. If you're a female, a clown or a goth, you should not wear make-up before your treatment or be a clown. Many foundations contain sun blocking substances (usually SPF) that will also block the red light.

Use it frequently enough for it to be useful. Once per day 10-20 minutes will be about right. Less than 3 times per week, then it's probably not worth using. Make sure you keep up the frequency and there's no need to do more than 20 minutes in a session. Don't expect red light therapy to give you an immediate cure. Results may take several weeks to a few months to achieve.

Don't press your skin against the light boxes. 12 inches or so is probably the right distance away, though there are no particular guidance details in the area.

Always wear light blocking (black out) goggles.

CHAPTER SUMMARY

- Red light therapy is red light and near-infrared light that delivers energy to cells by applying different ranges of visible and invisible wavelengths of light that penetrate the skin.
- Positive effects include: anti-aging, pain relief, fat reduction, clearer thinking, wound healing, reduced anxiety and depression, increased testosterone, increased muscle mass, increased bone density, and potentially reduced addiction to substances. It also reduces inflammation and increases mitochondria function.
- Red light clears up skin problems, heals wounds and helps to grow hair back. Near-infrared light penetrates deeper into the skin and provides pain relief, muscle healing, energizes the cells and provides anti-inflammatory benefits.
- To use red light therapy effectively, don't wear clothes, makeup or sunscreen. Use it in 10–20-minute sessions at least 5 times per week. Always wear light blocking goggles.

C hapter 13

HYPERBARIC OXYGEN CHAMBER THERAPY

"Your attitude, not your aptitude, will determine your altitude."

Zig Ziglar

Hyperbaric oxygen therapy (HBOT) is the medical use of oxygen in a pressurized environment, at a level higher than 1 atmosphere absolute (ATA). Increased pressure allows for oxygen to dissolve and saturate the blood plasma (independent of hemoglobin/red blood cells), which yields a broad variety of positive physiological, biochemical and cellular effects. This noninvasive therapy is the most trusted way to increase oxygen levels to all organs of the body. The typical treatment lasts for 60-90 minutes, during which the patient lies down and breathes normally. HBOT has been demonstrated in several clinical studies to enhance the body's innate ability to repair and regenerate. It is used as an adjunct therapy to complement and enhance the healing process in both chronic and acute conditions.

HBOT was first used in the early 20th century in the United States to treat near death influenza patients. It was then adopted in the 1940s by the United States Navy to treat deep sea divers suffering from decompression sickness. In the 1960s it was used to treat carbon monoxide poisoning, while it is still used for these conditions, it is also used to treat wounds, aid in athletic performance, boosts immune system function, help fight nerve pain and help regrow nerve cells, help treat traumatic brain injuries and help improve the lives of those on the autism spectrum. HBOT may also inhibit the growth of cancer cells and alleviate the side effects caused by chemotherapy and radiation treatments.

TREMENDOUS INFLAMMATION REDUCER

For long COVID and ME patients, getting increased amounts of oxygen into the bloodstream reduces proinflammatory cytokine release. You may recall that in COVID patients, especially those with robust immune systems, would suffer a major cytokine storm that caused massive inflammation leading to respiratory distress and death in many. HBOT also reduces inflammation in swollen and inflamed tissues, especially helpful for reducing lung inflammation.

LYME DISEASE

The type of bacteria that cause Lyme disease are anaerobic, meaning that they are unable to survive in oxygen rich environments. HBOT delivers very high concentrations of oxygen under a pressurized environment, killing bacteria and allowing the body's immune system to become more effective in dealing with the bacteria. Coupled with antibiotics, HBOT is a very effective treatment for Lyme, as not only does it help destroy bacteria, it also helps to relieve the symptoms of Lyme including joint pain, fatigue, inflammation, nerve damage and cognitive functioning. HBOT also helps to remove heavy metals and other toxins often present with Lyme. Furthermore, HBOT increases white blood cell count, helping to boost the immune system.

If you have Lyme and are struggling to beat the infection, then find your nearest HBOT center and book several sessions. Beware of the Herx effect (Jarisch-Herxheimer reaction), as oxygen kills of the *Borrelia* bacteria, toxins are flushed out of the body, but this entails suffering from headaches, fever and brain fog, as this toxic flushing increases inflammation in the short term. It may take several days to get over this flu-like period before considerable improvement is seen.

In a study undertaken in 1998 by W.P. Fife et al. (Google: "Fife HBOT Lyme" for the full report) found that fibroblasts (cells found in connective tissue) often protected the *Borrelia* bacteria from the effects of antibiotics. As HBOT provides high levels of oxygen under pressure, the oxygen is able to penetrate deep into the tissue to provide an oxygen rich environment where the bacteria are unable to thrive. The study looked at 91 patients and treated them with HBOT while they maintained their antibiotic treatment. The results showed that 84.8% of the patients had significantly improved symptoms as well as positive diagnostic changes in SPECT scans (3-D imaging of brain function).

HBOT FOR CFS AND FIBROMYALGIA

In a study titled "Hyperbaric Oxygen Treatment of Fibromyalgia: A Prospective Observational Clinical Study" 2019 by F Atzena et al., patients underwent 100% oxygen at 2.5 ATA for 3 days per week for a total of 20 sessions, each 90 minutes long. Pain, fatigue, quality of sleep, symptoms of anxiety and depression and health related quality of life were assessed before and after 10 and 20 sessions. Twenty-eight patients finished the 20 sessions and showed significant improvement for pain and anxiety (but not depression). Both fatigue and FM symptom severity scores significantly improved after 20 sessions. There was no significant change in the quality of sleep and there were no adverse side effects. (Google: "HBOT for fibromyalgia" for the full report.)

In a similar study for ME/CFS patients titled "The Efficacy of Hyperbaric Oxygen Therapy in the Management of Chronic Fatigue Syndrome," by S Akarsu et al. 2013, 16 patients received 15 treatment sessions over 3 weeks. The outcome measures included visual analog fatigue scale, fatigue severity scale, and fatigue quality of life score and were assessed before and after treatment. The patients' scores were found to be significantly improved on all three types of fatigue measurements. The results materially decreased symptoms of CFS and increased the quality of life of the CFS patients. (Google: "HBOT for CFS" for further information.)

If you have ME, fibromyalgia or Lyme, then please speak to your healthcare provider about starting HBOT. When speaking to them, be sure to cite the studies I have cited herein, as they will sway your case to ensure you get the treatment. Remember, many healthcare providers will be unaware that HBOT exists for anything other than decompression treatment! Don't be fooled into thinking that healthcare providers are educated into knowing all about a wide range of adjunct therapies, they may not be. They may not have been taught about HBOT at college unless they specialized in pulmonology. Remember to be your own health advocate, be firm and stand strong.

FURTHER BENEFITS OF HBOT

According to a study published in the American Journal of Physiology, HBOT increases the number of stem cells circulating in the body by an incredible 800%, this is the reason why HBOT is so effective at tissue regeneration. Stem cells exist in the bone marrow and can adapt to become parts of differing organs and tissues. The greater the frequency and duration of HBOT, the greater the increase in stem cell generation.

There are few downsides to HBOT, with those being the costs of treatment and the repetitive travel times to and from the clinic and the lengthy session times and frequency. With that said, the upsides are enormous including relief from CFS, fibromyalgia and Lyme disease.

However, the longevity of relief of fatigue is an unknown factor, as I failed to find evidence of permanence, so a long-term plan may be needed to be factored in.

WHAT TO EXPECT DURING HBOT

A HBOT chamber looks like a small submarine, a metal tube with a circular door and couple of round windows. You enter the chamber and either lie down or sit up (depending on the chamber's size and shape), you breathe normally, can meditate, or read a good book, like this one (not a joke, in case you were wondering). Sessions last from an hour or two depending on your particular ailment, and you may need 10 to 30 sessions.

You may feel some pressure in your ears, similar to what you experience as your plane is taking off or your spouse asks you to do the washing up, so you may have to equalize them by swallowing or blowing your nose (Valsalva maneuver). If you suffer from claustrophobia, this may be more challenging for you, so ask your medical provider if a sedative may be prescribed. Mild side effects can include headaches and temporary mild fatigue.

Do not have HBOT if you have the flu, a cold, or had recent ear surgery or ear trauma of any kind. Certain types of lung disease may be exacerbated in the short term and eye damage and sinus problems could occur. In very rare cases, oxygen poisoning can occur, leading to fluid in the lungs, lung failure, or seizures.

You if have the means, you can buy a chamber for the home. They are coming down in price, year after year. The cheapest I have found is on rehabmart.com for a class 4 Newtowne chamber, which is a soft chamber (allowing portability) with a 1.3 ATA pressure capability (known as mild HBOT) at $3,995 (refurbished). Most quality soft chambers with 1.4 ATA to 1.6 ATA cost over $10,000. Hard shell chambers offer up to 3 ATA but come with hefty price tag around the $100,000 range. Companies selling hard shell chambers state that soft shell chambers do not provide any therapeutic advantage as any pressure under 1.5 ATA cannot kill bacteria, but may enhance the growth of certain molds and aerobic bacteria; however, I cannot find any hard studies that support this. In fact, studies have shown that mild HBOT with lower pressures are actually more beneficial for chronic illnesses and neurological conditions.

However, there are some risks of having HBOT in the home including a fire risk if the chamber does not have an exhaust pipe leading to the exterior of the building. Both the chamber and the patient need to be grounded to avoid the risk of a static charge causing a flash fire. Only cotton clothing should be worn inside the chamber as synthetic materials can cause static build up and electronic devices should not be used inside the chamber. If you do decide to buy one for the home, check with your insurance company to find out whether having a chamber is allowed under your home insurance policy. In any case, you will have to have a doctors prescription in order to purchase a hard or soft chamber.

HBOT could be a key part of recovery for ME/CFS and potentially long COVID. A very recent study titled "Hyperbaric Oxygen Therapy for the Treatment of Long COVID: Early Evaluation of a Highly Promising Intervention," by Tim Robbins et al. 2021, produced very positive statistically significant results in reduced fatigue. The study was small with 10 patients receiving 10 sessions at 2.4 ATA over 12 days. Each session lasted 105 minutes, consisting of three 30-minute exposures to 100% oxygen, interspersed with 5-minute air breaks. (Google: "Tim Robbins et al. HBOT" for the full report.) (They should have called this study "Suretank Redemption"; they really missed a trick there.)

CHAPTER SUMMARY

- HBOT is the medical use of oxygen in a pressured environment, which allows oxygen to dissolve and saturate blood plasma.
- HBOT is used to treat decompression sickness, carbon monoxide poisoning, help wounds heal, aid in athletic performance, boost immune function, help fight nerve pain, help traumatic brain injuries, help regrow nerve cells, help those with autism and help with the side effects of cancer treatments.
- HBOT reduces inflammation and reduces proinflammatory cytokine release. It also reduces inflammation in swollen and inflamed tissues.
- HBOT helps to destroy the *Borrelia* bacteria that causes Lyme disease and helps remove heavy metals and toxins. A 1998 study showed that over 84% of Lyme patients had significantly improved symptoms.

- HBOT significantly reduces pain, reduces fatigue and increases quality of life for both ME/CFS patients and fibromyalgia sufferers.
- HBOT increases the number of stem cells by 800% and can help regenerate both tissue and organs.
- Side effects are short term in nature and may include headaches and short-term fatigue. Do not use if you have a cold, flu, or have had ear surgery or ear trauma.

C hapter 14

Cannabidiol (CBD)

"The winners in life treat their body as if it were a magnificent spacecraft that gives them the finest transportation and endurance for their lives."

Denis Waitley

CBD is one of many active ingredients that can be found in cannabis (AKA marijuana), though usually derived from the hemp plant. CBD does not include tetrahydrocannabinol (THC), the active ingredient responsible for getting high and the World Health Organization (WHO) have gone as far to say that CBD exhibits no effects indicative of any abuse or dependence potential. There have been no evidence of public health related problems with the use of CBD and it is not illegal to buy or consume, not even in Texas. Like other substances where there is no intellectual property to be exploited, CBD has not been involved in many high-quality human trials, due to lack of monetary return for such trials; however, there have been many academic studies, and anecdotal stories abound.

CBD appears to be very well tolerated and generally deemed safe to use, with potential minor side effects, including low blood pressure, dry mouth, dizziness, drowsiness, reduced appetite, and diarrhea. It can react with blood thinners and may alter liver enzymes used to process medications.

CBD comes in various forms including as an oil (to be used sublingually - under the tongue), as an oral spray, in capsule form, in gummies, in chocolate form, as a liquid for vape pens (to smoke) or as a topical cream for the skin.

Due to lack of clear evidence for treating a variety of potential ailments, there is wide controversy for CBD's effectiveness and I'm not going to get into the bones of the arguments, but there have been both academic studies and anecdotal reports of success treating the following:

- Chronic pain and inflammation, including neuroinflammation (potentially helpful to ME patients).
- Social anxiety disorder.
- Insomnia.
- Halting the growth of cancerous tumors.
- Reducing the incidence of epileptic seizures, especially in children.
- Reducing symptoms of multiple sclerosis.
- Reducing symptoms of Parkinson's disease.
- Reducing symptoms of Huntington's disease.
- Assisting with reduction in tobacco addiction.

As of the writing of this book, CBD has been approved by the FDA as an oral solution (Epidiolex) for two severe forms of epilepsy.

HOW CBD MAY HELP YOU

It has been postulated that CFS/ME patients suffer from a condition called endocannabinoids deficiency, that is low production of this lipid-based neurotransmitter that bind to cannabinoid receptors. The endocannabinoid system is a relatively new to the medical community in its discovery (early 1980s) and is still not well understood by the majority of physicians. It is considered, however, to be the largest network of neurotransmitters in the human body, responsible for regulating several functions. The endocannabinoid system functions to maintain homeostasis by regulating many physiological, homeostatic and cognitive functions including appetite, immune function, pain, metabolism, stress response, mood, energy balance and inflammation response. Symptoms of endocannabinoid deficiency include migraine, fibromyalgia, irritable bowel, and chronic fatigue. Fatigue is exacerbated by irregular sleep patterns which is perhaps the main symptom of this deficiency. The deficiency thereof can be caused by the following (apologies, another *science bit alert*):

- **An overabundance of metabolic enzymes.** An overproduction of enzymes breaks down the endocannabinoid compounds, so the endocannabinoid cannot bind to a receptor.

- **You may not have enough receptors.** Without sufficient receptors your body cannot connect available endocannabinoids, thus the signal cannot be transmitted to its designated area.

- **Your body not making cannabinoid compounds.** Without been able to synthesize sufficient endocannabinoids, these incomplete molecules can't make it to the receptors or can't attach themselves correctly.

While it may be very difficult to get a clear diagnosis of endocannabinoid deficiency, it may be prudent to assume one has the deficiency if headaches and waking at 3 am (without sleep aids) are endemic in your life. The simple solution is to use phyto cannabinoids, especially in CBD form just before bed. CBD creates an anti-inflammatory response by suppressing FAAH activity (fatty acid amide hydrolase) which controls the activity of N-arachidonoyl ethanolamine (AEA), which is a bioactive lipid (and also a championship-winning Scrabble word).

There is an enormous amount of scientific literature to wade through on this, and instead of wandering off further into science blurb land and boring you into a coma, you can learn more about this by googling: "endocannabinoid deficiency."

CBD can be bought just about everywhere, including your local pharmacy and on Amazon. Just to reiterate, CBD is not an illegal drug, it is non-addictive and safe to take. DO NOT CONFUSE IT WITH CANNABIS! However:

CAUTION FOR CANNABIS USERS

If you partake in smoking or ingesting cannabis, marijuana, grass, weed, herb, skunk, pot, ganja, doobage, Mary Jane, hash, doobie, devils' lettuce, magic dragon, or jazz cigarette (I think that covers it), then tread carefully.

Generally speaking, cannabis is going to chill you out, relax you, take away anxiety but is unlikely to give you energy. It may take away any motivation you may have to work on your fatigue and may keep you in a perpetual state of malaise. Of course, everybody reacts differently and you might respond like you've drank five cups of the richest Columbian coffee (THC reacts as both a stimulant and depressant). THC also acts to increase dopamine levels while reducing acetylcholine levels; that's why your heart may race while your memory becomes useless. It also makes you hungry for junk food, even Hershey's chocolate tastes great under the influence, though it's disastrous if you're following a particular diet and the inevitably high sugar consumption will lead to more inflammation.

If you enjoy cannabis and do not want to give it up, then it's best to consume prior to bedtime to help you sleep through the night, if that works for you, but don't take it every night. It may be helpful with fibromyalgia pain, but you will have to put up with being zoned out.

Ultimately cannabis is a personal choice and it depends on how you react to the substance; however, ME and COVID patients should generally stay away.

CHAPTER SUMMARY

- CBD come in various forms including as an oil (to be used under the tongue), as an oral spray, in capsule form, in gummies, as a liquid for vape pens (to smoke, don't do this, bad for your lungs) or as a topical cream for the skin.
- It has been postulated that CFS/ME patients suffer from a condition called endocannabinoids deficiency, that is low production of this lipid-based neurotransmitter that bind to cannabinoid receptors.
- The endocannabinoid system functions to maintain homeostasis by regulating functions including appetite, immune function, pain, metabolism, stress response, mood, energy balance, and inflammation response.

- Endocannabiniod deficiency causes an overabundance of metabolic enzymes, so the endocannabidiol cannot bind to a receptor. You may not have sufficient number of receptors and your body may not be making cannabinoid compounds.
- Symptoms of endocannabiniod deficiency include migraine, fibromyalgia, irritable bowel, chronic fatigue, and frequent waking through the night.
- Everybody responds differently to CBD oil, but it's certainly worth experimenting, in my opinion. Do not confuse CBD with cannabis, which may take away your motivation to beat fatigue and may make you crave junk food, which is disastrous for beating fatigue issues.

Chapter 15

EXPLORING OTHER INNOVATIVE THERAPIES

"Success is my only option, failure's not."

Eminem

So you've tried every single remedy that you possibly could without the desired results? You're on top of your depression and starting to get 7 or more hours a night sleep? You've tried exploring any spinal issues and had them fixed, tried nebulizing hydrogen peroxide and glutathione for several weeks without feeling more energized? You've taken high-dose vitamin D and some of the other supplements discussed in this book but still feel like a zombie? You've cut out most processed foods, sugar, fatty meats and eating a health plant-based diet without results? Then wow! You are a hard nut to crack, my friend, but don't despair, we have plenty of tools left in the shed to help you be the victor of your nemesis, fatigue. Here are some amazing therapies that have been shown to remedy fatigue issues in many people.

KETAMINE THERAPY

As referred to earlier in this book, ketamine therapy is used to help remedy treatment resistant depression. It is a medication used as an anesthetic for over 50 years and used by emergency responders to calm agitated patients, especially those who are suicidal. It is a psychotropic drug that it alters the state of mind and causes a dissociative experience with feelings of unreality and a host of visual and sensory distortions. A form of ketamine is now available in a nasal spray called Spravato, for treatment-resistant depression, which is provided under the control of physicians in a clinic setting. The risks associated with this form of ketamine include attention-deficit issues and unusual judgment or thinking problems.

More commonly, ketamine is available by specialist clinics via an intravenous infusion that last about 40 minutes to an hour or so and overseen by physicians. Most anecdotal reports confirm that the experience is an extremely positive and pleasant one. The treatment appears to be very effective for treating depression for those who suffer badly or suicidal. However, can it treat chronic fatigue? I first thought about trying ketamine as a potential therapy after I read a study undertaken in 2016 titled, "An Assessment of the Anti-Fatigue Effect of Ketamine from a Double-Blind, Placebo-Controlled, Crossover Study in Bipolar Disorder," by Saligan et al. The study included 36 people with treatment-resistant depression and participants were infused with ketamine hydrochloride or a placebo. The results showed that the ketamine group rapidly improved their fatigue levels compared with the placebo group up to 14 days post-treatment. However, the study did not follow up these groups longer than 14 days, so it was limited in scope.

Ketamine works through regrowing connections between synapses throughout the brain that have been broken over time. This reconnection appears to help reverse depression (and potentially fatigue), which may have been exacerbated by loss of these synapsis connections. Ketamine helps to increase the amount of a vital neurotransmitter called glutamate, which turns on glutamate receptors, thus literally changing the brain almost immediately.

I tried the therapy myself in January 2022 and can report the following. The therapy took place in a doctor's office in Del Mar, California, at the West Coast Ketamine Center. The initial consultation was over the phone to see if I was a suitable candidate for ketamine. When the doctor agreed that I might benefit from this therapy, I went in and had a longer consultation immediately prior to the first infusion. The infusion was given via an IV into the arm. I reclined in a lounger, put in my airpods and listened to slow beat electronic music. I quickly drifted away into a semi-conscious state and lost all sense of my physical body, essentially in a state of complete paralysis. Then the strangest, most incomprehensible feelings and sensations stormed through my brain, taking me on a wild trip through what felt like infinite space. I had my eyes closed, but I could see a vast array of geometric shapes completely filling up vast landscapes and voids as large as planets, with these shapes moving quickly in time to the beat and the electronic beeps of the music. I had times when I felt like I had some measure of control over the trip and I could comprehend my internal monologue, telling myself that I was okay. There were times in the trip where I had no control and honestly thought that I might die with a terrible sense of dread and panic. These moments were fast and fleeting and passed by quickly, with a sense of calm, exhilaration and euphoria coming in sporadic waves. My sense of time passing was nonexistent, with seconds feeling like minutes and minutes feeling like hours. I know that doesn't make a lot of sense, but the whole experience was insane. I would like to think I could make sense of it, but it felt like absolute randomness of feelings, emotions and senses. Waking up, I felt drowsy, dizzy and a little nauseous. The nurse gave me an antiemetic to relieve the nausea and I sat for 20 minutes or so before standing. The next morning, I felt absolutely wonderful, with more energy and a lightness of mood I hadn't felt in many months.

My second trip was far less scary, as I knew the medication was safe and effective, so I made my mind up to enjoy every minute of it. The second trip felt like the universe wrapped me up in a warm fuzzy blanket and showed me how stunningly beautiful the world could be with an overwhelming sense of calm, joy and euphoria. I felt like the atoms in my body had split up and were floating around in the ether calmly exploring light and shapes. I saw a giant skyscraper made up of billions of tiny green LED lights, which I flew up the side of until I reached the top. If you've seen the movie, The Matrix, you might get a sense of what I mean. It was if I had been uploaded to the matrix and free to move around the digital world as I felt so inclined. At the end of the session, I felt a sense of calm and happiness.

The third session was a little more challenging, as I was stressed by a busy morning, that led me to feel agitated. I calmed down enough before the session, but the agitation certainly bled through to my experience. The key to a successful ketamine therapy experience is to be very calm and positive immediately before the session. The remaining three sessions were wonderful experiences, with the major side effects of feeling much calmer, with a lighter mood and much more energy. I'm writing this shortly after my last session, so I cannot comment on its long-term effects yet. But I can say that it has completely changed my life, at least in the short term. I'm much calmer, happier and more optimistic about the future. This therapy is a real game changer and I urge you to seek it out and learn more.

THE LIGHTNING PROCESS

While there has been considerable scorn poured upon cognitive behavioral therapy (CBT), insinuating that chronic fatigue is all in the head (and quite rightly so), there is absolutely no doubt that your mental attitude is strongly correlated to whether you recover or not. A positive person with any ailment is more likely to recover than a negative person; but why is this true?

First, a positive person believes that they are going to get better and subconsciously the body is more willing and able to take on board medications and therapy. It is the reason that the placebo effect works in so many people in so many studies. You may recall the study of a new chemotherapy drug that was given to numerous patients, 30% of whom lost their hair, even though they had all taken a sugar pill.

Another amazing placebo effect study was undertaken in Japan on 13 people who were allergic to poison ivy. Each person was rubbed on one arm with a harmless leaf but were told it was poison ivy and touched on the other arm with poison ivy and told it was harmless. All 13 broke out in a rash where the harmless leaf contacted their skin.

If you believe a certain treatment will help you, it probably will. According to a report by the Harvard Medical School, the placebo effect isn't just a cognitive response, there are measurable physiological changes including heart rates, blood pressure and changes in blood test results. (Google: "Harvard Health placebo effect" for more information.) But the placebo effect only works if you believe the drug or treatment is real; that is why positive-minded people who believe they have taken a valid medication are more likely to get better than negative people.

The nocebo is also a very real phenomenon whereby a doctor tells you that the medication or surgery may have harsh side effects. Just being aware of the risks often increases the chances of the side effects occurring simply through the power of suggestion, but generally only for negative-minded people, who expect bad things to happen.

Second, positive people are more open to trying new things, such as many of the therapies extolled in this book, and thus increasing the chances of something actually working for them.

According to the deputy director of Harvard Medical School's Program in Placebo Studies, John Kelley, PhD:

Whenever you look at any randomized control trials, it's surprising how similarly the side effect profile for the placebo often mirrors the side effect profile for the active treatment. It's the power of the imagination. If you ask someone to imagine a visual scene in their minds, you can see on an MRI that their occipital lobes, the parts of their brains involved with vision, are activated. If you tell people to imagine doing some physical activity, you'll see the motor cortex showing activation. Just imagining something is happening is enough to activate those portions of the brain associated with that thought, or worry, or pain.

Being open-minded, and cognizant that I do not actually know everything (just don't tell my wife I said that), I am willing to try just about anything if I believe there is even an outside chance of it making a difference.

The lightning process is a cognitive behavioral program devised by fellow Brit, Phil Parker. I first came about this by chance on YouTube, where a woman suffering from chronic fatigue stated that her fatigue completely vanished after attending this program. I searched the internet and found a national network of practitioners in the United States and UK. At the time, late 2019, my fatigue was bad and my mood and demeanor were worse. My nearest practitioner was Jodie Goss, based in Los Angeles, so I thought, *What the hell, I have nothing to lose.*

The program is a three-day interactive seminar between the practitioner and a small group (or one-on-one if you desire), usually in the home of the practitioner.

The lightning process teaches you to recognize your psychological approach to your illness, to be aware of your response to your condition and teaches you ways to change your reaction. The system teaches you to spot when you are doing illness (they use a different spelling to differentiate, using a new word "du" instead of do, to highlight when you're purposefully being negative). They teach you to stop feeling fatigue by using the word *stop* as well as a concurrent physical action. They teach you to recognize when you're in the pit, a term used to highlight when you're being negative, such as saying, "I'm tired all the time" or "I hate my life." They teach you to self coach to train yourself to snap out of it. For this to work, you need to be somewhat open for suggestion and willing to take on the advice wholeheartedly. If you are generally a positive person this is truly worth your time.

I regard the lightning process as the very first step in my own recovery. It gave me the impetus and the energy to look after myself more competently and search for further answers. It's partly the reason I searched so hard for medications, supplements and therapies and gave me the motivation to start writing this book.

The lightning process is also used to help long COVID patients. According to testimonials from individuals on their website, the lightning process may help long COVID patients as well as chronic fatigue sufferers.

If you're unsure and would like more information before committing, you can get Phil Parker's book *Get the Life You Love Now: How to Use the Lightning Process Toolkit for Happiness and Fulfillment.* The book is available in paperback on Amazon for under $20. Also, for further information, go to www.lightningprocess.com.

MICKEL THERAPY

Mickel therapy is a consultant-based therapy that aims to help calm down an overstimulated hypothalamus (part of the brain which coordinates the autonomic nervous system and the pituitary controlling homeostatic systems including sleep and emotional activity). Their website (mickeltherapy.com) states that the therapy draws a distinction between the thinking brain and the core emotional mid-brain, which generates emotion independently of thought. The therapy teaches patients to translate their symptoms back into emotions and take corrective action so the symptoms no longer need to occur.

The therapy is provided by trained therapist either face to face (mainly in UK) or via Skype and sessions last about an hour or so. Patients are asked to take notes about frequency and situations when symptoms arise and given other activities to work on outside of sessions.

This therapy has been life changing for some. Please visit their website for further information and to check out individual testimonials.

CURABLE APP

Curable is an app used to help alleviate all types of pain and fatigue. The app teaches you to help yourself by using cognitive behavioral therapy exercises, visualizations designed for pain relief, graded motor imagery audio guides, expressive writing exercises, audio lessons on the neuroscience of pain, and meditations designed for healing.

Their website states that after 30 days of use, 82% of users report an improved quality of life and 68% report reduced physical symptoms.

They claim to be able to assist in the following: migraines, back pain, fibromyalgia, shoulder pain, knee pain, leg pain, hand pain, wrist pain, ME/CFS, CRPS, sciatica, nerve pain, IBS, and trigeminal neuralgia.

There are several testimonials from people who suffer from fibromyalgia, here is a notable one:

I've suffered with fibromyalgia pain and fatigue for ten years, and this has been the first time I'm hopeful that I won't be struggling with pain for the next several decades of my life! My pain has been reduced and my energy level has drastically increased through the exercises and meditation. It has also been wonderful to listen to and be a part of a supportive community who understands the experiences I've had. I'm not alone! - Brittany

I have not used this app, so cannot comment upon its efficacy. If you would like to learn more, then go to their website, <u>curablehealth.com</u>.

MYMEE.COM

This is website and app that states that they partner with you to identify lifestyle factors that contribute to autoimmune symptom flare-ups through personalized tracking, data analysis and health coaching.

They combine one-on-one sessions with a dedicated health coach, in app tracking and data analysis to create a personalized plan for managing and reducing your autoimmunity symptoms. They also offer lab work and specific supplements tailor-made to your symptoms.

Their website states that 76% of people see an improvement in fatigue, 70% see an improvement in pain, and 92% see an improvement in stiffness and mobility.

If you would like to find out more, their website is mymee.com.

FECAL MICROBIOTA TRANSPLANT

You may be aware of this interesting, slightly distasteful treatment, which consists of having somebody else's poop inserted into your colon, to help repopulate your microbiome with healthier bacteria. The treatment is often used to treat *Clostridium difficile* colitis (poor gut bacteria often caused by overuse of antibiotics), but it may be a promising treatment for COVID/ME patients with problematic gut issues, including irritable bowel syndrome, persistent diarrhea, etc.

In a research study of 42 patients with chronic fatigue, 30 of whom had IBS, half were treated with oral medication the other half were treated with fecal microbiome transplantation (by J.N. Kenyon et al., *Human Microbiome Journal* August 2019). The extract is as follows:

The gut microbiome comprises the community of microorganisms in the intestinal tract. Research suggests that an altered microbiome may play a role in a wide range of disorders including myalgic encephalomyelitis/ chronic fatigue syndrome (ME/CFS).

Methods

42 participants with ME/CFS with Irritable Bowel Syndrome (IBS) were allocated into one of two groups, 21 were treated with standard oral approaches, which centered around various nutritional remedies, probiotics, prebiotics, dietary advice and lifestyle advice. The second group who had mostly failed using oral approaches, were treated with Faecal Microbiome Transplantation (FMT). Each patient received 10 Implants, each from a different screened donor, and the Implants were processed under anaerobic conditions. The transplant is delivered via a pediatric rectal catheter, which is inserted through the anus to reach the lower part of the sigmoid colon.

The results were assessed on a percentage basis before and after treatment, 0% being no improvement, 100% being maximum improvement. An exact non-parametric Mann-Whitney (one-tailed) test was used to compare medians from those on FMT with those receiving oral approaches only. On clinical experience over many years, the only way to judge improvement in chronic fatigue syndrome as there is no test for chronic fatigue syndrome, is my clinical assessment.

Results

The median for the FMT group was found to be significantly higher compared with the oral treatment group (Mann-Whitney U = 111.5, p = .003). Therefore, the FMT group improved to a greater extent (z = −2.761).

Conclusion

This study shows that FMT is a safe and a promising treatment for CFS associated with IBS. Adequately powered randomized controlled trials should be carried out to assess the effectiveness of FMT in patients with CFS and IBS.

So, another person's poop may be a cure for IBS in CFS/ME patients, just don't tell your friends if you have one. Curiously, FMT may affect the gut to brain connection and may be a possible treatment for many neurological disorders, including Parkinson's, Alzheimer's, multiple sclerosis, epilepsy, autism spectrum disorder, bipolar disorder, hepatic encephalopathy, and neuropathic pain. If you would like to find out more, Google: "FMT neurological diseases."

Fun fact: Did you know you can make as much as $13,000 per year by donating your poop to a stool bank? On the downside, it's a bit of a shitty job.

On an interesting note, you may notice the British spelling of fecal is faecal. Not sure why Brits cling on to the Latin version of words, but my wife thinks traditional is better. I prefer the shorter version because it's more economical, but either way it's a crap argument.

Okay, I'll stop now.

OZONE THERAPY

Ozone is oxygen gas in its unstable O_3 form instead of the regular stable O_2 form (it is found in the upper atmosphere). It can be administered topically, as a gel, via gas bath or more usually, via IV infusion.

In 2019, the FDA deemed the therapy unsafe because they say that there have been no studies to assess its safety or efficacy. Rather curious as there have been literally hundreds of studies that have both shown efficacy and safety (and over 12,000 physicians use the therapy everyday), but I guess there's not much money in a cheap gas therapy, so thank you again, FDA. Why don't they say the same for Twinkies? There are thousands of clinics throughout the United States that offer this therapy. (Google: "ozone therapy near me.")

In bacteria, ozone disrupts the bacteria cell envelope through the oxidation process. In viruses, ozone damages the viral capsid and upsets the replication cycle by disrupting the virus to cell contact with oxidation. Without getting too deep into the science, ozone kills bacteria and viruses, while increasing red blood cell glycolysis rate. Ozone activates the Krebs cycle by stimulating the production of ATP (remember, those with chronic fatigue have trouble making ATP once it's spent).

In 2018 a study in Italy, 100 chronic fatigue patients were treated with IV ozone twice a week for one month and twice a month as maintenance. The study showed that 70 patients had significant increase in energy levels (70%) following full treatment. No side effects were found in all 100 patients treated. (Google: "Umberto Tirell ozone for CFS.")

There are several other benefits of ozone therapy, which include:

- Boosts the immune system and is anti-inflammatory.
- Reverses brain damage after a stroke.
- Lowers the risk of repeat heart attacks.
- Increases joint mobility.

- Removes toxins.
- Can ameliorate lower back pain (Google: "Magalhaes ozone lower back pain," for more information).
- May be able to assist stem cells reactivate into new cells.
- Can rejuvenate the skin and is anti-aging.

VIBRATION THERAPY

Vibration therapy is provided by either vibration machines (whole body) or localized devices. The whole-body machines are small platforms with chest height handles that vibrate while standing on them. The platforms vibrate in different directions, some just go side to side, but the better devices also go up and down, which helps produce rapid muscle contractions. The benefits of vibration therapy include increased bone density, increased muscle mass, improved circulation, reduced joint pain, reduced back pain, reduced stress levels and a potential boost in metabolism.

If you search for long enough you can find a research paper on almost anything. I found a study on vibration therapy for fibromyalgia and the results were interesting. In a review by Daniel Collado-Mateo et al. titled "Effects of Whole-Body Vibration Therapy in Patients with Fibromyalgia: A Systemic Literature Review," the authors came to the conclusion that whole-body vibration appeared to improve the outcomes, especially balance and disability index. The conclusion was that whole-body vibration could be an adequate treatment for fibromyalgia as a main therapy or added to a physical exercise program as it could improve balance, disability index, health-related quality of life, fatigue, and pain. If you would like to explore this therapy further, Google: "vibration therapy fibromyalgia."

ACUPUNCTURE AND MOXIBUSTION

As discussed earlier, acupuncture is the ancient Chinese art of sticking fine needles in various body parts. Moxibustion is the burning of mugwort leaves, a spongy herb that is thought to enhance the efficacy of acupuncture (and not a magic herb used by Harry Potter to attract girls). The herb is burnt close to the skin using a stick to apply heat to various areas. According to Chinese medicine theory, the purpose is to strengthen the blood and stimulate the flow of Qi (pronounced "chee"). The flow of Qi translates to the flow of energy, so low Qi means low energy. Now this may seem like a whole load of hocus pocus, flim flam, jibber jabber to our Western sensibilities, but there are some considerable studies showing efficacy of this therapy.

According to a meta-analysis (aggregate assessment) of 31 randomized controlled trials (by T. Wang et al., *BMC Complementary Medicine and Therapies*, Google: "T Wang acupuncture and moxibustion"), the study compared acupuncture and moxibustion (AM) with Western medicine (WM), traditional Chinese medicine (TCM), and sham acupuncture (SA).

The results were recorded using the method of total effective rate, and the conclusion states:

In this systematic review, we evaluated the treatment effect of acupuncture and moxibustion comprehensively which were found to be more effective than Chinese herbal medicine, Western medicine and placebo treatment (sham-acupuncture) in relieving symptoms. However, because of low quality evidence and heterogeneity, further studies are required to confirm this hypothesis.

For many, this therapy is believed to be very energizing. If you're an adventurous type, then this might be worth a try. I cannot comment upon its efficacy, as clearly I'm not that adventurous. Just kidding. I do intend to try this therapy soon.

HALOTHERAPY AND NEGATIVE IONS

Halotherapy entails breathing in salty air. This therapy originated from salt miners in the 1800s who found they were unusually healthy, they didn't get colds or flus, and rarely suffered from allergies. You can get this therapy at some spas: find the local salt cave (more likely salt room), but the most convenient way is to get a halo generator, a salt air machine (diffuser), a ceramic salt inhaler, or a salt lamp diffuser. I use halo generator by my bed and turn it on in the evening and mornings. The unit I bought is called the halo generator infinity (infinitysaltair.com) or you can Google: "halo generator for home use." I also use a Himalayan pink salt lamp on my desk ($15 on Amazon), so I'm inhaling salty air as often as possible.

Inhaling salty air has the following benefits: reduces mucus, prevents respiratory infections, reduces inflammation, reduces effects of allergies, reduces asthmatic symptoms, reduces effects of bronchitis, treats chronic obstructive pulmonary disease (COPD) and treats cystic fibrosis.

Furthermore, it is purported that salt increases levels of negative ions in the air, which naturally boosts the immune system and reduces fatigue.

Negative ions are particles with a negative net electrical charge with more electrons than protons, known as anions. They are generated in large quantities near moving water, as the water breaks down air molecules, so negative ions are greater near waterfalls, fountains, crashing waves and in rainstorms.

Once inhaled, negative ions reach the bloodstream and create a biochemical reaction that increases serotonin, the happy brain neurotransmitter, which also boosts daytime energy. They are also purported to increase the flow of oxygen to the brain, resulting higher alertness, decreased drowsiness and more mental energy. In a Columbia University study in 1995 by M Terman et al. (Google: "Columbia University negative ions" for the full study), they found that negative ion generators relieved depression as much as antidepressants for seasonal affective disorder.

I highly recommend getting a halo generator and setting up near your bed. I haven't tried a negative ions generator, but they can be found on Amazon and are relatively inexpensive.

NEW YORK CENTER FOR INNOVATIVE MEDICINE

I am highlighting this particular clinic as they offer a very wide array of interesting innovative therapies that are worth exploring. I have not attended the clinic nor tried any of the therapies they offer. If you live in the New York area, or don't mind traveling, then these therapies may be worth checking out. You can call the center on +01 (631) 377-5045 and discuss any that you think may benefit you. For further information, their website is nycim.com.

First up is **ACMOS Method Energy Balancing Therapy**. They state that this is an advanced form of energy balancing, comparable to acupuncture without needles. Their website goes on to explain:

The ACMOS method is a non-invasive specialty therapy for the balancing of a patient's energetic fields. This unique approach combines the wisdom of ancient traditional medicine with the scientific discoveries of modern molecular biology.

ACMOS is an acronym derived from the Analysis of the Compatibility of Matter on the Organism and its Synergy.

Each cell in our body vibrates at precise frequencies and exchanges information through the communication of these frequencies. With the ACMOS method, rather than needles, a practitioner has the ability to use highly specialized scientific bioresonance techniques and instruments to detect and correct bioenergetic imbalances in the body with precision.

The next therapy is **Airnergy, or activated oxygen therapy**, also known as spirovital or respiratory therapy, to deliver singlet oxygen. They go on to explain:

It utilizes a specialized device to continually convert oxygen in the air (triplet oxygen) into an active form of oxygen (singlet oxygen) that the body more easily absorbs.

193

This therapy is suitable for the regeneration of cellular functioning, and those suffering sleep disorders, infectious conditions, respiratory conditions, and many others. It also helps to strengthen the immune system, stimulate self-healing, regulate the capacity of the autonomic nervous system (ANS), and optimize metabolic regulation. Airnergy can also be used as a preventative treatment.

The user inhales the air via a comfortable cannula for about 20-30 minutes. As a result, it becomes easier for cells to utilize oxygen in the body. Patients will normally experience positive effects pretty quickly because improved oxygen utilization promotes (mitochondrial) cell activity and communication, regulates metabolism and releases new vital energy.

BioCharger therapy combines several therapies including pulsed electromagnetic fields (see the chapter on PEMF therapy), plasma gas technology, monochromatic light therapy, photon therapy and micro current technology. The goal of this therapy is to restore strength, stamina, coordination and mental clarity. They state that it improves cellular regeneration by reenergizing weakened cells and revitalizing the body's natural magnetic energy to align the mind and body.

Benefits of BioCharger therapy include: Increased energy levels, faster recovery from exercise, injury or stress related exhaustion, improved cellular regeneration.

Biofeedback Therapy works through heightening one's senses to how the mind interacts with the body scientifically known as psycho-neuro-immunology. The therapy uses electromyography, which measures muscle tension, thermal biofeedback, which measures skin temperatures and neuro-feedback or electroencephalography, which measures brainwave activity. They state that the benefits are:

- *Enhances and strengthens the mind-body (psychophysiological) connection*

- *Helps to identify tight muscles and helps to learn to relax those muscles*
- *Shows how the body reacts to stress and anxiety and helps to control these processes*
- *Helps women strengthen the muscles that control urinary incontinence*
- *Eases stress level and reduces headaches*
- *Reduces frequency and severity of tension and migraine headaches*
- *Improves control over heart rate variability and arousal of the sympathetic nervous system; a neuro-cardio combination responsible for many of the physical effects of someone's stress response*
- *Improves biorhythmic activity and sleep patterns*

The major appeal of biofeedback is that it pre-emptively teaches the patient a set of skills that can be used for life – without side effects. For example, it allows patients to identify early signs of stress so that corrections may be made before biochemical actions are triggered and physical symptoms occur.

Biomagnetic therapy uses pairs of magnets of opposite charges to depolarize areas in the body that might be affected by pathogens or other destabilizing factors. The main objective is to help balance the body's pH levels. To maintain good health, we must maintain a pH level close to 7.4. When your pH level is out of balance the body is more susceptible to cancer, viruses, bacteria, fungus, parasites and toxins, all of which will have a huge bearing on fatigue levels. A body that is too alkaline may be more susceptible to inflammation, pain and bacterial infections. A body that is too acidic may be more susceptible to viral and fungal infections. They state:

Clinical experience has shown that biomagnetic therapy may be used for a number of conditions and issues and that the benefits include:

- *Neutralizes pH and creates an environment that is inhospitable to pathogens.*
- *Correction of the intracellular energetic and ionic conditions.*
- *Completely natural, painless, easy, and non-invasive.*
- *No side effects and it may be easily used in conjunction with both conventional and alternative treatments.*
- *Targets the root cause of the pain/disease rather than only the symptoms.*
- *Results can be often seen in a few minutes, days or sometimes in a few weeks.*

Bioresonance Analysis of Health (BAH) is a system that evaluates a patient to help provide a specific, personalized program of treatments. The medical system uses quantum physics and other advanced scientific tools to help identify the roots of any disease or dysfunction. They state that this approach has yielded incredible results over the last 10 years in identifying complex chronic conditions. Furthermore they state:

A new paradigm of 21st-century biological medicine considers each person as a unique individual with incredible healing abilities. Bioresonance Analysis of Health accurately determines what medicines, supplements, remedies, and procedures will be most effective in the treatment of the patient in question. This system allows for great detail – from dosage and duration, and evaluates numerous integrative modalities and disciplines, piecing them together with great simplicity.

If you believe you have a longstanding undiagnosed illness that doctors have been unable to help you with, then this may be worth your time and effort, as a last ditch attempt.

Chelation therapy involves the use of compounds to bind to specific heavy metals to help remove them from the body. They state:

Chelation involves the use of compounds to bind to specific heavy metals, including mercury, lead, cadmium, and arsenic, and remove them from the body.

With the expanding use of heavy metals in manufacturing processes, these toxic substances are finding ways into the human body. Today, heavy metal toxicity is a growing problem. For instance, if many people have mercury fillings in their teeth, have been vaccinated, eat farm-raised fish or chicken regularly, consume processed food, or have gone through radiation and chemotherapy treatments, they may be experiencing heavy metal toxicity at this very moment. It is well known that heavy metals are difficult to remove from the system, and chelation therapy may be an excellent alternative to detoxify and restore the body.

Chelation therapy has shown promise in successfully improving the health of patients with such disorders as peripheral vascular disease, Alzheimer's disease, multiple sclerosis, amyotrophic lateral sclerosis, autism, and other chronic and complex conditions.

This may be a very useful therapy if you have had metal dental amalgams for a considerable period that you believe may have leached into your system. Obviously make sure you have any mercury, gold or silver fillings removed before the start of treatment.

Gerson therapy targets the microbiome by using nutritional therapy that involves juicing, diet restrictions and coffee enemas. They state:

Dr. Gerson reasoned that many common diseases were brought about by toxic, altered, and harmful food, water and air. Constant consumption and contact with these toxins lead to serious detrimental conditions. The Gerson therapy seeks to regenerate the body to health with a diet that consists of almost 20 pounds of organically grown fruits and vegetables daily as well as a progressive detoxification program using coffee enemas.

While every individual responds differently, the Gerson Therapy has been witnessed to have impressive results in patients suffering from the following diseases: melanoma, lymphoma, breast cancer, ovarian cancer, rheumatoid arthritis and systemic lupus erythematosus (SLE). Gerson

Therapy can be used as a complementary therapy to help achieve a better quality of life, even in cases where full recovery may not seem possible.

Benefits of Gerson therapy include:

- *Activates the body's extraordinary ability to heal itself through specific and selective dietary guidelines*
- *Implements fresh and organic products which help to detoxify and regenerate the liver.*
- *Boosts the body's own defense to fight disease with an increase in oxygenation.*

If you're unsure what a coffee enema actually is, then brace yourself. It's the act of inserting brewed, caffeinated coffee into your rectum in order to cleanse your colon. They are thought to increase bile flow and increase the production of glutathione (the master antioxidant) and a great solution for constipation. A coffee enema is also purported to provide a major boost of energy, so potentially useful for CFS patients. You can buy a coffee enema kit on Amazon, but don't try to do it yourself at your local Starbucks, they will call the police.

Also, an excellent way to give up caffeine. Once you have tried this, and witnessed the murky brown liquid draining into your shower pan, you will never want to drink coffee again.

Heartquest is a diagnostic system that monitors heart rate variability along with biorhythms by using electro-cardiac signals. They state it is used to follow indices of the autonomic nervous system, neurohormonal system, psycho-emotional state and brain electrical activity. They state:

Heart rate variability (HRV) is the physiological phenomenon of variation in the time interval between heartbeats. It is measured by the variation in the beat to beat intervals. A healthy heart rate variability is reflected by lots of variation in the time domain between successive heartbeats. This would indicate a very robust autonomic nervous system. Someone with less variation between one heartbeat to the next has low heart rate variability and indicates decreased autonomic nervous system regulation. The importance of heart rate variability is that it is controlled by the autonomic nervous system and therefore is a window into its function. The autonomic nervous system (composed of the sympathetic nervous system and parasympathetic nervous system) automatically influences the visceral organs, smooth muscle such as the blood vessels and glands and obviously a big influence on the heart.

With HeartQuest heart rate variability monitoring, one can discover how stress may be affecting the nervous system or cardiovascular system, and by extension-specific individual markers as well as overall health. In addition, the HeartQuest system goes beyond measuring only heart rate variability – it also determines the status of the neuro-hormonal system, brain waves, biorhythms and circadian rhythms, meridians and chakras, and overall vital force. Finely detailed and designed data displays are able to be shared with the patient in a simple to read manner, and HeartQuest is often utilized along with other evaluation methods as a supplemental diagnostic for the patient.

Low Level Laser Therapy (also called cold laser therapy, low power laser therapy) is the use of laser light with a very low intensity, which stimulates the cells and speeds up the healing process. This therapy is used for sports injuries, skin conditions, and, more pertinent for long COVID and ME patients, it treats chronic inflammation, increases ATP production and relieves fibromyalgia symptoms. It is also been studied for neurodegenerative disorders.

It is essentially the same as red light therapy, using infrared light wavelengths, but is used in a smaller, more direct beam for select areas of the body.

Matrix Regeneration Therapy has nothing to do with choosing the red pill over the blue pill; it is an advanced form of cupping to improve lymphatic drainage and regeneration. It is performed by a sophisticated medical instrument that offers cupping along with massage, acupuncture, and physiotherapy. They state:

MRT aims to detoxify the body and can be applied to many of today's common chronic diseases. With over 7 million environmental chemical toxins such as heavy metals, herbicides, and pesticides consistently around us, it is easy to see how the body becomes overwhelmed and uses its storage deposits (fatty or connective tissue) to temporarily hold toxins. The problem arises as these temporary holding areas become permanent. These substances stored in the body can cause a variety of disorders that range from a slight burden to total blockages and severe chronic disease.

Matrix regeneration therapy is an innovative and modern option for those that suffer from toxic "depot-clogging" ailments like rheumatism, gout, skin disorders, etc. The therapy is a combination treatment that aims to "unclog" these deposits effectively and safely. Indications include all forms of allergies, all chronic diseases, tumors, chronic intoxication/heavy metals, viral contamination, immune deficiency, chronic skin problems, and depression.

NanoVi Eng3 oxygen therapy is an advanced form of oxygen therapy that improves cellular activity. It is purported to counteract the negative effect of reactive oxygen species (ROS) aka free radicals. They state:

NanoVi is the first and only device to emit a verifiable reactive oxygen species-specific signal without the creation or use of harmful reactive oxygen species, and thus is augmenting the body's natural ability to repair cell damage. Oxygen is essential to the chemical process of cell energy production, but this process also produces reactive oxygen species (ROS). For the most part, ROS are damaging free radicals, but they also function as signaling molecules or secondary messengers. Over the last 15 years, scientists have confirmed that these secondary messengers are essential in triggering certain types of cellular repair. A single DNA, for example, is damaged more than 700,000 times per day and needs to be repaired as fast as possible. NanoVi bio-identical signaling technology relies on a ROS-specific signal to influence cellular repair mechanisms and consequently protect and improve cellular activity. Helping initiate the body's natural repair mechanisms improves cellular activity and the spectrum of free radical-damaged cellular functions is addressed. To create a signal that is bio-identical to what our bodies make, NanoVi creates a specific electromagnetic wave in the near-infrared portion of the electromagnetic specture that has precisely the same wavelength as the good (excited) ROS produces in our cells. Cell biologists, specifically scientists studying REDOX signaling, discovered how important this wavelength is in initiating cellular repair. In addition, testing at the physics department of the University of Washington confirmed the NanoVi produced wavelength that is needed to boost repair, antioxidants, and regeneration.

To enjoy the benefit, simply breathe in the NanoVi device's humidified air stream. The humidity transfers the signal to your body and, like many diagnostic or therapeutic signals, these signals immediately cascade throughout the entire body.

Neural therapy (aka therapeutic local anesthesia) entails injecting local anesthetics into specific areas of the body to treat a range of chronic conditions. They state:

Two doctors, the Huneke brothers of Germany, introduced neural therapy into medicine in 1928 when they rediscovered the therapeutic effect of local anesthetics. They introduced intra-and para-venous procaine injection therapy as a manner to eliminate interference fields. Interference fields are areas of chronic inflammatory material that cannot be removed or metabolized and which consist of the infiltration of lymphocytes/ plasmocytes and a disaggregation of the base substance. For example, scars create aberrant electrical fields which create confusion in the nervous system. Neural therapy works to take the aberrant signals and shut them down so the nervous system can reset itself, allowing the body to return to homeostasis. Neural therapy, as suggested by its name, aims to rectify the functioning of the autonomic nervous system of the body.

Neural therapy has been used in the treatment of hundreds of conditions, including depression, hormonal imbalances, dizziness, allergies, asthma, skin diseases, hemorrhoids, ulcers, chronic bowel problems, prostate and bladder problems, migraines, kidney disease, arthritis, back pain, as well other soft-tissue injuries.

The New York center for innovative medicine also offers:

EMDR therapy, which you will recall is vital if you carry emotional baggage (or PTSD) that plagues you every day.

Emotional Freedom Technique, which is a psycho-emotional therapy for emotional stress and a type of acupuncture but without the needles.

European Biological Medicine is a range of holistic therapies that include nutrient building infusions, neural therapy through injections and formulations, isopathy, anthroposophic medicine, spagyric medicines, homotoxicology, orthomolecular medicine, herbal therapies and acupuncture.

Family constellation therapy (aka Hellinger therapy), which is an emotional therapy to reveal unhappiness and suffering in generations of the family structure and aimed to help resolve these issues.

Gemmotherapy, which is the use of homeopathic medicines using extracts from various trees and buds to help detoxify the body.

Halo therapy, which is the use of biophotonic lights to harness the power of plants, herbs and amino acids to target the causes of diseases.

Ho'oponopono therapy (aka Self I-dentity), which is an ancient Hawaiian self-transformation technique for healing trauma.

Hydrogen peroxide therapy, which you should know all about by now. The clinic offers IV infusions.

Lecher antenna therapy, which is a scientific instrument for the detection of energy field's interactions to assess the bio resonance analysis of all-round health. (Google: "Ernst Lecher" for further information).

NAD/Brain Restoration Plus, as discussed in the supplements chapter later in this book, NAD (nicotinamide adenine dinucleotide) is an important coenzyme that is vital for the Krebs cycle to work efficiently (a fundamental problem for chronic fatigue patients). It helps transfer energy from the food we eat into our cells via mitochondria function. The clinic provides IV infusion as well as nasal spray application.

Neuro Emotional Technique (NET), which is a psycho-emotional therapy to help correct neurological imbalances related to the physiology of unresolved stress.

Organotherapy (mRNA therapy) is a therapy used to rectify diseased organs, glands and tissues through use of extracts such as insulin and thyroxin.

While many of these therapies may be seen as pseudoscience in nature, that should not necessarily diminish their importance or potential effects they may have on particular individuals. We are all different in both physical and mental composition and we all react differently to external (and internal) stimuli, whether that is pharmaceutical, botanical, magnetic or electrical. What works for one person may not work for another and I would not want presume that a particular therapy may not work because I feel it wouldn't work for me. So if you believe one of these therapies listed above might be of benefit to you, then you should follow your instinct and go with it, as it's is more likely to be efficacious if you believe it will help you.

I reiterate, I have not visited this clinic, nor do I have any association with it, but the therapies offered are innovative, varied and interesting, and who knows, maybe one of them might be life changing for you.

CHAPTER SUMMARY

- The lighting process is a seminar-based learning program that teaches you to recognize when you are allowing yourself to suffer from fatigue. It provides you with tools to think positive and to stay out of the pit. It is a worthwhile therapy that can help kickstart your recovery. For some people it can be a total cure.

- Ketamine therapy is a hot button therapy that can have remarkable results for reversing chronic depression and chronic fatigue. It is a psychoactive substance that is administered either through IV or nasal methods, that causes a dissociative experience. The positive effects can be felt as little as 24 hours after first treatment.

- Interactive apps/websites that provide cognitive support and advice may be worth your time include Curable (curablehealth. com) and Mymee (mymee.com).

- Fecal microbiota transplant (somebody else's poop inserted into your colon) may be a cure for irritable bowel syndrome, a common symptom of those with ME/CFS.

- Ozone therapy can help to kill viruses and bacterial infections and can increase red blood cell glycolysis rate. A 2018 study showed that ozone therapy increased energy in 70% of ME/CFS patients.

- Vibration therapy (via vibration machines) can improve circulation reduce joint pain, increase bone mass, increase muscle mass, reduce stress, and increase metabolism. It can reduce the symptoms of fibromyalgia.

- Acupuncture is the ancient Chinese therapy of inserting very fine needles into certain points in the body. Moxibustion is the burning of mugwort close to the skin. These therapies together may be energizing to some.

- Halotherapy is the act of inhaling salty air. The benefits include: reduces mucus, prevents respiratory infections, reduces inflammation, reduces effects of allergies, reduces asthmatic symptoms, reduces effects of bronchitis, treats chronic obstructive pulmonary disease (COPD), and treats cystic fibrosis. It increases the number of negative ions in the air, which boosts the immune system and reduces fatigue.

- The inhalation of negative ions increases serotonin, increases oxygen flow to the brain which increases mental sharpness and energy. Negative ions are generated in large quantities near moving water.
- The New York Center for Innovative Medicine offers a very wide range of therapies, including: ACMOS Method Energy Balancing Therapy, Airnergy Activated Oxygen Therapy, BIO Charger Therapy, Biofeedback Therapy, Biomagnetic Therapy, Bioresonance Analysis of Health, Chelation Therapy, Gerson Therapy, Heartquest, Low Level Laser Therapy, Matrix Regeneration Therapy, NanoVi Eng3 Oxygen Therapy, Neural Therapy, EMDR Therapy, Emotional Freedom Technique, European Biological Medicine, Family Constellation Therapy, Gemmotherapy, Halo Therapy, Ho'oponopono Therapy, Hydrogen Peroxide Therapy, Lecher Antenna Therapy, NAD Therapy, Neuro-Emotional Technique, and Organotherapy (amongst others).

Chapter 16

ANTI-INFLAMMATORY DIET

"A year from now you will have wished you had started today."

Anon

(DISCLAIMER: AN INDIVIDUAL DIET PLAN WILL VARY FROM PERSON TO PERSON BASED UPON THEIR MEDICAL HISTORY, PLEASE REFER TO YOUR DOCTOR OR NUTRITIONIST BEFORE A MAJOR CHANGE IN DIET RECOMMENDED HERE OR ANYWHERE ELSE).

First, I don't believe there should be such a thing as going on a diet. What you eat IS your diet; therefore going on a diet doesn't make much sense because it implies a temporary change, and a temporary change in diet is pointless because you regress immediately when you eat your normal diet again. This is why going on a diet to lose weight simply doesn't work. If you are going to change the types of food you eat, then make it a permanent change or a lifestyle change; anything else is a waste of time and effort.

If there is only one thing you take away from this book (though I sincerely hope there is more than one), then it is do whatever it takes to reduce inflammation, or I should say the causes of inflammation.

No doubt we are all aware that eating healthier is vital for a long and healthy life; however, if you have long COVID or ME, then the importance of eating healthy food is ten times more important. My CFS specialist told me that ME is likely to shorten my life span and to enjoy the days I have left (his bedside manner was not particularly comforting). Well, that is unacceptable to me. I plan on living to 100 just to annoy my kids and I've decided to do whatever it takes to beat this insidious affliction and achieve my goal.

But the unvarnished truth is changing your diet from a Western diet to an anti-inflammatory diet is not easy. Truth be told, most of us are completely and utterly addicted to sugar, and breaking the addiction cycle is extremely challenging. Sugar provides a dopamine rush (in the nucleus accumbens part of the brain, the same area of the brain responsible for addiction to drugs) and is at least as addictive as cocaine. Sugar controls the brain's reward system, which was useful when mankind were cavemen and calories were in short supply, but in our world of abundant processed food, it is disastrous. Furthermore, the more sugar you consume, the more tolerant to its effects you become, requiring more and more to become satiated. The average American consumes between 22 and 30 teaspoons per day, the daily recommended allowance is 6 teaspoons for women and 9 teaspoons for men.

'Yeah, yeah, but I'm not addicted to sugar', I hear you say! But think about it, have you ever gone one week without eating sugar? That includes no ketchup, no salad dressing, no processed food, no carbs (pasta, potatoes, rice, etc.) and the obvious: no candy, cakes and pastries, etc. Probably not, but the joys of the fourth or fifth week, when the cravings pass by are well worth the effort and the no-carb, no sugar flu symptoms pass. You will have more energy than you thought possible. Brain fog will disappear and this will help provide you the motivation to continue your life without sugar or sugar substitutes (refer to the chapter on motivation and positive thinking later in this book). However, temptation is everywhere and the addictive nature of sugar will certainly test your will power to the max. This is exacerbated by the short-term sugar withdrawal symptoms of severe cravings, headaches, lack of energy, muscle aches, nausea, bloating, cramps, irritability and anxiety. Sounds like a bundle of fun, but here are some tips for getting through that period. Start slowly! If you drink soda, swap it out for water, tea or decaf coffee for a couple of weeks. Then swap out your sugary cereal for yogurt or the Boyce breakfast (see later in this chapter for details). After another 2 weeks, cut out all processed food. Two weeks after that, cut out all sugar including all carbs, salad dressing, ketchup, and sauces on meat. If you're still not convinced that sugar is your number one enemy, read on.

SUGAR IS POISON AND HIGHLY INFLAMMATORY (ESPECIALLY FOR CHRONICALLY ILL PEOPLE)

One of the symptoms of CFS/ME is difficulty regulating blood sugar (glucose). Some people may have very high glucose levels and others very low. If you have very low blood sugar your food cravings will be extreme, you may have dizzy spells when standing up too quickly. High blood sugar can drive even more sugar cravings through the get high, then crash cycle. It can also lead to low testosterone in men (increasing insulin resistance and diabetes) and high testosterone in women leading to polycystic ovarian syndrome (PCOS), which exacerbates chronic fatigue, leading to a nasty negative cycle.

Sugar also suppresses the immune system and stimulates yeast overgrowth in the intestines, known as *Candida* overgrowth.

CANDIDA AND AUTOIMMUNE DISEASE

If you are too partial to sugar and carbs there is a high likelihood that your consumption is leading to *Candida* overgrowth which exacerbates autoimmune response. If we can rid ourselves of *Candida* overgrowth, then maybe we can reduce or even eliminate our autoimmune disorder. Of course, if you don't eat sugar or carbs, then you can skip this bit....

WHAT IS *CANDIDA*?

I thought you'd never ask. It is a fungus that is naturally found in your mouth and intestines and in normal amounts helps you to absorb nutrients and is vital for your digestive health. A diet high in sugar and carbs, including medications such as birth control pills and antibiotics can disrupt the balance of bacteria allowing *Candida* to grow out of control. The symptoms of *Candida* overgrowth are long, so deep breath, here they are:

- Fungal infections of your skin and nails, such as toenail fungus, athlete's foot, and ringworm.
- Oral thrush, vaginal infections, vaginal itching, urinary tract infections and rectal itching.
- Brain fog, difficulty concentrating, lack of focus, poor memory, ADD/ADHD.
- Skin conditions such as psoriasis, eczema, rashes, hives, and tinea versicolor.
- Digestive issues, including bloating, constipation, or diarrhea.
- Mood issues, such as anxiety, depression, and mood swings, tiredness, feeling worn out, chronic fatigue, or fibromyalgia.
- Strong cravings for sugar and refined carbohydrates.
- Itchy ears.
- Severe seasonal allergies, nutrient deficiencies.
- Recurring sinus infections.
- Autoimmune diseases such as Hashimoto's disease, rheumatoid arthritis, lupus, ulcerative colitis, scleroderma, or multiple sclerosis.

Do some of these symptoms sound familiar? There are many crossovers with long COVID and ME symptoms, so identifying whether you have *Candida* overgrowth can be tricky. If you do eat a lot of the sweet stuff and have many of the above symptoms, then you likely have *Candida* overgrowth. Even if you eat a moderate amount of sugar and feel awful after eating sugar, you may have also candida overgrowth.

Candida breaks down the walls inside your intestines (all 4,000 sq ft of it!), which are only one cell thick and leads to leaky gut syndrome (AKA increased intestinal permeability). Your intestines are supposed to form a tight barrier that controls what gets absorbed into the bloodstream. Leaky gut allows partially digested food and toxins to enter the bloodstream and triggers our old friend INFLAMMATION.

We know that increased permeability causes Celiac's, Crohn's and irritable bowel syndrome, but scientist now believe that it exacerbates lupus, type 1 diabetes, multiple sclerosis, arthritis, allergies, asthma, acne, obesity, mental illnesses, CHRONIC FATIGUE AND FIBROMYALGIA.

So as the toxins, undigested food and bacteria pass through your intestinal wall into your bloodstream, your immune system sees them as outside invaders, going into overdrive and sending antibodies to fight them, which is the cause of the inflammation. As time goes on, your immune system becomes confused and stressed, as these foreign invaders keep on coming leading to worsening symptoms and full blown autoimmune disease. Due to cell mimicry, any foreign body that is floating around your bloodstream gets attacked by your immune system, but it also attacks healthy cells that it mistakes for that foreign invader leading to further problems.

Do you need any more motivation to quit sugar?

But it's not just sugar that causes *Candida* overgrowth, it's alcohol too. If you have CFS/ME, you are probably intolerant to alcohol, so this may not be an issue for you. If you do partake, then you will need to cut back substantially. You will also need to cut back fruit, grains and legumes, to no more than one cup per day.

There are also a few supplements that are worth a look that are specifically used to reduce *Candida* in your intestines. You can find many different brands on Amazon but the key ingredient to look for is caprylic acid. Caprylic acid is a medium-chain fatty acid found in coconut oil and is both antibacterial and anti-inflammatory. Scientists think it is effective at reducing *Candida* because it can break down the membranes of *Candida* cells.

KEEP A FOOD JOURNAL

Keeping track of what you eat can help you enormously. You can track your progress in cutting out sugar and processed foods and can monitor how you feel day to day or even hour to hour. You can see how you respond to a sudden intake of sugar (a moment of weakness) or how you respond to potential allergens such as gluten or lactose. You can monitor how you feel after five days of eating salads, which is a very useful test, as I guarantee you will have more energy and feel lighter on your feet.

Keeping a journal or diary creates a state of awareness (or mindfulness) of what you eat and when you eat, which may provide you with more motivation to keep going in the right direction. It can help you remember what you've eaten that day so you don't eat the same foods the next day. As the English poet William Cowper said, "Variety is the spice of life."

Keeping a journal will help you count calories (if you want to) and will help you see if you are overeating or not getting enough. You may be able to tell whether you are eating out of sheer boredom rather than out of need.

When you're writing your entries, write down how you're feeling at that time of the day (write down the time of your entry also), but keep it short in order to save time. Make sure you write the size of the serving as well as the type of food you're eating, small, medium or large will suffice.

FOOD JOURNAL/NUTRITION APPS

There is an app for everything nowadays and food journalling is no exception. If you want to use an app to write your food journal, then here is a list: Nutrients, MyFitnessPal, MyNetDiary, Myplate Calorie Counter, Nutrition Facts, Calorie Counter, Waterlogged, Shopwell, Fitocracy Macros, Diet Tracker, Protein Tracker and Superfood.

NOOM

Noom is worth a special mention as it is quite an impressive app that uses psychological tricks to help keep you on the healthy food track. Their website states:

Noom uses the latest in proven behavioral science to empower people to take control of their health for good. Through a combination of psychology, technology, and human coaching, our platform has helped millions of our users meet their personal health and wellness goals. While we started with weight management, now we're working to expand our behavior change platform to help people with chronic and non-chronic conditions, such as stress and anxiety, hypertension, and diabetes, and build a healthier world for all. Our products are developed using evidence-based approaches and scientifically-proven principles, such as cognitive behavioral therapy (CBT) to help people build sustainable habits that last a lifetime. We're constantly innovating and fine-tuning our products to ensure our users have access to the most effective healthcare tools in the market. Noom users are matched with one of our thousands of trained coaches to help guide them along their health journeys and provide the support needed to achieve their goals.

You can check out their website, noom.com, or Google: "Noom user reviews" to find out more information.

EAT ORGANIC ONLY

Mass farming techniques rely on a myriad of pesticides, fungicides, weedkillers and insecticides on crops, hormones and antibiotics in animal products. It is absolutely vital to avoid mass farmed products due to the toxic load they place on the digestive and immune systems. While some organic farmers do use pesticides they are primarily derived from natural substances. Organic food has no artificial flavorings or colorings and although food producers can use 40 different synthetic substances, this is substantially less than the thousands of chemicals that can be legally added to conventional food.

Organic foods have better quality, denser nutrients and antioxidants than conventionally grown foods. They are packed with vitamins, minerals, micronutrients and enzymes. A 10-year study completed in 2008 at the University of California (Google: "pubmed 17580007") found that organic tomatoes have almost double the concentration of a beneficial flavonoid called quercetin compared with conventionally grown tomatoes on an adjacent field. Furthermore, conventional foods are often grown in sewage sludge, containing a whole host of nasty, hazardous materials, including the contents of flushed toilets. Regulations pertaining to organic foods prohibit the use of sewage sludge and irradiation (which is food exposed to ionizing radiation to reduce microorganisms, with an unknown risk of cancer).

Also, eating organic is the only way to avoid genetically modified organisms (GMOs), which should be avoided at all costs. Ever wondered why most European countries completely banned GMOs? Yet Americans said, *Yeah OK please experiment on me, that's just fine.* There was no way to know if GMOs caused diseases or long-term health issues when they were introduced into the American food chain in 1994 when Calgene first introduced its delayed-ripening tomatoes. While GMOs are probably safe, we really don't know for sure and people with ME are not in a position to be test subjects.

'Yes, yes, but are organic foods worth the extra cost?' I hear you ask. Yes they are because not eating organic foods will inevitably lead to very expensive healthcare bills. For UK readers, I know your healthcare is free, but still eat organic as it will help reduce fatigue issues. If you simply can't afford to buy all organic food, then at least try to cut out the dirty dozen. The Environmental Working Group released its 2021 dirty dozen, which includes strawberries, spinach, kale, collard greens, mustard greens, nectarines, apples, grapes, cherries, peaches, pears,

Bell and hot peppers, celery, and tomatoes. More than 90% of these produce tested positive for residues of two or more pesticides. Bell and hot peppers tested positive for over 115 different pesticides.

DRINK MORE WATER

Dehydration causes fatigue with everybody. You don't have to be Einstein's more intelligent brother to figure out that dehydration makes chronic fatigue far worse. Your body contains about 70% water, so drinking water is extremely important for general well-being. It helps maintain electrolyte balance, blood pressure, helps detoxify, lubricates joints, promotes cell health, regulates body temperature and reduces the frequency and duration of headaches.

So, you keep forgetting to drink water? Here are some handy tips to help you drink more. Buy a large reusable water container, such as a hydro flask. A large quantity container will make it easier to drink more. Drink a glass of water when you wake up, this will help to stop a headache in its tracks. If you haven't already got one, install a water filter to your kitchen faucet. It's a good idea to replace other types of drinks with water, such as soda, milk, fruit juice and coffee. Yes, I know it's boring, but so is chronic fatigue.

If water really is too boring for you to drink constantly, then try adding effervescent electrolyte tabs or electrolyte powder, especially on warm days. Electrolytes are chemicals that conduct electricity when mixed with water, they help to regulate muscle function and hydrate the body. Electrolytes can help to stave off headaches and provide a mild energy boost. They are vital to take if you are outside in hot weather.

Stop drinking caffeine! One cup of coffee or tea first thing in the morning is okay, but more than that will affect your nervous system and add to potential dehydration (depending upon your particular sensitivity). Never drink energy drinks! They are full of nasty chemicals, sugar and way too much caffeine that may stay in your system until the wee hours, making a good night's sleep almost impossible.

KETOGENIC DIET

The keto diet first came to my attention a few years ago when a doctor recommended, I try it as a way to help cut out sugar. It is a high fat, low carb diet that uses body fat as the body's main energy source rather than glucose. The diet has many potential beneficial side effects including losing weight! Eliminates risk of diabetes, cancer, epilepsy and Alzheimer's.

The process is known as ketosis as your body burns ketones, a water-soluble molecule produced from fatty acids secreted by the liver. The ketones are transported into tissues where they are converted into acetyl-CoA, which is then used in the citric acid cycle and oxidized for energy.

It only takes 2-4 days to enter ketosis if you eat virtually no carbs and no sugar. It helps to fast within this period and undertake some physical activity if you are able. The easiest way to find out if you are currently in ketosis is to test your ketones using a blood ketone meter (search Amazon for "ketone meter"). Once you have a meter, your blood ketone levels need to be above 0.5 mmol/L to be using ketones for fuel. Once you are using ketones, they will drop after the initial rise as you start burning them up.

There is also a new tech device that claims to make it super easy to check whether you are burning ketones called lumen (www.lumen.me). The device measures CO_2 concentration by inhaling a fixed volume of air through the device, holding your breath for ten seconds, then exhaling. The company states that the device will provide daily data as to whether you are burning fat or glucose and will improve your metabolism by showing you how your body shifts between using fats and carbs as a source of energy.

While it is a certain fact that you will feel better and have more energy on a keto diet, it is particularly difficult to stick with it. There can be no cheat days as consuming more than 50g of any carbohydrate will kick you out of using ketones for energy and back to using glucose (if you must cheat, then eat less than 50 g in in any day). Once your body starts using glucose, you will immediately be in the glucose crash cycle leading to sugar cravings again. It will then take several days to get back to ketosis, with the struggle of fighting off sugar cravings over this period.

So what are the keto-friendly foods? They are: low carb vegetables such as peppers (check you're not allergic to nightshades), broccoli, asparagus, avocados (great source of healthy fats), mushrooms, spinach, zucchini (courgettes in the UK), cauliflower, green beans, lettuce, garlic, kale, cucumbers, Brussel sprouts, celery, tomatoes (again, check nightshade allergy), onions, eggplant (aubergines in the UK), cabbage, artichokes, radishes (yuck, still yuck, in UK). Actually, just to clarify, in the United States the word meaning distaste is yuck; in the UK, "one shall not partake, thank you kindly."

Other keto foods include eggs, cheese, coconut, olive oil, avocado oil, plain Greek yogurt, and all meats and poultry.

Choose organic meat which has been grass fed. Grass fed animals produce meat with higher amounts of omega-3 fats, antioxidants and conjugated linoleum acid. Grass fed animals produce leaner meat that contains less monounsaturated fat. Whereas grain fed animals produce meat with much higher levels of omega 6 fatty acids, which are very inflammatory. Remember, we are trying to avoid inflammation at all costs.

Grain fed animals eat a base of either soy or corn usually supplemented with dried grass and usually given antibiotics and growth hormones such as estrogen, estradiol, progesterone, trenbolone acetate, and testosterone. These hormones have been shown to transfer into the human body, and estrogen in particular can result in cancer.

Low carb cheeses include blue cheese, brie, camembert, cheddar, chèvre, colby jack, cottage cheese, cream cheese, feta, goat cheese, halloumi, havarti, limburger, manchego, mascarpone, mozzarella, muenster, parmesan, pepper jack, romano, string cheese (if you must), and swiss.

Fun things to eat on keto diet include popcorn, peanut butter (again check for allergies, almond butter (more delicious and healthier than peanut butter). Low carb "French fries" include vegetables you can cut into strips such as zucchini, carrots, green beans, turnips, parsnips, asparagus, eggplant, portobello mushrooms, which you then cover in olive oil, avocado oil or coconut oil, add salt and then roast in the oven.

All seafood is allowed on the keto diet (however, seafood is becoming increasing contaminated with pollutants, the major toxin being mercury, so take it easy.)

Avoid "dirty keto" products, which are becoming more available by the day. Keto-friendly cookies, protein bars (etc.) are still a form of junk food, so don't get suckered into the marketing nonsense.

However, the keto diet does come with some side effects that can include low blood pressure, kidney stones, constipation, increase risk in heart disease (if you over increase your red meat intake). Anybody with conditions regarding their pancreas, liver, thyroid or gallbladder may want to avoid the keto diet.

Needless to say, make sure you discuss any major dietary changes with your doctor.

THE PALEO DIET

Paleo, short for paleolithic, referring to the caveman or stone age era where the main type of foods were only plants and animals. The diet excludes all dairy, processed foods, grains, sugar, legumes, salt, alcohol and coffee. The premise is that the human digestion system has remained relatively unchanged over time and is better suited to consuming natural foods that were eaten for hundreds of thousands of years rather than the bunch of chemicals that make up our current Western diet for the last 50 -70 years. The diet is based on a sound concept, but has been criticized because participants tend to eat too much meat leading to a potential risk in heart disease. So, if you do want to try the diet, increase the vegetable intake and go easy on the meat.

I have not personally tried the paleo diet; however, it is quite similar to the keto diet with a few subtle differences. Both diets include Meat, seafood, eggs, nuts, vegetables. Unlike keto, the paleo diet does not include dairy or sugar-free sweeteners (though you should definitely avoid these on any diet). Paleo includes natural sweeteners such as honey and agave, most fruits, and starchy vegetables including potatoes.

BUSH GROUND TREE (BGT) LIFESTYLE CHANGE

If you decide that you simply cannot stick to any particular diet, then just do this. Eat anything that comes from a bush, tree or grows out of the ground (subject to allergies). Limit meat and dairy (however, eat natural yogurt and eggs) and avoid sugar, artificial sweeteners, processed foods, carbs and alcohol. Simple to remember and a recipe for a healthy and happy life.

Whatever diet you choose, try to stick with it. The keto diet can be a real game changer that can provide a real energy boost that can propel you straight onto the road to recovery.

American ME/CFS Society has useful information regarding diet. This is a useful extract from their website:

Diet is one of the most obvious places to begin making the necessary accommodations to the demands of a chronic illness. However, it is not always the easiest. For many people with chronic fatigue syndrome and myalgic encephalomyelitis (ME/CFS), devising a workable diet poses numerous difficulties. About two-thirds of ME/CFS patients have gastrointestinal symptoms such as heartburn, gas, nausea, diarrhea, constipation, and cramps. In many cases, these symptoms are caused by food sensitivities. Others may have concurrent conditions such as interstitial cystitis or migraine headaches that require certain dietary constraints.

Even those who do not suffer from GI problems still have the demands of a chronic illness to contend with. These patients need to maintain as wholesome a diet as possible, simply to help their ailing bodies to heal. Problems caused by disruptions in cell metabolism, malabsorption, and food sensitivities make it all the more important for chronic fatigue syndrome and myalgic encephalomyelitis patients to maintain an appropriate diet – that is, following a diet that will maximize the nutrients available to a healing body while minimizing any harmful effects that specific foods or food additives may produce.

*"**What should I eat?**" is a question asked by most Chronic Fatigue Syndrome and myalgic encephalomyelitis patients, and although the question makes a great deal of practical sense, it is not easily answered. Diet is an important consideration for anyone who is ill; in the case of ME/CFS, however, what constitutes an appropriate diet?*

This question has no simple answers. ME/CFS patients react to foods with the same frustrating inconsistency as they do to medications. Whereas one person can maintain a vegetarian diet, another needs to eat meat at every meal. Some feel significantly better after cutting back on carbohydrates and eliminating fruit. Because each person's digestive system reflects one's own unique case of ME/CFS – complicated by allergies, food sensitivities, bladder sensitivities, blood sugar problems – there is no single "best diet" for patients.

But finding a good diet, even in the most difficult circumstances, is not impossible. Most people proceed by trial and error, noting which foods make them feel better or worse. The following are some simple guidelines that may be helpful in devising your particular ME/CFS diet.

*****Listen to your body.*** This is the most important rule for people with ME/CFS. If a particular food item makes you feel worse, don't eat it, even if it is supposed to be "good for you." Even "good" foods, such as broccoli, nuts, fruit, and spinach can do harm if you cannot digest them. Your body will, in most cases, give you clear signs when it can't.*

Nausea, insomnia, headaches, anxiety, gas, diarrhea, and constipation are some of the side effects produced by the digestive system when it can't digest the food you have eaten.

Eat sensibly. *Patients with ME/CFS need to consume a healthy, balanced supply of nutrients to provide the basic raw materials required to make them well. For those whose choices are not already restricted by food sensitivities, maintaining a broad, varied diet will provide the best basis for improvement.*

Eat simply. *Try not to mix a lot of different ingredients in one dish. This will help with digestion and make it easier for you to identify food reactions. Use plain fresh vegetables, starches, and proteins.*

Eat wholesome foods. *Avoid all processed foods, as these contain artificial additives (even when advertised as "natural"). Buy organic foods, whenever possible, to eliminate the extra burden of pesticides, hormones, and antibiotics abundant in most commercial produce and meats.*

Some foods should be avoided, because in most patients they will exacerbate symptoms. chronic fatigue syndrome and myalgic encephalomyelitis physicians and clinicians advise avoiding the following five foods.

1. **STIMULANTS (coffee, tea, caffeinated sodas, cola, some herb teas, including mate, and ma huang).** *For healthy people stimulants, such as coffee, tea, or energy drinks provide a temporary boost, enabling them to get through a hard day or a crisis. However, because stimulants cause the adrenal glands to work harder, stimulants will exacerbate ME/CFS fatigue. Caffeine also produces insomnia, which is a perennial problem for ME/CFS patients.*

2. **ALCOHOL (wine, beer, hard liquor).** *Alcohol intolerance is almost universal among ME/CFS patients. Most people with ME/CFS discover early in the illness that even a small glass*

of beer or wine makes them quite ill. The reasons for alcohol intolerance are multifold: (1) alcohol acts on the central nervous system, which in ME/CFS patients can be hyper-reactive, (2) alcohol is toxic to the liver, (3) alcohol interferes with the methylation cycle, (4) alcohol is a vasodilator, which will exacerbate vascular symptoms (e.g., NMH and POTS). Because many ME/CFS patients have suboptimal liver function, ingestion of alcohol should be rigorously avoided. Those who are especially sensitive should also avoid herbal tinctures and alcohol-based mouthwashes.

3. **SWEETENERS (sugar, corn syrup, sucrose, glucose, dextrose, brown sugar, fructose, aspartame, saccharin).** *Many people with ME/CFS crave sweets, especially when blood sugar levels fall in the late afternoon. Researchers have proposed that sugar-craving is due to faulty carbohydrate metabolism and subsequent low levels of ATP and blood glucose. Eating foods loaded with simple carbohydrates (sugars), however, only exacerbates the problem. Blood sugar levels rise after the consumption of carbohydrates, which leads to an increased production of serotonin. Serotonin inhibits the release of cortisol, the hormone responsible for reducing inflammation and releasing stored glycogen from the liver. When cortisol is inhibited, inflammation increases. The problem becomes even more complicated in ME/CFS patients because carbohydrate metabolism is disturbed and not enough glucose is formed from carbohydrates to maintain blood sugar levels. After the temporary elevation caused by the flood of sugar, blood sugar levels plummet. The result is a vicious cycle of physical and mental exhaustion. Dried fruits, especially dates, and starchy vegetables should also be avoided, particularly in the evening, because they may worsen insomnia.*

4. **ANIMAL FATS.** *Liver and gallbladder function, which are vital for breaking down fats, can be impaired in ME/CFS patients,*

especially those with low blood volume. ME/CFS patients have also been shown to have deficiencies in the transport molecule acylcarnitine, which enables the body to use fats at the cellular level. Eat fats in moderation and avoid rich foods and sauces. If you eat meat, use very lean cuts and remove the skin from chicken and other fowl.

5. ***ADDITIVES (artificial colors, artificial flavors, preservatives, MSG).*** *Sensitivities to petrochemicals and their by-products are common in ME/CFS patients. People may not realize that many food additives are derived from petrochemicals. Allergic reactions such as inflammation, itching, pain, insomnia, depression, hyperactivity, and headache caused by common food additives can be severe and can contribute to ME/CFS flares. Although all synthetic food additives should be avoided, the following are particularly problematic for patients with ME/CFS.*

Artificial colorings (tartrazine, AZO dyes, FDandC, or "coal tar colors"). These are derived from petroleum, and although described as "food" colors, are primarily used to dye cloth.

MSG and MSG-containing substances (monosodium glutamate, monopotassium glutamate, hydrolyzed vegetable protein [HVP], hydrolyzed plant protein, sodium caseinate, calcium caseinate, and Flavorings). Because glutamate acts as an excitatory neurotransmitter, a number of neurological and allergy-like symptoms can result from consuming MSG, including sneezing, itching, hives, rashes, headache, asthma attacks, acid stomach, excessive thirst, bloating, restlessness, balance problems, chest pain, joint pain, and severe depression.

Food sensitivities can produce such a wide array of symptoms – restlessness, anxiety and panic attacks, migraine, joint pain, insomnia, nightmares, rashes, and malaise – that they might not be recognized in a person with the usual broad spectrum of chronic fatigue syndrome and myalgic encephalomyelitis symptoms. For some patients, reactions may be so severe that food intake is drastically restricted.

Fortunately, eliminating a few offending foods from the diet can improve symptoms dramatically.

Dr. Robert H. Loblay and Dr. Anne R. Swain, two clinicians working on ME/CFS research in Australia, discovered that about one-third of their patients considered themselves "much better" after eliminating offending foods from their diets. These patients reported significant improvement in specific symptoms such as headache, muscle pain, malaise, depression, and irritability after adopting a modified diet. Treatment surveys conducted by a DePaul University research team and by Dr. Fred Friedberg also confirm that about one-third of patients who adopt anti-allergy diets experience moderate to major improvement in ME/CFS symptoms.

The task of identifying offending foods is made easier by the fact that most food sensitivities tend to fall into groups that are fairly predictable. The following list, compiled with the help of numerous individuals with ME/ CFS, may help you to identify the most common symptom-producing foods.

NIGHTSHADE FAMILY (eggplant, pepper, tomato, potato). *All members of the nightshade group contain atropine, an alkaloid that is an anticholinergic (inhibits acetylcholine) and produces inflammation.*

MILK PRODUCTS. *Many patients, especially children, have sensitivities to milk products. Lactose intolerance can produce bloating, gas, and discomfort. In addition, milk thickens mucus, which can worsen symptoms for patients with allergies.*

FRUITS. *Fruits contain large amounts of fructose. People with severe problems from defective carbohydrate metabolism experience less fatigue and general malaise with a fruit-free diet. Patients with fewer GI problems often find they can digest fruit better when eaten after a meal rather than on an empty stomach.*

GAS-PRODUCING FOOD (onions, cabbage, Brussels sprouts, broccoli). *People with gastrointestinal problems should avoid gas-producing foods.*

SPICY FOODS (black pepper, curry, garlic). Many people with food sensitivities seem to do best with a bland diet, especially in the acute phase and during relapse. Avoid spicy foods if you have gastrointestinal problems.

RAW FOODS. Even though salads provide necessary fiber, many ME/CFS patients experience discomfort after eating raw vegetables. Eating well-cooked vegetables and grains usually reduces digestive problems.

YEAST-CONTAINING FOODS (brewer's yeast, fermented products, mushrooms, aged cheese, some B vitamins). Molds, in general, can produce strong reactions in people with ME/CFS.

ACID FOODS (fruits, tomatoes, vinegar). Patients with interstitial cystitis or recurrent gastritis should avoid acidic foods, as these can exacerbate symptoms.

NUTS. Nuts should be avoided because they contain large amounts of arginine, the amino acid needed for herpesviruses to replicate.

SOY PRODUCTS. Soy products sometimes provoke reactions such as headache or gastrointestinal pain in sensitive individuals.

Anything you can do to lessen work in the kitchen will help you improve your diet because you will have more energy to plan and eat meals. If you are acutely ill or bedbound, make it a priority to get some help in the kitchen. People who feel too tired or sick to cook may not eat, which creates problems above and beyond those caused by chronic fatigue syndrome and myalgic encephalomyelitis. If friends offer to help, ask them to prepare meals. If you are alone, try some of the following suggestions to cut down on your work load.

Prepare meals in advance. Cook during periods of higher energy or ask someone to prepare food and freeze it in individual portions.

Buy frozen food. Frozen organic and natural foods are available from health food stores as well as many supermarkets in urban areas. You can also purchase frozen organic meats and main dishes that do not contain artificial additives.

While there is an enormous amount of excellent information in this extract, you may have noticed one small problem. If you eliminate all the foods they recommend, then what on earth is left to eat? Snails? The key is to try the elimination diet to isolate the effect of suspected intolerances. Use your food journal. Remember the BGT diet. It's simple to follow, is anti-inflammatory and will keep you healthy. Make sure most vegetables are cooked and assess how you feel after eating fruit.

ELIMINATION DIET

Before you even start with the elimination diet, you should see an allergist, have a blood test and find out if there are any biomarkers in your immunoglobulin E (IgE) that point to any food allergy. There are now home tests you can take that make the whole process more convenient and cheaper. There is a company called Curex (getcurex.com) that have a home kit that can cover most types of allergen including pet, dust, mold, pollens, etc., as well as many types of food. (Other companies exist too. Google: "home allergy tests").

The first step is to cut out all refined sugars immediately, as we are all, to some extent, allergic to sugar because it is essentially poison to COVID and ME patients. This is a given and a must.

The obvious place to start is to cut out the likely suspects, such as all processed foods, gluten, and lactose. When you cut out sugar, you will find that you will eat less gluten anyway, as they are usually combined. Glutenous carbohydrates, such as pasta, bread, pastries etc., turn to sugar in the digestive system, which is quickly dumped into the bloodstream, so I would recommend cutting out gluten immediately if you have not already done so. If you need more persuading, gluten is a major cause of inflammation for people with a thyroid condition and is also a known accelerant for autoimmune disorders.

So after cutting out glutenous carbs and sugar, try cutting out lactose for two weeks. Lactose intolerance has become extremely common in recent years, partially due to increase in awareness and self-diagnosis and arguably because of an increase in over processing of dairy products. Lactose intolerance is caused by not having enough of the enzyme lactase, which is required to breakdown lactose, the sugar found in milk. It can also be triggered by Crohn's disease or gastroenteritis leading to less lactase being produced in the small intestine, which also happens naturally as we age.

Next is to cut out other known allergens such as eggs, tree nuts, peanuts, seeds, shellfish, fish, artificial sweeteners (you should cut these out regardless!) nightshades (tomatoes, peppers, eggplant, potatoes) one by one to isolate any sensitivities.

Be patient, take your time and try to figure out which food groups you may be allergic to. Cut out any offending food groups for at least six months before you slowly introduce them again, if you desire to do so. But if cutting out a food group makes you feel a lot better, then don't bother reintroducing them if you can live without them happily.

THE BOYCE SUPERFOOD BREAKFAST

While I am not a great cook and I am not going to provide a detailed menu with amazing recipes (apologies, but it really is for the best), I will provide you with my superfood breakfast I invented. It is incredibly delicious and packed with goodness.

Get a bowl and add:

Half cup of quick oats, quarter cup of chia seeds, quarter cup of golden flax seed (ground), sprinkling of both cacao powder and cacao nibs, quarter cup shaved coconut, handful of pumpkin seeds, then add a plethora of your favorite nuts (though check you're not affected by nuts using your elimination diet first). I add almonds, macadamia nuts, walnuts, pecans and a small amount of brazil nuts. I also add blueberries, blackberries, and a sliced banana. Mix it all together and add almond milk. Eat and enjoy!

It sounds like a lot of work, but you can make it in large batches and store it in a container in the fridge. I eat it at around 10am to ensure I have fasted to 16 hours. I make sure I eat a large bowl and this usually keeps me going until to dinner time.

FASTING

Fasting is both a useful short-term hack for exhaustion periods and a long-term strategy for overall health and wellness. Fasting gives your digestive system a break, which uses a considerable amount of energy in order to digest food. That's why we feel sleepy after a very large meal. Fasting is not trendy and should not be seen as a short-term gimmick.

So if you are having an exhausting episode, try not to eat anything for 24 to 48 hours. Use every ounce of your will power to get through the hunger pangs and you will find that your energy levels will rise by the next morning. The benefits of fasting are huge. Studies have shown that it is an effective way to extend your life span. In one study, rats that fasted every other day lived 83% longer than rats that ate every day.

But most important for ME patients is that fasting reduces inflammation and, if you're still unaware, inflammation is the major cause of chronic fatigue and a major reason long COVID lingers.

A 2019 study by Mount Sinai researchers found that fasting reduced the release of proinflammatory cells called **monocytes**.

"Caloric restriction is known to improve inflammatory and autoimmune diseases, but the mechanisms by which reduced caloric intake controls inflammation have been poorly understood," said senior author Miriam Merad, MD, PhD, Director of the Precision Immunology Institute at the Icahn School of Medicine at Mount Sinai.

"Monocytes are highly inflammatory immune cells that can cause serious tissue damage, and the population has seen an increasing amount in their blood circulation as a result of eating habits that humans have acquired in recent centuries," said Dr. Merad.

"Considering the broad spectrum of diseases that are caused by chronic inflammation and the increasing number of patients affected by these diseases, there is an enormous potential in investigating the anti-inflammatory effects of fasting," said Stefan Jordan, a postdoctoral fellow in the Department of Oncological Sciences at the Icahn School of Medicine at Mount Sinai.

INTERMITTENT FASTING

Intermittent fasting is a must and an important part of your recovery.

The 16/8 intermittent fasting regime is surprising easy to follow and will do wonders for your energy levels and overall health. The 16/8 diet is simply not eating for 16 hours and eating within an 8-hour window. You can pick your window that works well for you based on your sleeping habits or daily routine. I start eating at 10 am and stop eating at 6 pm. It takes a couple of weeks to get used to it, but after that it really does become easy. If I slip up because of a restaurant booking or party and eat at say 7 pm, then I simply don't eat again until 11 am next day.

If you need further convincing to start fasting, there are myriad benefits other than a reduction in inflammation. Fasting controls blood sugar levels because it reduces insulin resistance. By decreasing insulin resistance your body becomes more sensitive to insulin allowing it to transport glucose from you bloodstream to your cells more efficiently. As a consequence, keeping your blood sugar steady will keep your blood sugar levels from spiking and crashing, making it easier to overcome sugar addiction. In concert, fasting becomes far easier after you have broken the sugar addiction cycle.

In addition, fasting may improve blood pressure levels, which inevitably enhances heart health. In one study conducted in 2010 (Surabhi et al., University of Illinois), a meagre 8 weeks of alternate-day fasting reduced LDL cholesterol by 25% and blood triglycerides by 32%. (Google: "Surabhi et al. heart disease" for the full report.)

In animal studies it has been shown that fasting can increase the generation of nerve cells in the brain to increase cognitive function and reduce neurodegenerative disorders.

Fasting also increases metabolism as it increases the neurotransmitter norepinephrine, which aids in weight loss. It also increases human growth hormone, which is a key hormone in muscle growth, weight loss and efficient metabolism.

So to recap, fasting helps reduce triglycerides, stabilize blood pressure and blood sugar levels, increases cognitive function, reduces inflammation, increases muscle growth and increase life span! Need any more reasons to start?

If you still need help here, there are many apps that can help you with intermittent fasting including:

Window - An app that notifies you of when your eating window opens and closes and syncs to your apple devices including the apple health app. The app is free unless you want to access the premium version, which provides fasting plans and promises to keep you motivated using visuals.

InFasting - Has features including a journal where you can share your feelings and emotions, calendar to record your body transformation, daily logs to track progress, and reminders to help you hit your goals.

Fastic - More health oriented and has 400 healthy recipe ideas to get the most out of your eating window. Also provides access to communication with others fasting to help provide motivation to keep going.

Zero - Is a time tracking app that will allow you to track your eating window with a dashboard to help you analyze your eating habits over time. It's a useful app if you use another fasting app that doesn't alert you to your window start and finish times.

Fastient - Another tracking app with more features including a way to maintain a record of your food intake. Useful if you're a particularly anal individual.

Bodyfast - This app provides ten different types of fasting plans, with coaching and meal planning tips. Useful if you like your hand to be held throughout the process.

Vora - Has a fasting tracking component but also provides community support from others to provide emotional support. If you have a friend also fasting you can communicate through this app.

FastHabit - Useful if you like to change up the types of fasting you do. This one syncs with apple health app and the apple watch.

Life Fasting Tracker - This app is useful if you're also on the keto diet as it will track how long you've likely been in ketosis. You can also contact friends through the app to help with motivation.

Whist there are many more positive aspects to fasting than negative ones, fasting does come with some warnings. First, there are the obvious hunger pangs and cravings. You may give in a few times to begin with and hate yourself afterwards. Quite right you pathetic excuse for a person! People died in wars so you could starve yourself, so pull yourself together and just do it. Also, you may become irritable for the first few days, otherwise known in my house as "Mr. Grumpy Pants" (my wife's charming nickname for me), a period where you shout at the kids and kick the dog for no apparent reason. But don't worry; this period will pass as you get used the process and the dog will forgive you. Your kids will never forget and eventually dump you in a retirement home. If you live that long, which you will if you follow the advice in this book.

THE GUT MICROBIOME

It is common knowledge that 70% of our immune system resides in the gut, that's why taking on the dietary changes in this chapter are so important.

You are no doubt aware that there are both good and bad bacteria fighting for space in the gut and what we eat (and touch) determines which one wins the daily battle. You may not win every battle but it is imperative that you win the war.

In COVID patients, increasing evidence appears to show an interaction between the gut microbiome and COVID, which can affect the longevity and severity of the virus. A recent study has shown that profiling of the gut microbiome (via a poop test) can predict the future severity of COVID. (Google: *Frontiers in Medicine*, The unique impact of COVID 19 on human gut microbiome research" for further information.) Furthermore, a disrupted gut microbiome may contribute to the cytokine storm, which causes a proinflammatory environment throughout the body. **So, balancing your microbiome through eating a healthier diet coupled with an increase in consumption of fermented foods and probiotic supplements, may reduce the severity and longevity of COVID.**

The gut microbiome is also affected by environmental factors such as the bacteria we physically touch and inadvertently ingest on a daily basis. The increase in the use of hand sanitizers and disinfectants has reduced the variety of bacteria in the microbiome of the general population. The massive reduction in national and international travel throughout the pandemic and beyond has further reduced our exposure to important types of bacteria that help feed our microbiome. These factors combined with stay-at-home workers, increased sedentary living, increased antibiotic use and overall poorer diet has led to a sea-change shift in the health balance microbiome in both the general population and more importantly, those suffering from long COVID and other chronic conditions.

With regard to ME/CFS, a study has shown an unusual profile of the microbiome with **high levels of glutamic acid and argininosuccinic acid with a decrease in alpha-tocopherol** found in the feces of ME patients. Glutamic acid is an amino acid that is used to form proteins and helps nerve cells in the brain to send and receive signals to other cells. High levels of glutamate (glutamic acid turns to glutamate in the body), disrupts energy metabolism, causes inflammation and can increase anxiety. Ingesting glutamate, usually in the form of monosodium glutamate, common in processed foods and Chinese foods, also leads to frequent headaches, increased blood pressure, obesity and increased sensitivity to pain, a possible cause of fibromyalgia. An increase in argininosuccinic acid can increase ammonia in the blood (hyper ammonia), which leads to... you guessed it, fatigue. A decrease in alpha-tocopherol (low vitamin E levels) leads to malabsorptive syndromes and cystic fibrosis.

Without going into greater detail on these issues (please Google them for further information), **eating more probiotic foods such as kimchi, sauerkraut, pickled cabbage, natural yogurt, and kombucha coupled with probiotic supplements is vital to maintain a healthy biome and immune system and vital weapon in the war against fatigue.**

CHAPTER SUMMARY

- First step in reducing inflammation is to cut out as much sugar in your diet as you possibly can, including empty carbs, pasta, potatoes, rice, and all treats and sugary drinks.
- Reduce your sugar intake slowly but consistently, as sugar withdrawal symptoms can be severe including headaches, nausea, irritability, muscle aches, bloating, and increased anxiety.
- Reducing sugar should eliminate chronic inflammation and *Candida* overgrowth, a fungus that grows in the gut and thrives on sugary foods. *Candida* exacerbates fatigue issues for COVID and ME patients and causes a veritable laundry list of nasty

symptoms including many digestive problems, skin problems, brain fog, severe reaction to seasonal allergies, sugar cravings leading to more Candida and a whole host of autoimmune diseases, including MS, Hashimoto's, lupus, rheumatoid arthritis, and ulcerative colitis, among others.

- Keep a food journal to track your progress as it creates awareness of how much you eat, what you eat and how often you eat. It can help you eliminate certain foods by motivation and allows you to write down how you feel in response.

- Eat organic foods only to help eliminate ingestion of pesticides, fungicides and insecticides on fruit and vegetables and eliminate ingestion of hormones and antibiotics in animal products. (Remember that glutathione is vital for combatting these annoying but inevitable additions to our food supply). Organic foods have denser nutrients, antioxidants and have more vitamins, minerals, micronutrients and enzymes than nonorganic. Try to avoid genetically modified foods, while probably safe, there is no evidence that they actually are.

- The ketogenic diet can be excellent for ME/CFS patients, as it reduces reliance on using sugar (glucose) for energy, which is not metabolized properly by ME patients and converts energy production from sugar to fats.

- A simpler and easier to follow diet is to eat anything that grows on a bush, tree or grows out of the ground. Take it easy with meat and dairy and avoid sugar, artificial sweeteners, processed foods and carbs.

- The Boyce superfood breakfast is very filling and very nutritious. Mix small amount oatmeal, ground flax seeds, chia seeds, shaved coconut, cacao powder, cacao nibs (if you like chocolate taste), pumpkin seeds, your favorite nuts, then add your favorite berries. Top it all off with almond milk (or cashew milk or oat milk) and enjoy.

- Fasting is both a short-term hack to get energy and a long-term strategy for health and longevity. If you're having an energy crash, try not to eat for 24 hours and monitor how you feel. Fasting is a proven way to extend life span, and it reduces proinflammatory cells called monocytes.

- Intermittent fasting is very important for both COVID and ME patients. The 16/8 time frame (fast for 16 hours, eat within an 8-hour window) is surprisingly easy to stick to and allows your body to rest and conserve energy, while helping to regulate blood sugar and reduce insulin resistance. Intermittent fasting helps to reduce triglycerides, stabilize blood pressure, reduces inflammation, increases muscle growth and may increase life span.

- Eat probiotic foods and take both prebiotic and probiotic supplements and make sure you look after the balance of your gut microbiome.

C hapter 17

Supplements and Medications

"Most great people have achieved their greatest success just one step beyond their greatest failure."

Napoleon Hill

In this chapter I discuss the most effective supplements that I take in order to achieve constant, strong energy levels. I also provide a brief review of medications for ME, acute COVID and long COVID.

Please don't be too alarmed by the number of supplements I take. Most have little to negligible side effects and are vital to kick start your recovery.

Some doctors are not keen on recommending different types of supplements for a wide variety of reasons. They may be unaware of the wide range of supplements available, perhaps they are reticent to recommend a substance that has not gone through the pharmaceutical FDA channels and it's just not the doctor thing to do. There is also the litigation issue that is unique to doctors in the United States, which forces them to err on the side of caution (and take out incredibly expensive indemnity insurance policies, the cost of which is passed onto patients and one of the main reasons US healthcare is so expensive compared with that of other countries).

Furthermore, you will not find large-scale double-blinded clinical studies for most supplements available today. The reason is one of money and lack of regulatory oversight. Large trials are prohibitively expensive and only viable if there is a period of market exclusivity (intellectual property opportunity) in order to recoup costs of running a trial. Most supplements are generic (not protected by patents) and thus there is no financial incentive for organizations to spend on such trials, especially in lack of regulatory requirement by the FDA. This does not necessarily mean that supplements don't work for their reputed therapeutic targets, though we have to rely on small studies by scientific or governmental institutions coupled with anecdotal reports.

It is true that not all supplements are not made equal. Some can have major side effects and the quality between brands varies wildly. It is very important to do your own research on the best brands with the purest ingredients and naturally, the more expensive, the better the quality, generally speaking.

If you tell a doctor that you're taking ten or more supplements every day, this is a possible exchange:

"Did you say you take ten different supplements every day?"

"Yes, Doc, that's what I said!"

"Honestly, Patient X, I don't think that is entirely safe and I can't recommend you keep taking that many."

"It's sexy X if you please, Doc."

"I do not."

"The supplements are vital to my recovery and are much safer than the hardcore antidepressants, acid reducers and sleeping tablets you've prescribed to me over the last two months."

"But the cross indications of that many supplements must be causing you some gastrointestinal problems?"

"Not really, no. Actually, I was going to ask you about an old supplement with a mass combination of chemicals I was going to take when I get home today. The ingredients are, amongst others: Reduced iron, niacin, thiamine mononitrate, riboflavin, folic acid, fructose corn syrup, animal shortening, soybean, cottonseed, canola oil, beef fat, dextrose, modified corn starch, glucose, sodium acid pyrophosphate, baking soda, monocalcium phosphate, sweet dairy whey, soy protein isolate, calcium and sodium caseinate, salt, mono- and diglycerides, polysorbate 60, soy lecithin, soy flour, cornstarch, cellulose gum, sodium stearoyl lactylate, Sorbic Acid, yellow 5, red 40. I hear good things about this combination of chemicals."

"You shouldn't take all that stuff in one go, I've never even heard of polysorbate 60 or sodium acid pyrophosphate, sounds dangerous."

"But you've already consumed these chemicals yourself earlier today."

"No, I haven't! That's ridiculous!"

"They're the ingredients of a Twinkie. I see the empty wrapper sitting on top of your trash bin. So, before you lecture me about putting a variety vital body and brain nourishing nutrients that I can't get from our wonderful food supply, you should take a long hard look at the poison you're putting in your own body, Doc!"

"Mmm, I see you're making quite a good point here. Now get lost and never darken my door stoop again, X."

"It's sexy X."

"GO!"

The point I'm trying to make here is that we are willing to ingest a whole host of chemicals when they are packaged together and cleverly marketed as treats, but many are reluctant to take a variety of supplements that are actually beneficial to health. That simply makes no sense.

The following supplements are focused on providing one of two things (or both). First, increasing mitochondria functioning to help cells derive energy from the food you eat and, second, reducing inflammation wherever possible. Please speak to your healthcare provider before starting any supplement regimen, especially to ensure there are no cross-indications or possible adverse reactions with any medications you might be taking.

WATER

Yes I know, not exactly a supplement but fairly useful if you want to live for more than a couple of days. The quality of the water you drink is extremely important. If you drink straight out of your kitchen tap (faucet), make sure you at least analyze the water first. I got a TDS digital water tester (on Amazon for less than $20) that told me my water was pretty much undrinkable. I bought a reverse osmosis filter that takes all the impurities and toxins out. If you find one of these a little pricy then you can buy a Brita filter or something similar for a fairly low price.

Carry a hydro flask or similar (at least 40 oz) and keep it filled with filtered water everywhere you go. This will reduce the risk of minor dehydration which will exacerbate your symptoms surreptitiously. This is my daily routine:

Fill the water bottle and add one scoop of electrolyte, one scoop of D ribose (5 g) and one scoop of acetyl L-carnitine (500 mg). This will give you a power lift to start your day (explanation below).

ELECTROLYTE POWDER

Electrolytes (potassium, magnesium, and sodium) are minerals found in your blood. They help to balance your pH levels and move nutrients in and out of your cells. They help to keep your salt levels from dropping, which causes a loss in blood volume (a major issue for chronic fatigue patients). They help to regulate blood pressure and muscle contractions. Many powders you can buy have the addition of certain vitamins. If you live in a warm climate or sweat a lot, then electrolytes are vital. The flavored versions make water more interesting, but make sure the sugar content is low.

D RIBOSE

D ribose is a hugely underrated supplement and is EXTREMELY IMPORTANT for those with chronic fatigue. Ribose is a sugar and carb and is a component of ribonucleotides from which RNA is constructed. More importantly, it is an essential component of adenosine triphosphate (ATP) the power source to our cells. We know that those with chronic fatigue cannot produce ATP fast enough once depleted, which leads to major energy crashes and exacerbates post exertion malaise (PEM).

In a 2012 study published in *The Open Pain Journal by J Teitelbaum,* showed the **daily consumption of D ribose, 5 grams, 3 times a day over 3 weeks, resulted in an average boost in energy in 61% of patients with CFS and fibromyalgia.** The study included 257 people with CFS and fibromyalgia. Furthermore, the study found:

- 37% increase in overall well-being
- 29.3% improvement in sleep
- 30% improvement in mental clarity
- 15.6% decrease in pain.

Side effects are minor, potentially being diarrhea, nausea and headaches. It may cause low blood sugar if combined with diabetes drugs. Avoid D ribose if you have low blood sugar issues. I took a high dose of 20 g per day for 2 weeks, then dropped it to 10 g per day, which has been life changing, but I would start with a low dose and work up, as diarrhea can be a problem! Google: "Open Pain Journal Teitelbaum" for the full report.

ACETYL-L-CARNITINE AND PROPIONYL-L-CARNITINE

L-Carnitine helps to transport long chain fatty acids from foods into the mitochondria for conversion into cellular energy. This is one of the most important supplements for CFS/ME patients, as it helps to reverse mitochondria dysfunction. Approximately 98% of your L-carnitine is stored in the muscle, with trace amounts in the liver and blood.

There are different types of L-carnitine, the most common being acetyl-L-carnitine and propionyl-L-carnitine. Acetyl-L-carnitine is a common supplement, which is purported to enhance cognitive function.

There was a study in 2004 entitled "Exploratory Open Label, Randomized Study of Acetyl and Propionyl-L-carnitine in Chronic Fatigue," by Ruud Vermeulen et al., that compared acetyl-L-carnitine and propionyl-l-carnitine (and both combined) in in three groups of 30 CFS patients. The results were measured by three different tests including multidimensional fatigue inventory, McGill Pain Questionnaire and Stroop Attention Concentration Test. Scores were assessed 8 weeks before treatment, at randomization, after 8, 16, and 24 weeks of treatment.

Clinical global impression of change after treatment showed considerable improvement in 59% of the patients in the acetyl-l-carnitine group and 63% in the propionyl-l-carnitine group, but less in the acetyl-l-carnitine plus propionyl-l-carnitine group (37%). Acetyl-L-carnitine significantly improved mental fatigue and propionyl-l-carnitine improved general fatigue. Attention concentration improved in all groups, whereas pain complaints did not decrease in any group. Two weeks after treatment, worsening of fatigue was experienced by 52%, 50%, and 37% in the acetyl-l-carnitine, propionyl-l-carnitine, and combined group, respectively. In the acetyl-l-carnitine group, but not in the other groups, the changes in plasma carnitine levels correlated with clinical improvement. (Google: "Vermeulen acetyl-l-carnitine" for further information.)

Either acetyl-l-carnitine or propionyl-l-carnitine Combined with electrolytes and D Ribose, makes for a powerful fuel boost. I use acetyl-l-carnitine and mix these ingredients into my daily water bottle. Side effects are minimal, but it can interfere with blood thinning medications, so skip it if you are taking them.

MAGNESIUM

Magnesium is the fourth most abundant mineral in the human body. Woo hoo I hear you say. Yes indeed. Your body can't produce magnesium, so we have to get it from our diet, but as we consume the good ole Western diet, we don't get anywhere near enough. According to the USDA, 68% of Americans do not consume the daily recommended intake for magnesium. So, what can magnesium do for chronic fatigue?

Well, in 1991 The Lancet reported a randomized, double-blind, placebo-controlled trial of 20 ME/CFS patients in the UK and found that the subjects with CFS had lower red blood cell magnesium than healthy controls. Patients treated with intramuscular magnesium sulphate for six weeks had higher self-reported energy levels, better emotional state and less pain than when compared with placebo.

On further investigation, I found an excellent article summing up the reasons why magnesium is so vital on www.prohealth.com.

An article by Dr. Mildred Seelig observed an overlap with ME/CFS and many of the symptoms of latent tetany syndrome, a medical condition resulting from magnesium deficiency leading to sleep abnormalities, vertigo, mitral valve prolapse, headaches, and anxiety. She proposed that ME/CFS patients would improve with the treatment used for LTS, namely magnesium. Dr. Seelig concluded: "The evidence that magnesium deficiency causes a variety of both humoral and cellular defense disturbances, among which are several that have been identified in CFS and fibromyalgia, is a reason to suspect that either magnesium deficiency or its abnormal utilization might be a pathogenic factor in CFS."

Dr. Martin Pall's work supports Dr. Seelig's conclusion. Dr. Pall speculated that, given the likelihood that people with CFS/ME are marginally deficient in magnesium before falling ill, magnesium deficiency may actually contribute to the pathogenesis of the illness. In his book, "Explaining Undiagnosed Illnesses," Dr. Martin Pall presents a compelling argument implicating oxidative stress in the etiology of CFS/ME. An important part of the cycle of oxidative stress typical of multi-system illnesses like CFS/ME, FM and Gulf War Syndrome is the chronic excitability of NMDA receptors. This over-excitability results in a hyperactive nervous system – along with cell damage, inflammation, and lowered production of ATP. Magnesium is one of the principal inhibitors of NMDA activity, which makes it a valuable treatment for any illness involving chronic oxidative stress.

In addition to its contribution to oxidative stress, Dr. Myhill believes that low magnesium levels in CFS/ME patients are a symptom of mitochondrial failure. When mitochondria fail, calcium leaks into cells and magnesium leaks out. According to Dr. Myhill, this leakage explains why it is useless to test serum levels of magnesium. As she puts it, "Serum levels are maintained at the expense of intracellular levels. If serum levels change this causes heart irregularities and so the body maintains serum levels at all cost. It will drain magnesium from inside cells and indeed from bone in order to achieve this." Dr. Myhill's explanation not only accounts for why serum levels of magnesium are inconsistent in CFS/ME, but why magnesium supplementation is so effective.

Take 400 mg of magnesium first thing in the morning. The only side effect might be diarrhea. If you get this, halve the dose immediately and build up to the full dose slowly. Magnesium supplements have helped me enormously. If you really don't want to take it in supplement form, then you will have to eat larger quantities of leafy greens, fish, nuts, seeds, and dried fruits (though dried fruits are high in sugar, so consume small amounts).

Magnesium has been used to treat such diverse conditions as diabetes, cardiac disorders, migraines, asthma, and major depression and can reduce high blood pressure to boot. More easily absorbed versions are glycinate, malate and L-threonate. Avoid versions such as oxide or citrates as they are poorly absorbed. Don't skip this one!

CoQ10

Coenzyme Q10 is a compound that is created by the body and stored in the mitochondria in the cells and help to produce energy. It also protects cells from oxidative cell damage, bacteria, and viruses. CoQ10 is present in every cell in your body.

Is it possible for ME patients to have lower CoQ10 levels than healthy people? Low levels of CoQ10 can exacerbate mitochondrial diseases and increase demands on muscle tissue. As previously discussed, ME patients cannot produce adenosine triphosphate (ATP) as fast as healthy people and CoQ10 can help generate ATP.

Oxidative cell damage can be caused by excessive amounts of free radicals, which inhibit proper cell functioning, so it is vital that your levels of CoQ10 are at or higher than regular levels.

Apart from being absolutely necessary to raise energy levels it has many other positive benefits including, prevention of heart failure, increases fertility, decreases the chance of cancers, reduce headaches, increases exercise performance, reduces blood sugar levels, increases cognitive functions, increases lung function and reduces inflammation.

Take CoQ10! But take the ubiquinol form as it is the most absorbable form. I take 500 mg daily. Later in this chapter I refer to a study recently undertaken using CoQ10 combined with NAD to treat chronic fatigue. The results were very encouraging. Please read on.

BAKING SODA

A 2018 study in the *Journal of Immunology* (Google: "Sarah C Ray et al.," www.jimmunol.org) focused on a theory that baking soda may assist in creating an anti-inflammatory environment in the body. Scientists found that regularly drinking a mixture of baking soda and water was helpful in reducing inflammation associated with conditions like rheumatoid arthritis. Specifically, the study found that after two weeks of drinking the baking soda with water, the baking soda appeared to direct immune cells (known as macrophages) to work on reducing inflammation, instead of prompting it. In other words, baking soda helped boost the body's anti-inflammatory response, putting out a calming signal instead of an emergency attack signal.

This could be a potential game-changer for people with autoimmune diseases, including ME and long COVID sufferers.

Experts suggest starting by mixing 1/8 teaspoon of baking soda with a glass of water, and drinking it a few times a week. Keep track of any improvements noticed to discuss with your doctor. Because the study only evaluated baking soda intake for two weeks, it's likely best to keep your baking soda consumption to a minimum, say no longer than a month. Needless to say, always talk to your doctor before starting a new supplement routine, or using baking soda for any type of health condition.

There are a few side effects to be aware of when consuming baking soda. Most commonly, short-term use of baking soda could lead to stomach issues, such as nausea, cramps, vomiting, or diarrhea.

To help reduce the chances of these side effects, don't drink on an empty stomach. Don't try this elixir if you have high sodium (salt) levels as baking powder is high in sodium.

OMEGA-3 FISH OIL

There has been a lot written and discussed about this very popular supplement and many studies have extolled its benefits for joint lubrication, eye health, depression and anxiety, reduce risk of heart disease, reduce ADHD in children, reduce insulin resistance, potential slowing of Alzheimer's disease and reduced fat in liver. However, important for ME sufferers, omega-3 fish oil is purported to reduce inflammation and autoimmune conditions.

Fish oils is derived form several types of fatty fish like anchovies, mackerel and salmon. There are two types of fatty acid known as eicosatetraenoic acid (EPA) and docosahexaenoic acid (DHA). Both types have shown to be beneficial to heart and brain health. The other type of fish oil is derived from krill, tiny sea creatures that are the main staple for whales, seals, penguins and some other sea birds. So, should you take fish oil or krill oil? The simple answer is krill oil. Fish oil fatty acids are digested as triglycerides, whereas krill oil acids are found in the form of phospholipids, which experts believe helps increase absorption and effectiveness over triglycerides. Perhaps more importantly krill is at the bottom of the food chain, whereas fish eat other fish, which eat other fish. This increases the likelihood of toxins being passed through the food chain to the larger fish. Krill are filter feeders that eat tiny phytoplankton. krill oil is also purported to contain more antioxidants (called astaxanthin) than fish oil and may be better for heart health. On the down side krill oil is more expensive than other forms of omega 3's, so you pay your money and take your choice.

If you don't want to consume any fish-based products, then you can get omega 3's from ground flaxseed, flaxseed oil, chia seeds, walnuts, canola oil and soy oil. You can also get omega-3 from plant-based supplements such as IWI omega-3 algae based soft gels (www.iwilife.com). The company states that their proprietary blend is clinically proven to help your body absorb 50% more omega-3's than fish or krill oil. Their product also contains chlorophyll, phytosterols, omega-7, carotenoids, and other antioxidants.

Beware that some omega-3 oils may affect blood clotting, so check with your doctor if you are taking blood thinning medications.

MULTIVITAMIN

Should you take a multi vitamin? Probably yes, as there are a multitude of ingredients that you're probably not getting from your food supply. While I could run through the list of ingredients, I suspect it would bore you into a coma and I think I've pushed the risk of that to the limit already. Suffice to say, do your own research as there are thousands of brands available. It is worth paying for a more expensive brand, as more money usually equals better quality. I take one mega multivitamin per day with a meal.

PHOSPHATIDYLSERINE

Phospha what? I hear you say. It is a fatty substance called phospholipid (same as krill oil) derived from soy (used to be derived from cows, but discontinued due to mad cow diseases aka Creutzfeldt-Jakob disease). The phospholipid surrounds braincells and helps keep memory sharp. It helps keep memory sharp. Did I just say that? I can't remember; maybe I need to take more. Animal studies suggest that phospholipid decreases with age, especially problematic for ME patients who suffer from brain fog. It is being used to help Alzheimer's disease patients along with those with multiple sclerosis. It is also used for muscle soreness in athletes that overtrain and may be useful for you if you do have the energy to work out.

This supplement is considered generally safe up to the recommended daily allowance of 600 mg but for no more than 10 days. After 10 days, drop to 300 mg or less. Side effects are minimal, with the main ones being gas, stomach upset and sleeping issues. Always take this supplement first thing in the morning. If you believe your sleep is being disturbed, then stop taking it. Like krill oil, if you are taking blood-thinning medications, talk to your doctor before taking it.

BETAINE HCL

Betaine hydrochloride is used to treat a whole smorgasbord (favorite word ever) of ailments including anemia, asthma, low potassium, atherosclerosis (hardening of arteries), yeast infections, food allergies, gallstones and thyroid disorders. It is mainly used as a stomach acidifier and digestive aid, while it does provide hydrochloric acid, there is no scientific consensus as to whether it actually increases acid in the stomach.

What we do know is that lack of stomach acid leads to bacterial overgrowth in the small intestines (that is why antacids are such a bad idea). A UCLA study of 52 ME patients found that bacterial overgrowth occurred in 90% of the patients. The regular treatment is antibiotics, but as you are probably aware, antibiotics wipe out both good and bad bacteria that inevitably leads to more problems.

A regular amount of stomach acid is required to help extract vitamins and minerals from food, and Betaine HCL is purported to help these vital nutrients to be absorbed.

The dosage is a little tricky; it depends on whether you have sufficient acid already. If you're like the 90% of ME patients who have too little acid, then taking the supplement may be a good idea. If you take too little, you might get a burning sensation of acid reflux, because there may not be enough acid to trigger the release of food into the small intestine. If you take the right dose for you, then you should not suffer acid reflux again, there will be enough acid to trigger the processing of food into the small intestine. However, if you take too much you might get diarrhea. So, it really is a case of trial and error.

TRANS RESVERATROL

Resveratrol is a polyphenol, a compound derived from plants and is found in grapes, blueberries, cranberries, mulberries, peanuts and pistachios. It is also found in red wine; however, that does not warrant drinking three bottles of it a day to derive the benefit as my wife would lead me to believe.

While there is still no scientific consensus, it is thought to prevent cancer, heart disease, neurodegeneration and, importantly for COVID and ME patients, reduce inflammation.

Ideally, we are looking for reduced inflammation in the brain, fortunately a study in mice has shown that resveratrol may reduce inflammation in the hippocampus part of the brain. It appears to interfere with protein fragments called beta-amyloids, which causes plaque buildup and may cause Alzheimer's diseases.

There are purportedly many other benefits of taking resveratrol including reducing blood pressure, increasing insulin sensitivity (thus reducing potential complications for diabetes), reduce joint pain, potentially suppress cancer cells from multiplying, may help increase the good HDL cholesterol levels.

Perhaps most intriguingly, it may extend life span. In animal models it has shown to change how genes express themselves and may activate certain genes that reduce the diseases of aging, similar in effect to calorie restriction.

NMN AND NADH SUPPLEMENTS

NMN stands for nicotinamide mono nucleotide, a basic structural unit of the nucleic acid RNA and the precursor of the essential molecule nicotinamide adenine dinucleotide (NAD), possibly a question you've never asked or wanted to know. However, you would die without NAD, so it may be worth your attention. NMN supplements have shown to improve insulin activity and insulin production, which provide metabolic benefits as well as increased glucose tolerance.

NAD is the most abundant molecule in the body besides water, it is used to repair DNA and is vital for the Krebs cycle to work. You may recall the Krebs cycle is the cycle of mitochondria burn and refuel using ATP to ADP to AMP and the slow rebuild back to ATP. Boosting NAD can help speed up the process of building back ATP and thus reducing fatigue times. NAD also play a very important role in regulating inflammation and cell survival during the immune response.

NADH (the H stands for hydrogen) can be taken intramuscular (IM) or intravenous (IV) injection for a healthcare provider or can be taken in supplement form or via a transdermal patch. As alluded to earlier in this chapter, a recent study titled, "Effect of Dietary Coenzyme Q10 Plus NADH Supplementation on Fatigue Perception and Health Related Quality of Life in Individuals With ME/CFS: A Prospective, Randomized, Double-Blind, Placebo-Controlled Trial," by Jesus Castro-Marrero et al., at Vall d'Hebron University in Barcelona, produced the following results. The study aimed to examine if CoQ10 and NADH ingested orally over 12 weeks improved fatigue and sleep in 207 patients. The study group received 200 mg of CoQ10 and 20 mg of NADH once daily. The endpoints were simultaneously evaluated and the study group showed **significant improvement** in both reduced fatigue levels and higher quality sleep over control (placebo) group. (Google: "Marrero et al. ME/CFS" for the full report.)

Should you take NMN supplements or NADH supplements? The answer is that you should take both, as combining these supplements may provide more benefits than taking either one alone. Combining the supplements is slated to create a much faster path to promoting cell metabolism. Make sure you add CoQ10.

NAD and COVID

A recent scientific article (2020) titled "Influence of NAD+ as an aging related immunomodulator on COVID 19 infection: A hypothesis" (Google: "Journal of Infection Influence of NAD" for more information) postulated that supplementing with NAD can minimize the effects of the cytokine storm that plagues COVID victims, especially the elderly. The article hypothesizes that NAD has a direct inhibitory effect on PARP-1 (enzyme involved in DNA repair) and can prevent proinflammatory cytokines from overreacting. As a side effect, NAD may stabilize telomeres (see the longevity chapter later in this book for explanation), which slows down the aging process and has a positive impact on immune cells function.

MITOPURE

Mitopure is a relatively new compound made by a company called Timeline Nutrition. It is molecularly identical to Urolithin A, which is a nutrient found in pomegranates and is very useful in optimizing mitochondria function. In some people it is metabolized in the gut microbiome (about 30%-40%) and belongs to a class of organic compounds known as benzo-coumarins. As you are aware ME/CFS patients suffer from mitochondria dysfunction, which is the leading cause of post exertion malaise. Any compound slated to optimize the functioning of mitochondria and potentially repair the Krebs cycle, demands our full attention.

The company state that each sachet of mitopure powder delivers the same amount of urolithin A as 6 glasses of pomegranate juice. I am currently taking a 2-month supply and have not experienced any side effects.

SUPER B COMPLEX

B vitamins are absolutely essential for cellular energy, blood cell formation and protein metabolism. Super B complex contains most essential B vitamins including thiamine, riboflavin, niacin/niacinamide, vitamin B_6, B_{12}, folic acid and pantothenic acid. Some may also contain vitamin C, vitamin E, biotin and zinc. B_{12} deficiency is of particular significance, especially if you are a vegetarian or just trying to eat healthier, as B_{12} is found in meat and fortified processed food, which you must avoid at all costs, so supplementation is vital.

There was study in 1999 by JC Leap et al. in the *Journal of the Royal Society of Medicine* (Google: "JC Leap JRSM" for more information), whereby CFS patients showed preliminary evidence of reduced functional vitamin B in their systems, especially pyridoxine (vitamin B_6).

Take a super B complex every day or B_6 and B_{12} (methyl cobalamin form as it is better absorbed by the body than the synthetic cyanocobalamin). Ask your functional doctor/naturopath for B_{12} shots if you think you need them.

PHARMACEUTICAL MEDICATIONS

CT38 by CORTENE INC.

An interesting drug in development is CT38 by Cortene Inc, which is a peptide agonist aimed to overstimulate a neural pathway known as

CRFR2, which they believe is the pathway that causes a wide variety of long COVID and CFS symptoms. To overstimulate the pathway appears strange, as you would think they would rather block the pathway; however, they believe that this counterintuitive approach causes the pathway to downregulate without the need for chronic treatment.

I have already discussed how the drug works in chapter 2, so please refer back for further information.

The trial infused CT38 subcutaneously for varying periods to a maximum of 10.5 hours in 14 patients. Several different dosing regimens were tried, until they found an optimal dose based on results. There was a significant reduction in mean 28-day total daily symptom score (TDSS), and follow-up data 1 to 2 years after the drug was taken suggested long-term changes in the CRFR2 pathway, leading to improvements in sleep, cognitive symptoms, appetite and fewer energy crashes. The drug is still a long way from market. A larger trial is needed to confirm the early positive results, so keep looking at their websites for updates corteneinc.com. You may even be able to get into their next trial if you so desire by contacting them directly and expressing interest.

AMPLIGEN

Ampligen (AKA Rintatolimod) is an anti-viral drug made by AIM Immunotech (formerly Hemispherx Biopharma) and has been studied for treating ME/CFS for severely debilitated patients over one year, as well as HIV, Ebola, H1N1 (swine flu) and some cancers.

In clinical trials Ampligen has been shown to help lift brain fog and increase exercise tolerance, while decreasing the viral load of HHV-6 and decreasing RNase L activity (anti-viral activity). The company states that in trials, 80% of its patients improved and 50% improved significantly. Side effects may include flushing, increased heartbeat, anxiety, sweating, nausea, diarrhea, liver enzyme level changes, itching, low blood pressure, rashes, potentially lower white blood count, dizziness, and confusion.

Unfortunately, Ampligen failed to get FDA approval, though it can be prescribed in limited numbers for special cases (check with your CFS specialist or functional doctor as to whether you might be a candidate). If you fancy a trip to Argentina, where the drug is approved and available, you can get a doctor to prescribe it for you there. However, the company are still trying to get US FDA approval and approval in Europe for other indications. Check their website, Aimimmuno.com, for updates. You may be able to get it for off label use in the future.

VALCYTE

Valcyte (AKA Valganciclovir) in another anti-viral medication used to treat cytomegalovirus in those with HIV/AIDS and organ transplant patients. This drug, made by Genentech, is FDA approved, but not for CFS; however, it has shown to be effective for treating it.

You may have heard of Jose Montoya, a former Stanford professor who was leading several studies on CFS before he was fired for misconduct issues. One of those studies was about the effect of Valcyte on CFS, "Response to Valganciclovir in Chronic Fatigue Syndrome Patients with HHV6 and EBV IgG Antibody Titers." Here is an abridged abstract from the study. *(Science bit alert).*

*Valganciclovir has been reported to improve physical and cognitive symptoms in patients with chronic fatigue syndrome (CFS) with elevated human herpesvirus 6 (HHV-6) and Epstein-Barr virus (EBV) IgG antibody titers. This study investigated whether antibody titers against HHV-6 and EBV were associated with clinical response to valganciclovir in a subset of CFS patients. An uncontrolled, unblinded retrospective chart review was performed on 61 CFS patients treated with 900 mg valganciclovir daily (55 of whom took an induction dose of 1,800 mg daily for the first 3 weeks). Patients self-rated physical and cognitive functioning as a percentage of their functioning prior to illness. Patients were categorized as responders if they experienced at least 30% improvement in physical and/or cognitive functioning. **Thirty-two patients (52%) were*** *categorized as responders. Among these, 19 patients (59%) responded physically and 26 patients (81%) responded cognitively.*

Baseline antibody titers showed no significant association with response. After treatment, the average change in physical and cognitive functioning levels for all patients was +19% and +23%, respectively (P < 0.0001). Longer treatment was associated with improved response (P = 0.0002). No significant difference was found between responders and non-responders among other variables analyzed. Valganciclovir treatment, independent of the baseline antibody titers, was associated with self-rated improvement in physical and cognitive functioning for CFS patients who had positive HHV-6 and/or EBV serologies. Longer valganciclovir treatment correlated with an improved response.

Ask your doctor if you feel Valcyte might benefit you.

LOW DOSE NALTREXONE (LDN)

LDN is an oral medication created 50 years ago to treat opioid and alcohol abuse, by blocking the opioid receptor (the euphoric effect of endorphins). The dose for this indication is 50 to 150 mg per day, but scientists have found that much lower doses of 3 to 5 mg per day works differently in the brain and provides pain relief and anti-inflammatory properties in the nervous system.

Science bit alert.

LDN targets the non-opioid antagonist pathways, including the toll-like receptor 4 (TLR 4) that are found on microglia (types of macrophages, central nervous system immune cells). Microglia causes inflammation that leads to pain sensitivity, fatigue, sleep disorders, mood disorders, cognitive disruption and general malaise. If the microglia are activated, they release cytokines and interleukins that may become neurotoxic, leading to these debilitating symptoms. LDN is believed to disrupt this process and block the TLR 4 from becoming activated and stops the microglia in its tracks.

Scientist have found a way to make LDN more potent (higher tolerated doses without affecting the opioid pathway), by changing its formulation through a stereoisomer of naltrexone called dextro-naltrexone, which has shown to have zero activity within the opioid receptors but is active in the microglia receptors.

The increased frequency of treatment response of LDN and excellent safety profile, confirms the feasibility of LDN in potentially alleviating ME/CFS symptoms. (Google: "Polo et al. LDN" for further information.)

GENTLE LDN (GENTLELDN.COM)

Discuss with your functional medicine doctor to prescribe you LDN, if you feel this will be of benefit to you. If you want to act in a faster manner, go to gentleldn.com, a site that states that you can consult with their physicians online and receive a personalized treatment plan, and LDN will be delivered to your door.

I am in the process of taking LDN….

Their protocol (they state built by Harvard and Stanford trained physicians) entails:

- Complete a survey for eligibility screening and schedule your intake visit.
- Receive a customized plan based on a 15-minute tele-health session with their clinician.
- Get LDN delivered to your home. It is delivered from a trusted compounding pharmacy.
- Follow up via surveys and tele-health sessions at regular intervals.

Side effects of LDN are minimal and it has been shown to be well tolerated; however, some side effects that may occur include: stomach pain, blurred vision, discomfort while urinating or increased frequency of urination, hallucinations, mood changes, and ringing in the ears.

COVID MEDICATIONS

The vaccinations are the most important thing you can do to protect yourself, your family and your community. However, if you already have long COVID or know somebody who suffering from acute COVID then please read the following:

REMDESIVIR (BRAND NAME VEKLURY)

Remdesivir is an anti-viral drug that has been FDA approved for COVID patients, made and distributed by Gilead Sciences. Unfortunately, recent, more robust trials have shown that the drug may not be as effective as earlier trials may have indicated coupled with the fact that it has a very short half-life and quickly degrades in the bloodstream. It can only be administered intravenously in a cycle of repeated dosing up to 10 days, requiring costly hospitalization. The World Health Organization (WHO) have issued a recommendation against the use of Remdesivir regardless of diseases severity. However, Gilead have partnered with Georgia State University to help create a modified version in oral form that may be more effective. There is no evidence that it may be effective for long COVID. Notwithstanding, there are two newer drugs that have shown greater promise.

MOLNUPIRAVIR and PAXLOVID

Molnupiravir is an oral, antiviral medication still in development by pharma giant Merck (and Ridgeback). Initial trial results are promising, with the company stating that Molnupiravir can cut down the number hospitalizations and COVID deaths by 50%. The drug is for those with mild to moderate COVID and has clearance to be used in the United States and Europe.

Paxlovid is another antiviral drug made by another pharma giant, Pfizer, who have stated that their oral drug reduces the risk of hospitalization and death by 89% (no deaths in patients who received the drug compared with 10 deaths in the placebo arm - Ouch! Karma was not on their side the day they enrolled in the trial). This was also recently approved in the United States and Europe.

Both of these drugs may save millions of lives in the future from acute COVID, and in due course, may prove to be effective in long COVID patients, assuming both companies undertake the necessary trials. It will be worth your while to Google both of these medications regularly to see if they are in trials for long COVID.

HYDROXYCHLOROQUINE AND IVERMECTIN

Hydroxychloroquine (let's call it HDQ, it takes ages to type) is an anti-malaria drug also used to treat autoimmune diseases including lupus and rheumatoid arthritis. Ivermectin, originally intended for animals to treat parasites, has been FDA approved to treat parasites in humans. Many have taken animal doses that are highly toxic and potentially fatal. A study in Egypt showed potential efficacy, but the trial was not controlled and deemed flawed. Further trials are underway as I write this, so it may still prove to be effective, just not proven right now. Check the Merck website for updates on their trials.

A lot of hot air has been spouted about HDQ and all relevant government agencies (FDA, CDC, NIH) have agreed that it is completely ineffective for COVID or long COVID patients. Based on the trial data it appears not worth taking for COVID or CFS patients.

ANAKINRA (BRAND NAME KINERET)

Anakinra is not a Russian porn star, it is a recombinant interleukin (IL)-1 receptor antagonist. I bet that sentence has never been written before. It is an immunosuppressive drug used to treat rheumatoid arthritis and neonatal-onset multi system inflammatory disease distributed by Swedish biopharma company Sobi. The drug has a history of being relatively safe, and the company are in the process of running trials. Initial results look promising, especially for those who have an extreme inflammatory response to the virus. Again, this could prove very useful to long COVID and ME/CFS patients in the long run, so keep monitoring its progress (sobi.com).

POTENTIAL LONG COVID DRUGS

LYT 100 - DEUPIRFENIDONE

A small biotech company called PureTech, has started a phase II trial of their drug LYT 100 (deupirfenidone). The trial is to test the drug for its anti-fibrotic and anti-inflammatory effects associated with Long COVID respiratory conditions.

A company spokesperson said, "We believe that the respiratory complications of Long COVID are being driven by residual inflammation and fibrosis, or scarring, in the lungs. So, we believe that the dual mechanism, anti-inflammatory and anti-fibrotic, is ideally suited to address the issues in long COVID respiratory complications," he said. "We see this as a major unmet need, and that includes the respiratory complications component of long COVID. So far, these respiratory complications are among the most common symptoms or problems that Long COVID, long-haulers are experiencing."

The initial results are slated to be ready by the end of 2021, so check their website puretechhealth.com for updates.

ZOFIN

Another biotech company called Organicell Regenerative Medicine is using the power of nanoparticles in their drug, Zofin, in phase I/II trials for Long COVID. Zofin is a biologic therapeutic derived from perinatal sources (discarded tissues at birth, such as placenta, umbilical cord, etc.).

A patient in an early trial was a healthy doctor and marathon runner who had been struck down with COVID and hospitalized for 7 weeks. He was treated with 3 doses of Zofin. A company spokesperson stated,

"Between the second and the third infusion, he already saw changes in his shortness of breath, fatigue, and muscle aches that he was experiencing, and he was ready to go back to work after 3-4 weeks. He went from totally debilitated to going back to the OR. We understand that this is a single case. We have done 4 of those single cases and have seen the same results, where patients go back to having less shortness of breath, less muscle aches, less fatigue. That is what drove us to actually file for an IND."

They don't appear to have a website, so Google "Organicell" for updates.

VIROLOGIX

Virologix (leronlimab) is a experimental drug under development by CytoDyn Inc, which is a monoclonal antibody drug for long COVID. They are further down the road than the other biotech companies cited, as they are in phase III, which they have recently completed.

Virologix is a viral entry inhibitor against the CCR5 receptor and originally intended as a HIV drug. It has fast track designation from the FDA and results should be imminent. Please check their website, cytodyn.com for updates.

CHAPTER SUMMARY

- Make sure the source of your water is clean. Buy a TDS water tester if you think your water is not pure. If it is not pure, make sure you get a filtration system, even if it's a simple Brita filter.
- D ribose is an essential component of adenosine triphosphate (ATP), the power source for all cells. A study of 257 people with CFS showed that D ribose supplements of 5g, 3 times per day over 3 weeks resulted in an average boost of energy in 61% of subjects involved.
- L-carnitine helps to convert food into cellular energy and helps to reverse mitochondria dysfunction. In a study on 90 CFS patients 59% of acetyl l carnitine group and 63% of the propionyl l carnitine group showed considerable improvements in energy.

- Add electrolytes, 5 g of D ribose and 500 mg of acetyl-L-carnitine (or propionyl-L-carnitine) to your water bottle every morning.
- Low magnesium levels indicate potential mitochondria dysfunction. Take the more easily absorbed versions including glycinate, malate, and L-theonate magnesium.
- CoQ10 is stored in the mitochondria of the cells and help produce energy. They also protect cells from oxidative stress, bacteria and viruses. Low CoQ10 levels can exacerbate mitochondria dysfunction. The ubiquinol form is the most absorbable.
- Taking baking soda in small amounts may help reduce inflammation.
- Krill oil may be the cleanest and most effective way to take omega-3 oil. Omega-3 oil reduces inflammation as well as providing a plethora of health benefits.
- Take a multivitamin every day. Make sure you do some research to find a good quality one.
- Phosphatidylserine is a supplement that is particularly useful if you suffer from brain fog. It can also reduce muscle soreness if you do have the energy to work out.
- Betain HCL supplements are primarily used as a digestive aid and are purported to assist in the absorption of vitamins and minerals in food.
- Resveratrol provides a multitude of positive health benefits, but also can reduce inflammation. Animal studies have shown that resveratrol reduces inflammation in the hippocampus part of the brain.
- NMN and NAD supplements work to help to speed up the process of building back ATP thus reducing fatigue times. combining NMN with NAD increases cell metabolism. Studies show that combining these with CoQ10 increases energy levels.
- Mitopure is a supplement made by Timeline Nutrition and provides a digestible form of urolithin A, which helps in optimizing mitochondria functioning.

- Super B vitamin complex is essential for cellular energy, blood cell formation, and protein metabolism. A past study showed ME/CFS patients are low in B vitamins.
- Pharmaceutical medications in development for chronic fatigue include CT38 by Cortene Inc, Ampligen by AIM Immunotech, Valcyte (Valganciclovir) by Genentech.
- Low dose naltrexone is available now (gentleldn.com) and can reduce inflammation in the brain.
- Acute COVID medications include remdesivir and soon to be fda cleared, molnupiravir and Paxlovid. Ivermectin is in trials for COVID, as is anakinra. These drugs may be useful for long COVID in due course.
- Long COVID drugs under development include LYT100—Deupirfenidone for reduced inflammation in the lungs. Also, Zofin by Organicell and Vyrologix by CytoDyn.

C hapter 18

EXERCISE IS POSSIBLE

"The greatest discovery of all time is that a person can change his future by merely changing his attitude."

Oprah Winfrey

Is exercise possible? If you've read about the treatment evolution of CFS you probably came across the large study in the UK undertaken by NICE (anything but) National Institution of Clinical Excellence. Known as the pace trial, a poorly designed, poorly executed study whose main recommendations were graded exercise therapy (GET) and cognitive behavior therapy (CBT). This recommendation caused misery for millions of patients worldwide, demeaning and belittling the severity of these patients' problems and making recovery very difficult. Naive doctors worldwide drank in this crap and dismissed patients with disdain and served them up antidepressants by the truckload. Shameful. A special shout out to Professor Peter White, the leader of this trial: thanks for nothing and glad you've retired now. Please spend your retirement writing apology letters to all those you have hurt.

NICE has backtracked since, stating that cognitive therapy should be used only as a supportive therapy and graded exercise therapy should not be used at all.

The fact is graded exercise therapy doesn't work; it makes fatigue so much worse. However, that didn't stop me trying to figure it out. The problem is that not exercising at all is going to shorten your life span and cause further health issues down the line. So how can we do it?

At first, walking a hundred yards might seem like a feat of endurance. If you are bed bound, then exercise is not viable until you follow most of the protocols laid out in this book. Your level of fatigue will dictate what your body is capable of. If you have changed your diet and are following some or most of the therapies and supplements laid out, then you should be in the right place to start exercising. One of the main goals of this book is to get you to a point where you can start to exercise again.

OXYGEN IS THE KEY TO EXERCISING. Generally speaking, there are two types of oxygen deficiency caused by exercise; aerobic exercise, running, swimming, tennis etc (aerobic means with oxygen) and anaerobic exercise such as heavy weight training (anaerobic means without oxygen). I could go into the differences between the two, but it would probably bore you to sleep. Ahh, maybe I should talk about that in the chapter about sleep! Anyhow, suffice it to say EXERCISE WITH OXYGEN THERAPY WILL ALLOW YOU TO START EXERCISING AGAIN.

EXERCISE WITH OXYGEN THERAPY (EWOT)

You probably scoffed when you saw the title of this chapter, exercise is possible. Trust me: exercise is possible with the aid of a pure oxygen supply while undertaking mild exercise.

There are several companies that provide the right equipment to allow you to use EWOT (discussed below). The equipment includes an oxygen generation unit, which is attached to a large bag or bladder that is hung form a large rack. The oxygen generator fills the bag which has a hose attached linking it to a face mask worn by the person exercising. You then ride a bike or walk/run on a treadmill while breathing pure oxygen through the mask which is under some mild pressure provided by the bag.

As you may recall ME patients suffer from lasting lactic acid build up, which doesn't clear as fast as in healthy people. As you're using energy through exercise, the body burns through your ATP (adenosine triphosphate) to ADP (adenosine diphosphate) to AMP (adenosine mono-phosphate). You then need to convert the molecule back to ATP from scratch, which is a very long and slow process causing exhaustion and multi day crashes. When you use EWOT, oxygen is increased to all the cells in your body increasing ATP production, which separates blood cells that stick to each other allowing more oxygen to be absorbed.

Even without suffering from ME, we slowly lose the ability to absorb oxygen into our cells over time. As we age, the pressure of oxygen absorption decreases from 100 mmHg of arterial oxygen pressure when we are in our twenties to 60 mmHg when we reach the age of seventy. EWOT raises the arterial pressure back up to higher levels we enjoyed in our youth or before we had ME. A useful analogy might be to think of an old house where all the plumbing pipes have become narrow over time and won't allow enough water to flow through. That is similar to our micro vessels that won't allow enough blood oxygen to pass through, which can cause pain and proliferate chronic conditions.

EWOT VS HYPERBARIC OXYGEN CHAMBER THERAPY (HBOT)

Hyperbaric oxygen chamber therapy is fantastic therapy if you have the financial means and the time for the treatment and the trips to and from the clinic. (Please refer back to the chapter on HBOT). Of course, you can buy a unit for the home, but will need a prescription and be able to spend a hefty amount. HBOT is a relatively slow process and you cannot exercise inside a chamber. This is a better system than EWOT if you absolutely cannot exercise at all and cannot get your heart rate up.

However, the benefits of EWOT are similar to hyperbaric chamber therapy but can be used in your own home and considerably cheaper and faster to use. Increasing your heart rate allows you to make more carbon dioxide than in HBOT which allows more oxygen reach your capillaries and micro vessels. EWOT is likely to provide much faster results in feeling good with an uptick in energy. HBOT used for a long duration is excellent for fighting neurodegenerative diseases, wounds, serious infections and increasing life span. EWOT improves circulation, restores blood flow and increases ATP production immediately. Furthermore, increasing blood oxygen levels every day is likely to reduce your risk of cancer over time (Google: "EWOT and cancer").

I am using EWOT every day for 15 minutes and it provides me with a rush of energy. It is also allowing me to use my lungs again! To use my leg muscles and start the process of getting back to some semblance of aerobic fitness. I bought my system from a company called MAXX O2 (EWOT.COM) for about $3,000. Expensive? Yes, but worth every penny to get my fitness back, which has been missing for the last 15 years.

A person suffering from Lyme for over 21 years who used their EWOT system stated this on their website:

Finding the Maxx O2 system was a true blessing for me. After one session, I received noticeable improvements in my vision, walking and thinking. I was able to start with 5 minutes of EWOT and received benefits right away. I have been doing EWOT now for 3 months, and I can take a walk on the beach with no problem. EWOT is not just for athletes, it's for anyone who wants to improve their quality of life. Once you get Maxx O2 system set up, it's very simple to use. I have recommended it to everyone I know.

I am not recommending any one system, like any consumer product, there are many on the market with a range of costs and benefits. Here are a few other websites to explore:

- LiveO2 -www.liveo2.com
- Hypermax Oxygen - www.hypermaxoxygen.com
- Sajune Ozone and EWOT package - www.promolife.com

If you are thinking of skipping this therapy because you think you simply cannot exercise, get it anyway and use it just to breathe pure oxygen. Even standing up and walking around in circles, you will get oxygen to areas of your body that you couldn't previously. Maybe after a week of standing or walking for 15 or 30 minutes, you can do just one or two squats while wearing the mask. Then maybe a week later three or four more squats. It's amazing the progress you can make while breathing in the oxygen. I've been using the therapy for several weeks now and have not suffered from sore muscles after exercise. I have even dared to let lactic acid build up in my muscles to see if I crashed the following day, but no! Nothing. I can't recommend this therapy highly enough. It might just be the key to getting your life back and extending your precious years on this planet.

ULTRA LIGHT WEIGHT TRAINING

Whether you have EWOT or not, you can try this method of anaerobic exercising to start to get back your fitness levels. The key to ultralight weight lifting is not to let your muscles build up lactic acid to the point of pain and/or muscle failure. We're not trying to challenge for the Mr. Universe title so taking it super-duper easy is the key to starting. Even if you're extremely frail and fatigued most of the time, just lifting two cans of baked beans fifty to a hundred times will help you to build muscle and strengthen bones. There have been studies that show that you can build muscle with light weights as long as the reps are high enough (Google: "Nicholas Burd, Maastricht University") for the relevant study. Again, I'm not advocating exhausting oneself with each session; that is simply not going to work. Trust me. I've tried it over and over again with the same crashing results. But using super light weights and not reaching exhaustion or letting lactic acid build up will work for you.

Aerobic exercise is trickier to monitor correctly in terms of calculating how much energy you can or should expend in one session. As you are no doubt aware going for a walk can either be easy or absolutely exhausting depending on how you feel and how far you've walked. Sometimes you can walk or run and feel just fine, then wake up the next day completely exhausted. The best advice is to undertake about half as much as you think you can, and keep doing that each time you undertake any form of aerobic exercise.

However, using EWOT with light weights or short treadmill time will make exercising far easier, more enjoyable and with a much lower risk of a major energy crash.

CHAPTER SUMMARY

- Exercise with oxygen therapy entails undertaking mild exercise while breathing pure oxygen through an oxygen generator hooked up to a large bag. When you use EWOT, oxygen is increased to all the cells in your body increasing ATP production. As we get older oxygen absorption decreases from 100 mmHg of arterial oxygen pressure when we are in our twenties to 60 mmHg when we reach the age of seventy. EWOT raises the arterial pressure back up to higher levels we enjoyed in our youth or before we were sick.
- Websites where you can explore include: ewot.com, live02.com, hypermaxoxygen.com, promoife.com.
- Ultralight weight training entails lifting very light weights with multiple reps, but without building up lactic acid. The key to ultralight weight lifting is not to let your muscles build up lactic acid to the point of pain and/or muscle failure.
- Aerobic exercise is tricky to measure, so only do about half as much as you think you can stand. This should reduce the risk of crashing the next day.

Chapter 19

EMERGENCY PLAN FOR A NO ENERGY DAY

"If you can't fly then run, if you can't run then walk, if you can't walk then crawl, but whatever you do you have to keep moving forward."

Martin Luther King Jr

We all have days like these. It's your son's or daughter's wedding day. It's your own wedding. It's a work commitment you simply can't miss. But you're in the middle of a crash. You can barely walk to the bathroom and somehow you have to be somewhere and function like a regular person. These are truly dreaded days. I've been there a few times; I know your pain. But there are short-term hacks that can help you get through a short time span with enough energy and cognizant fervor to fool most people.

This is the plan:

1. Wake up, drink a cup of coffee take one modafinil.
2. 5 minutes of slow, deep breathing.
3. Add 5 g of d-ribose powder and 500 mg of acetyl-L-carnitine powder to 40 oz of water along with a packet or sachet of electrolyte powder.
4. 10 minutes of nebulizing 2% food grade hydrogen peroxide.
5. Rinse out nebulizer and nebulize 2 ml of reduced glutathione.
6. Take a cold plunge. Either jump in a cold pool, bathtub or take a cold shower. More deep breathing.
7. Wear an ice cap for as long as you can stand.

8. Eat nothing the day before and a light no carb, no sugar meal just before your event.

This is how it all works:

ADHD (ATTENTION DEFICIT HYPERACTIVITY DISORDER) DRUGS FOR FATIGUE

I used to take Adderall for emergency use (I now take Modafinil, see below). Adderall is an amphetamine and a powerful stimulant that increases focus, clears brain fog and provides a day long burst of energy. I liken it to the fictional drug NZT-48 as taken by Bradley Cooper's character in the movie *Limitless* (highly recommended if you haven't seen it), which provides his character with superhuman cognitive powers and takes him (spoiler alert) from bum to presidential candidate. While not quite that effective, it feels magical, especially if you have severe brain fog.

Take it as early as you can in the morning, as it lasts all day and can encroach on getting to sleep at night. Side effects can include irritability, increased anxiety, headache, nausea, dry mouth, loss of appetite and diarrhea.

You're probably asking yourself can I take it all the time? I find that they provide you with false energy, your brain writes checks that your body cannot cash. If I take them for 4 days straight, I crash for 4 days after. Not much fun. Also I find they stimulate the sympathetic nervous system, which is the exact opposite of what we are seeking for a long-term solution. So best advice is to keep them for emergency use only.

A better type of stimulant worth checking out is called Modafinil (brand name Provigil). It is used to keep people awake during the day to combat narcolepsy. There are many anecdotal stories of this drug being life changing for many. Similar to Adderall in effect, it has fewer side effects and appears to be less addictive. I now use this instead of Adderall for emergency days. I have also tried it for a period of five days. It provides excellent cognitive function and, for me at least, it had fewer side effects as I felt less wired and more focused. It also doesn't appear to affect the SNS quite as much as Adderall; however, it still provides a false sense of having energy reserves you cannot truly spare. It still comes with a crash one or two days after use. Of course, everybody is different and this might work out better for you. Side effects include headaches, nausea, anxiety, dizziness and dry mouth. It must be taken as early as possible in the day to avoid the effects of encroaching on sleep. It is advisable to avoid taking this if you are taking other pharmaceuticals due to potential interactions.

Could micro-dosing modafinil be a short to medium term solution for fatigue? The FDA states that modafinil is prescribed at 200 mg per day for all its approved indications; however, it is also available at 100 mg dose. I am sure some people have used 50 mg or even as low as 25 mg per day to stave off fatigue. I cannot find any studies or anecdotal stories regarding the potential of micro-dosing, though I'm sure there are anecdotal stories out there.

NEBULIZE 2 ml OF 2% - 3% FOOD GRADE HYDROGEN PEROXIDE FOR 5 -10 MINUTES

Please go back and read the chapter on hydrogen peroxide therapy if you need reminding how important this is for recovery. Small amounts in small bursts can be hugely beneficial to kick starting your day.

DEEP BREATHING FOR FIVE MINUTES

Go to YouTube and search "Wim Hof breathing." He has an 11-minute video that has been viewed 24 million times. The guided breathing session entails breathing in quite hard and fast for about 15 breaths, then holding your breath for quite a few seconds and breathing out slowly. The deep breathing certainly is stimulating and can make you feel a little light headed. If you don't get an EWOT system, then this method of breathing can help you if you try the exercises immediately before trying any physical exercising.

ELECTROLYTE WATER DRINK WITH D RIBOSE AND ACETYL L CARNITINE.

This isn't just for emergency days, but should be consumed every day. Many people with CFS have low blood volume exacerbated by low sodium. Electrolytes contain potassium, magnesium and sodium.

COLD PLUNGE

As stated earlier, the cold plunge really does work, bringing short term relief if you do it infrequently and longer-term relief if you do it frequently. Before you balk at the idea and scream "shiver me timbers," let's take a re-run through the benefits of cold therapy. It is proven to do the following: Improve immune function, improve quality of sleep, REDUCE INFLAMMATION, increase pain tolerance, improve adrenal function, may stop food cravings, lowers blood sugar, improve sexual performance (you might want to warm up first; seriously), increase hormone levels and last but not least, helps reduce body fat.

Take a cold shower. If you really can't stand to be cold, then fill up your sink with cold water, add ice and dunk your head in it until you get brain freeze, similar to when you eat ice cream too quickly. Remember that encephalomyelitis means inflammation of the brain and spinal cord? The ice water reduces inflammation very quickly and can make you feel somewhat lightheaded. Repeat the process two or three times, dry off and take a few more deep breathes. You might be surprised as to how much better you feel. When you become reassured that this treatment is extremely beneficial and tolerant after a short time of practice, you might want to invest in a plunge tank or a chest freezer specifically used for plunging (always unplug before getting in). The bathtub with cold water and ice is a more practical alternative for most people. If you don't have a bathtub, buy a regular large garbage bin (with wheels) fill with cold water and ice. You probably won't need to add ice in the winter months.

USE AN ICE CAP OR HEAD WRAP

Buy an ice cap or head wrap, can get them on Amazon or possibly your local pharmacy chain. They are hats that have gel packs that are inserted in them that are left in the freezer until you have a headache. Well, that's what they're designed for, but ME users should use them frequently. I always use a gel cap if I have to go somewhere and I have to be compos mentis. I bought two and keep them stored in the freezer, so when one of them warms up, I have another to use.

FASTING FOR 24 HOURS THE DAY BEFORE.

Fasting for energy might seem a little counter intuitive, but it works. Fasting for a day gives your entire digestive system a break from slaving away all day like it normally does. Your digestive system draws a lot of your energy to process and digest food. This energy which is usually used up by the digestive system is conserved and your metabolic rate becomes far more efficient.

When you fast your body stops using glucose for energy, which makes your cells resort to other means to create energy. Your body will then start gluconeogenesis, which is a process of your body producing its own sugar. Instead of burning carbs for sugar, your liver helps by converting non-carbohydrate material like lactate, amino acids and fats into glucose for energy.

CHAPTER SUMMARY

We all have times when we must be somewhere and must appear cognizant and energetic. Try this protocol when you absolutely must be there!

- Don't eat anything the day before. On the day, drink a cup of coffee take one Adderall, Dexedrine, Ritalin, or modafinil. Sit up in bed and try 5 minutes of deep breathing through your nose.
- Get a water flask and add 5 g of d-ribose powder and 500 mg of acetyl-L-carnitine powder and a packet or sachet of electrolyte powder.
- 10 minutes of nebulizing 2 to 3 ml of 2% to 3% food grade hydrogen peroxide.
- Rinse out nebulizer and nebulize 2 ml of reduced glutathione.
- Take a cold plunge. Either jump in a cold pool, bathtub, or take a cold shower. More deep breathing. Wear an ice cap for as long as you can stand.

C hapter 20

HOW TO STAY MOTIVATED AND THINK POSITIVE

"I have not failed. I've just found 10,000 ways that won't work."

Thomas Edison

Perhaps the greatest challenge of dealing with both ME and long COVID is to stay motivated to beat it. It's all so easy to throw your hands up in the air and say, "to hell with it, I'm drinking an eight pack, eating a giant bowl of ice cream and not move off the sofa for three days." It's the mental struggle that is so hard to stay on top of. You may feel that you deserve alcohol, drugs or sugary treats to balance out the fatigue, malaise and depression that you may be suffering. It's only natural, and part of our human nature to gain pleasure from whatever sources we can when we're suffering. But as you are aware, these things always make you feel worse and you always regret it soon after. So how can you avoid this negative cycle?

Well, first, you can start as many as the positive protocols laid out in this book. Just making positive steps, no matter how small will set you on the right path to success and increased energy that will, slowly over time, will provide you with more positive energy to make more positive steps. It's the first step in the positive loop cycle. As defined in Chapter 4, beat depression first. Go and read this chapter again if you're feeling depressed. If you're OK but need a push in the positive direction, then try these strategies. Have a notebook by your bed and write down all the positive things that you did in the day. Small things like you cooked your own meal, had a pleasant conversation with a stranger, hugged a loved one, laughed at a TV show. Then write a list of things you are thankful or grateful for, such as the love of others, your home that is keeping you warm and dry, your pets that show you unconditional love, etc.

Showing gratitude helps to put things into sharp perspective. A day in bed may bring you down mentally, so read a positive book, even if you only have the energy to read for thirty minutes or so. Stare out of the window and appreciate the trees, flowers etc. It's an amazing planet and we're all privileged to live on it. Reflect on these things when you're otherwise incapacitated. It will get you through the darker days.

There are many great books on positive thinking such as the classics, "Success Through A Positive Mental Attitude" by Napoleon Hill, "The Power of Positive Thinking" by Norman Vincent Peale, "The Secret," by Rhonda Byrne. Also there are modern books such as "The Subtle Art of not Giving A F**k" by Mark Manson, "You Are A Badass" by Jen Sincero, "Unf**k Yourself" by Gary John Bishop. Not sure why it's a prerequisite for modern positive thinking books to use curse words, but hey I guess I shouldn't give a f***.

Having a negative day? Try listening to positive music, whatever the genre you prefer, but make sure it is upbeat and happy. If you like pop music, then here is my playlist that will make you smile and get you through the day without losing your mind:

Beautiful Day - U2

Don't Stop Me Now - Queen

Days Like This - Van Morrison

Feeling Good - Michael Bublé

You Are the Sunshine of My Life - Stevie Wonder

Three Little Birds - Bob Marley

Here Comes the Sun - The Beatles

What a Wonderful World - Louis Armstrong

Happy - Pharrell Williams

Walking On Sunshine - Katrina and the Waves

Lovely Day - Bill Withers

I Gotta Feeling - Black Eyed Peas

Groove is in the Heart - Deee-Lite

Wake Me Up Before You Go Go - Wham!

Can't Stop the Feeling - Justin Timberlake

Tubthumping - Chumbawamba

Cake By the Ocean - DNCE

Daydream Believer - The Monkees

Mr. Blue Sky - ELO

I Got You (I Feel Good) - James Brown

Don't Worry, Be Happy - Bobby McFerrin

Of course, there were some songs that almost made the cut such as "F**k You" by Lily Allen, fantastic happy melody, but thought the lyrics weren't quite positive enough. For the death metal fans out there I tried to find positive songs, but the best I could find were "Hammer Smashed Face" by Cannibal Corpse, "Every time I Die" by Children of Bodom and "Forced Gender Reassignment" by Cattle Decapitation. You don't even want to know about the negative songs.

And yes, keep laughing and stupid stuff and make other people laugh. It won't do you any harm and makes life an all-round more pleasant experience. Which leads me onto…..

THE POWER OF A SMILE

Even when you don't feel like it, smiling can help change your mood and give you a mild boost in energy. Smiling produces endorphins and reduces cortisol and adrenalin and helps calm the sympathetic nervous system. Even fake smiling can can cause these metabolic changes just by your brain reacting to the movement of face muscles, which it recognizes as a smile. So, when nobody's looking, just smile. When you wake up in the morning lying in bed, just smile. Smile when you're in the shower or driving, what harm can it do?

DEALING WITH FAILURE

Have you ever failed at anything? If no, then well done you are an alien or superhero, if yes, then you are probably a human being. Everybody fails at something, repetitively, it's how we learn and grow as an individual. It's not what you fail at, but how you respond to that failure that counts and that includes failing at recovery. I've had so many health crashes after I thought I had nailed my illness, I lost count, but I didn't give up trying. Sure, I had a couple of days feeling sorry for myself, but I got straight back on the internet searching for solutions. The Thomas Edison quote at the beginning of this chapter reflects how very important it is to bounce back from failure. It may have been many more years before the light bulb was invented if Edison gave up after his seventh or eighth-hundredth try. Use failure as motivation to do something else, to get better and remember everybody, absolutely everybody fails at something and failing at your own health is no different.

HOW TO DEAL WITH OTHERS

It's undoubtedly hard to deal with other people when you're low on energy, especially if they have little empathy for your condition. The key is to keep interacting without taking on their stress or becoming stressed yourself. There are two ways to go about this. First, try to only see the good in other people and ignore the bad stuff. This might be a little easier than you think, just write down or say three good things about the person in question and repeat them just before you meet that person. Second, make sure it is not you who is the difficult party. If you know you can be abrasive, difficult or emotional, then make an effort not to be, because your actions are usually reflected in how people deal with you. Be the good that you can see in other people and this will help reduce your stress load. If you find that some people still completely drain your energy, then kindly tell them you will be out of contact until you recover. If they like you, they will wait. If not, they probably weren't good friends in the first place. If the people you are having difficulty with are your family and you're stuck with them, then make sure you communicate how you feel regularly, making sure they understand how receptive you are.

TRY TO MEET OTHERS LIKE YOU

Camaraderie and companionship of others that share your interests is one great way to keep positive and stay motivated. There are many online support groups that you can join, just Google: "long covid support group or ME/CFS support group." Meeting others with the same issues can help you learn more about how they cope, what therapies, drugs and supplements they use. If that doesn't sound like your cup of tea, getting in touch with people regarding more fun activities can help brighten your world.

THE LAW OF ATTRACTION

First off there is no scientific evidence for the law of attraction and it is considered to be a pseudoscience. So why have I decided to even acknowledge it? Well let's define what it is supposed to mean first. It is the supposition that positive thoughts help to bring positive outcomes and negative thoughts help to bring negative outcomes. While it is nonsense to state that the universe delivers these positive or negative things (the universe is made of an infinite amount of atoms that do not care about your feelings) the essence of the statement is undeniably true. Imagine you state one of the following when you wake up, "today I'm going to have fun, have energy, enjoy my food and have a great time with my spouse" or "I hate my life, I think I'll stay in bed all day and hide." You do not have to understand metaphysics or be particularly spiritual to understand that one of these statements will lead to a better day than the other one. Every action you take is always preceded by a thought. The quality and frequency of those thoughts shape how you feel, affect your health day to day and ultimately shape how successful your life is. So, every day when you awake, say something positive that you are going to do or achieve that day. The law of attraction may not be a statutory law or a law of physics, but it does make sense if you believe that a positive thought precedes a positive action. So how can you use it everyday? Positive affirmations is the answer.

POSITIVE AFFIRMATIONS

Positive affirmations are simply positive phrases you repeat over and over in order to establish a positive mindset and lead you down the path that you want to be on. Remember thoughts always precede actions and positive thoughts create positive actions. There's some solid science to show efficacy of this psychological trick. According to a 2016 study by Cascio et al. titled "Self-affirmation activates brain systems associated with self-related processing and reward and is reinforced by future orientation" (Google: "Cascio et al. 2016" for the full report), MRI evidence showed that certain neural pathways are created during self-affirmation practice. The study states that this neural activity went on to predict changes in behavior reflecting the affirmation in response to a separate physical intervention.

Even without the science, common sense would dictate that if you say you're going to do something, you're more likely to do it than if you never had the thought in the first place. The more times you repeat a thought, especially out loud to yourself (verbalize the thought), the greater the chance of the thought becoming a reality.

On the flip side, you may now understand how negative self-talk can be so detrimental to your mental and physical health. It's pointless being your own worst enemy, so why do it?

Make up your own affirmations about getting healthy that are relevant to you and make them short and to the point. I've written some examples below. Remember, nobody needs to know you're doing these, so self-consciousness need not be an issue.

- I'm getting healthier every minute of every day.
- My energy is increasing all the time.
- I'm feeling healthy and strong today.
- I'm in total control of my health.
- I'm calm, relaxed and happy every day.

You can use a variety of different affirmations for things other than just your health, such as success in relationships, success in your choice of profession, success in achieving wealth etc. There is really no downside to using affirmations, so what have you got to lose?

MONITOR YOUR INTERNAL MONOLOGUE

One of the great challenges of beating ME and long COVID is to maintain the hard work of treating yourself with the recommended therapies, supplements and medical devices etc. The way to keep working on doing the right things is to make everything habitual, rather than doing things as random chores. In combination with positive affirmations, you can use habits to better yourself for every part of your life including relationships and finances as well as your health. **Your outcomes in life are a lagging measure of your habits.** Your weight is a lagging measure of your eating habits. Your bank balance is a lagging measure of your financial habits. Your energy levels are a lagging measure of your desire to undertake the therapies promoted in this book!

The first step is to carefully monitor your inner monologue. Saying negative based definitive statements out loud (or even in your head) can be incredibly damaging to your wellbeing. Simple statements such as, "I'm tired all the time" or "I just can't resist chocolate" or "I'm a low energy person" can slowly ruin your life through negative reinforcement. The more often you say them, the truer they become to you. Let's say you wake up tired and you say to your spouse, "Oh God, I'm tired all the time." Your brain interprets those words as *yes we should be tired today, because it's what we are.* The truth is you're not tired all the time. You have had many days in your life that you felt perfectly fine. If you feel tired today, then say to yourself, "I'm a high energy person, I have lots of energy." It may be contrary to how you feel right now, but you're unconsciously setting yourself up for success in future days. Difficult? Maybe. Impossible? Definitely not. What have you got to lose?

HOW TO CREATE A HABIT

Make your new therapy connect to an existing habit. For example, you're dedicated to taking a new range of supplements that you have learnt about in this book and that you know will provide you with more energy, but you have to remember to take them every day. Tie them to something you do in your morning routine, such as brushing your teeth. Have your supplements bottles block your toothpaste, so you have to physically move the bottle to get to your toothpaste. Make sure you have a glass of water by your sink and hey presto! You should not have to even think about taking them. Say to yourself, "I can't have my morning cup of coffee until I've had 15 minutes of red-light therapy." Use post-it notes to leave yourself reminders to do things and put them where you will definitely see them, like on your bathroom mirror or on top of your toilet.

There are three things to keep in mind when creating a new habit:

- **A TRIGGER.** A visual cue such as placing your toothpaste behind your supplements, or an alarm on your phone to go off the same time every day.
- **MOTIVATION.** Write a post-it note saying, "take your supplements to provide more energy," and stick it on your bathroom mirror.
- **REWARD.** A cup of coffee or breakfast only after you've taken your supplements.

You can use a similar routine for a whole variety of positive changes that you want to make. Think about it and get creative.

CHAPTER SUMMARY

- Write down or mentally recall all the positive things that happen to you each day, no matter how small or trivial.
- The power of a smile can change your mood, even if it's a fake smile. Keep laughing, even at the stupid stuff.
- It's OK to fail at things, it's one of the most important aspects being human. Failing at recovery by forgetting to take meds or not bothering to do therapy is OK and not worth beating yourself up over. Just be sure to get back on the horse the very next day.
- Try to stay away from people who increase your stress levels. Stay close to people who make you feel better and see the good in others and yourself. Meet other people who have similar interests to yourself.
- Positive thoughts lead to positive actions and negative thoughts leads to negative actions. The frequency of positive or negative thoughts creates the sum of the quality of your life.
- Positive affirmations can help you make positive changes and assist you in making sure you do the therapies and take the necessary supplements etc.
- Make doing your therapies a habit by creating a trigger (visual cue), motivation (write it on post-it note) and give yourself a reward (breakfast). Remember your outcomes in life are a lagging measure of your habits.

C hapter 21

LONGEVITY STRATEGIES

"If you're not comfortable with being laughed at, ridiculed and tormented, you shouldn't try to bring the world anything new or interesting."

Anon

The most disturbing conversation I had with a CFS doctor was the time he said my life will be cut short by having ME. In retrospect, I'm glad he told me this as it inspired me to seek out every possible remedy and made this book happen. It is true that life expectancy of ME suffers is less than healthy people (partly due to the high suicide rate); however, I firmly believe that taking an active approach and following the protocols laid out in this book will go a long way in extending your life span. With that said, we should explore other ways to extend life span, to give us the very best chance of living to triple digits and really annoying our kids.

First, let's quickly look at several factors (outside of ME/COVID) that will naturally shorten our lives.

1. **THE MODERN DIET** - You are no doubt aware by now that eating a Western diet high in sugars, artificial sweeteners, preservatives, antibiotics, hormones, saturated fats, and a whole host of chemicals the FDA allow food manufacturers to put into the food supply chain are killing us quickly. Heart disease is the number one killer in the west and diabetes is catching up. Not to keep ramming home this point but switch to the anti-inflammatory diet as set out earlier in this book. It will reduce you fatigue symptoms and reduce or eliminate the risk of heart

disease, diabetes and many cancers. Also try to get your body mass index (BMI) below 25, anything above that statistically shortens life span (depending on degree over that number). If you are particularly motivated to live longer, then give up animal protein. Meats are now consensually agreed upon by the scientific community to reduce life span by causing all sorts of cancers as well as increasing BMI and hugely increasing the risk of heart disease. The argument that you won't get enough protein is nonsense. How many vegetarians have been admitted to the ER for lack of protein? Absolutely none. Remember gorillas and horses have excellent muscle mass eating many pounds of leaves every day.

2. **STRESS** - Everybody has it, everybody has to deal with it. Uncontrolled stress levels will shorten your life. In a nutshell, manipulate your life to reduce stress. Cut out people that make you feel stressed, take up meditation (as discussed in this book) and if you have the energy, do yoga. Don't watch or listen to the news. Terrible things happen around the world every day, if you take on the emotional baggage of these terrible things, it will stress you out and shorten your life span. By stressing about the plight of the Afghan people, the current COVID situation or starvation in Ethiopia isn't going to help you and it isn't going to help them either. Unless your job is being a politician, envoy, or diplomat (and it does pain me to say this), then bury you head in the sand and become more insular. I understand that most people desire to be in touch with the world, to be able to debate with friends and colleagues the trials and tribulations of the human race, and I understand it's part of what makes us human. But if you have a chronic illness, the stress just isn't worth it and you have to put your health first in this case. Don't watch cable news networks. They use your own bias and fears, amplify them by 10 through use of manipulation, exaggeration and half-truths. Don't be an unwitting pawn in their game, this is a fast track to getting

needlessly stressed. Of course, you should be aware as to whom you should vote for based on your personal principles, but limit your exposure to that. If you're carrying a childhood or adult trauma with you every day, then be proactive, see a therapist and ask for EMDR therapy to rid yourself of any stressful baggage once and for all. Reread the chapter on positive thinking and take on the points raised seriously.

3. **SMOKING, DRUGS, AND ALCOHOL ABUSE.** They will shorten your life span in a heartbeat. I'm not going to get into a long diatribe on this, you know what to do.

4. **ENVIRONMENTAL TOXINS.** We are increasingly exposed to toxic substances every day, and one of your primary concerns is to reduce your and your family's exposure. Do the following: Wash your hands frequently with natural soap, eat fresh or frozen instead of canned foods, eat organic whenever possible, **always filter your tap water**, buy only natural cleaning ingredients, make sure your home is cleaned regularly, buy natural shampoo, conditioners etc free of parabens, phthalates and sulfates. Parabens are used as preservatives in cosmetics, food and drugs. Parabens can penetrate the skin, then affect the endocrine system creating havoc with hormonal production and can even mimic estrogen. This can lead to all sorts of reproductive and developmental issues and, as you are aware, hormonal imbalance may be one of the causes of chronic fatigue. Phthalates are used to make plastics more pliable and can be found in soap, shampoo, cosmetics, detergents, plastic pipes and vinyl flooring among other things. This substance can also cause problems with the endocrine system and has been banned in Europe. It is still used widely in the United States, so make sure it is not in the products you buy. Sulfates help shampoos and soap lather up and become soapy. While not as dangerous as the other two substances mentioned, it will strip the skin of natural oils leading to skin irritation and can breach the skin barrier, assisting the

absorption of other compounds. Parabens can be avoided by looking in the ingredient list for the words, methylparaben, propylparaben, isoparaben or butylparaben. Phthalates are often listed as an acronym such as DHEP or DiBP. Sulfates are usually listed as sodium laureth sulfate or ammonia laurel sulfate. Other ways to reduce exposure to toxins include: stop using plastic water bottles, use a HEPA filter on your vacuum cleaner, and take shoes off before entering the house.

5. **PHYSICAL INACTIVITY** - This is a tough one for both long COVID and ME sufferers, but inactivity is a known life-shortener and one of the main reasons why ME sufferers do not live as long as non-sufferers. We must move with enough force to supply blood, oxygen and nutrients to our body's extremities to function properly. As we get older, inactivity can lead to osteopenia (loss of bone mass), sarcopenia (muscle loss), hip fractures, depression, dementia and stroke. However, don't despair, please reread over the chapter "Exercise Is Possible." EWOT (exercise with oxygen therapy) and ultra-light weight training can you get you started on the road to recovery and moving once again. Couple this with the anti-inflammatory diet, the correct supplements, hydrogen peroxide therapy, glutathione therapy, PEMF, and red light therapy, and you should be moving around again with some vigor in the not too distant future.

FASTING

I've already discussed intermittent fasting in the anti-inflammatory diet chapter, and it will do wonders for your energy levels. But if you want to really boost longevity, then a more serious look into fasting should be on your menu. In animal models, fasting is the only proven strategy to increase life span. The following is an extract from the NIH report "Fasting increases health and life span in male mice." (Google: "NIH fasting in mice.")

Studies have suggested potential health benefits from long-term calorie restriction. In long-term calorie restriction, average daily caloric intake is kept below what is typical or habitual, but without malnutrition or deprivation of essential nutrients. Calorie restriction can be achieved through simply eating less overall, or through specific periods of fasting.

One decades-long study in rhesus monkeys found an extension of life span with calorie restriction. However, another did not. Differences between those two studies—including the type of food used—made comparisons difficult.

Researchers from NIH's National Institute on Aging (NIA), led by Dr. Rafael de Cabo, wanted to better understand if the type of food eaten, and when it is eaten, alters how calorie restriction affects the body. They divided almost 300 male mice into two diet groups. One group was given a diet low in sugar and based more on whole foods. The other group's diet was higher in sugar and more processed.

Within these two groups, the researchers divided the mice into three feeding regimens. One had access to a food dispenser at all hours of the day (ad libitum, AL). A calorie restricted (CR) group received 30% less food than the AL group, placed into their cage once a day at the same time. A meal fed, or MF, group was given the same amount of food as the AL mice on average, but were fed only once a day. The mice were monitored over the course of their natural lives. Mice that died were examined for evidence of disease, including cancer and liver damage. The results were published on September 6, 2018, in *Cell Metabolism*.

The researchers had expected that mice eating the whole foods-based diet would have a survival advantage when calorie restricted. But this is not what they observed. Diet composition did not affect health and life spans. However, the periods of fasting did.

Mice in the MF groups quickly learned that they would not have 24-hour access to food and developed the habit of eating quickly. Mice in the CR groups also finished their smaller meals rapidly. Therefore, the mice in these groups had extended periods of time without food.

Compared with mice in the AL groups, mice in the MF groups lived about 11% longer, even though their total food intake and body weights were similar. Mice in the CR group lived about 28% longer. Mice in the CR and MF groups also developed disease later than mice in the AL groups. Increasing daily fasting times, without a reduction of calories and regardless of the type of diet consumed, resulted in overall improvements in health and survival in male mice. "Perhaps this extended daily fasting period enables repair and maintenance mechanisms [in the body] that would be absent in a continuous exposure to food," Cabo says.

Studies in female mice, as well as in other animals, are needed to confirm these findings. More work will also be needed to explore how different lengths of fasting impact health. Finally, the impact of fasting on human health may differ in important ways.

The research is certainly fascinating and there are many other rat and mice studies that have confirmed that calorie restriction extends life span. There are different ways to fast, such as eat one meal per day, eat regularly but skip eating for one day per week. I have a friend that doesn't eat on Tuesdays, he said he finds it very easy to do after a few weeks and he is super healthy.

BLUE ZONES

Blue zones are particular areas around the world where the average age of death is much higher than in other places. The blue zones include Okinawa, Japan; Sardinia, Italy; Nicoya, Costa Rica; Ikaria, Greece and Loma Linda, California.

Research of blue zones allows us an insight into the lifestyles of the super elderly who not only live a long time, but in good health through their nineties.

Obviously, food is an important factor. Blue zoners (let's call them that, it sounds cool) eat mainly a plant-based diet, they stop eating at 80% full, they tend to eat their smallest meal in late afternoon or dinnertime and drink alcohol moderately.

A quick dietary run through:

- **OKINAWA, JAPAN.** They eat from the land and sea including 60% vegetables including bitter melons, garlic, shitake mushrooms, seaweed, kelp, bamboo shoots, radish, cabbage, carrots, okra, pumpkin, green papaya. Grains include millet, brown rice, wheat and noodles. Soy foods include tofu, miso, natto, and edamame. If you're wondering what natto is, then wonder no longer. Natto is a traditional Japanese food made from soybeans that have been fermented using the bacterium *Bacillus subtillis*. It has a strong smell and is slimy and sticky in texture. Natto is a superfood but can smell like aged cheese, so it may be considered an acquired taste.

- **SARDINIA, ITALY.** The Sardinian diet comprises flat bread (high protein, low gluten durum wheat, similar to the ingredients in Italian pasta). The bread is high in fiber and low in complex carbs, so it does not spike sugar levels in the blood like our Western bleached white flour-based bread does (thus reducing risk of type 2 diabetes). They also bake sourdough bread and instead of yeast to make the bread rise, they use live lactobacilli, which helps convert the sugar and gluten into lactic acid, lowering the bread's glycemic index. They also eat lots of veggies and beans including lava beans, chickpeas and tomatoes. They generally cook the tomatoes to reduce lectin load. They also consume mastic oil, which is derived from a resin (mastic gum) from a plant called pistacia lentiscus. Mastic oil may protect the lining of the stomach and may kill bad bacteria and even freshen breath. They also drink lots of goat's milk, which is high in good bacteria, which is excellent for the gut.

- **NICOYA, COSTA RICA.** Their diet consists of black beans, plantains, papaya, squash, corn tortillas, yams, and pejibaye. The latter is a savory fruit from a specific type of palm tree (the type that also produces hearts of palm) that can be eaten on its own or used as an ingredient in a number of sweet or savory dishes. This fruit is highly nutritious, packed with vitamins B_1, B_2, B_6, B_{12}, C, A and E. They eat black beans almost every day with white rice and corn tortillas. The tortillas are specially made using a process (to release the niacin) that helps to absorb vitamins and minerals from other staple foods. Yams are high in vitamin B_6 and papaya has vitamins A, B, and C and also contains an enzyme that fights inflammation. Squash has high levels of carotenoids, which are organic pigments known for decreasing the risk of certain cancers. Nothing they eat is processed or contains preservatives, and all are locally grown and freshly prepared.

- **IKARIA, GREECE.** Their diet includes lentils, chickpeas, black-eyed peas, and horta, which is a leafy green plant. They also consume goat's milk, yogurt, and cheese with whole grain bread and locally sourced honey (mixed with herbal tea). They eat little meat, usually about once per week, but do eat fish, olive oil, nuts, berries and drink red wine in moderation. They eat a range of herbs to flavor their food including mint, garlic, rosemary, artemisia, sage and dandelion. This typical Mediterranean diet includes locally produced, fresh foods devoid of any preservatives and processed food.

- **LOMA LINDA, CALIFORNIA.** The general community in Loma Linda are 7th day Adventist, a denomination of protestant Christian church known for their emphasis on diet and health, adhering to kosher food laws and strict avoidance on what they consider to be unclean foods. They believe that their bodies are holy temples and should only be fed the healthiest foods. They generally follow a vegetarian diet devoid of alcohol and caffeine. They eat beans, lentils, chickpeas, peas, leafy greens, sweet potatoes, carrots, onions, parsnips, brown rice, oatmeal, popcorn, whole wheat bread, buckwheat and millet. They also eat large amounts of raw nuts. They avoid cow's milk and other full fat dairy products.

If you would like to follow a blue zone diet, there are a few specialized diet books, including *The Blue Zones Kitchen: 100 Recipes to Live to 100* by Dan Beuttner, *The Blue Zone Cookbook* by Tyler Peter, *The Blue Zones Mediterranean Diet Cookbook for Beginners* by Lyle Christensen, and *The Ultimate Blue Zone Diet Cookbook* by Derrick Nathan.

So what is the takeaway from blue zone diets? You may have noticed that most of the diets are plant based with very little meat consumed. They consume zero processed foods and no sugar except sugar found naturally in fruits and vegetables. Most of the foods they eat are grown locally, which increases the likelihood of those foods being fresh, containing maximum vitamins and minerals. They consume very little alcohol, tobacco, dairy products or caffeine. The alcohol they do consume is generally red wine, high in polyphenols and resveratrol. All five blue zones DO eat eggs, on average 2 to 4 times per week.

So, if you want to live to 100, become a vegetarian, give up sugar, processed foods, dairy, tobacco and alcohol and stop eating when you're 80% full. Easy peasy. If you do the exact opposite, you will be lucky to reach 80 and much less if you have a chronic condition. Is an extra 20 or 30 years on planet earth worth the sacrifices? That's a tough, personal decision only you can make.

OTHER SIMILARITIES OF BLUE ZONES

They all have incredibly strong social structures. The elderly are not shipped off to the nearest retirement home, they're revered, loved and kept within the home. This keeps them engaged with their families and local communities, which provides them a reason to get out of bed in the morning. None of them have crazy work out routines, but they all move around a lot, walking around their communities, gardening and other chores. Many live in areas with steep slopes benefiting heart health and most people generally walk to work.

Not only do people in blue zones get enough sleep, they make sure they nap in the day if they need to do so. However, these naps are generally very short in nature of 30 minutes or less.

LIVE LONG ENOUGH TO LIVE LONGER

Don't underestimate the ingenuity of mankind to to seek out and develop brand new medicines, therapies and devices to help turn back the sweeping hand of time. The longer you live, the greater chance you will live to see greater and greater life extension advancements, continually compounding, increasing your chances of living even longer. The famous futurist Ray Kurzweil, has stated that we will reach a point around 2029 when new, innovative medical technologies will add one additional year to your life expectancy every year. You don't need to be a math whiz to figure out this potentially means immortality? Maybe his prediction is a tad optimistic, but living a very long time is on the cards for the human race, assuming another more virulent, deadly virus doesn't come along and wipe us all out. The trick is to remain healthy enough to live long enough to benefit from these future advancements in longevity. These advancements may include tissue rejuvenation, stem cell technology, regenerative medicine, molecular repair, nanotechnology, gene therapy and artificial organ transplants.

You should use the anticipation of these future technologies to motivate yourself to follow as many of the therapies laid out in this book as possible and make the change to a healthier diet.

If you have the time, I can recommend Ray Kurzwiel's and Terry Grossman's book *Transcend: Nine Steps to Living Well Forever*. They go into great detail as to how you can take advantage of future biotech and nanotech advances. It's a fascinating read.

TELOMERES

Telomeres are a string of proteins found at the end of linear chromosomes. The best analogy would be to imagine the plastic aglets at the end of a shoelace that hold the fabric together and stop it fraying. Telomeres are like aglets, in that the shorter they get, the less protection they provide the chromosome from cell destruction known as senescence. Human cells can't copy telomeres (lack sufficient telomerase), so every time a cell divides the telomeres become shorter. Therefore, the accumulation of senescent cells over time contributes to many age associated illnesses and diseases. By slowing down or even reversing the shortening of telomeres may provide an important aspect of life extension and lower incidences of disease progression.

Scientist from the Faculty of Medicine and Neuroscience at Tel Aviv University in Israel have recently announced that for the first time in human trials, they have reversed the shortening of telomeres by using a special protocol in hyperbaric chamber therapy. The study, part of a comprehensive research program targeting aging as a reversible disease, has been published in the peer review journal *Aging* titled "Hyperbaric Oxygen Therapy Increases Telomere length and Decreases Immunosenescence in Isolated Blood Cells: A Prospective Trial."

The trial included 35 adults over the age of 64 who received 60 HBOT sessions over 90 days. Their blood samples were collected prior to treatment at the 30th and 60th sessions and two weeks after the last session to test telomere length and senescence.

The study lead, Prof. Shai Efrati, stated, "After dedicating our HBOT research to exploring its impact on the areas of brain functionality and age-related cognitive decline, we have now uncovered for the first time in humans HBOT's biological effects at the cellular level in healthy aging adults. Since telomere shortening is considered the 'Holy Grail' of the biology of aging, many pharmacological and environmental interventions are being extensively explored in the hopes of enabling telomere elongation. The significant improvement of telomere length shown during and after these unique HBOT protocols provides the scientific community with a new foundation of understanding that aging can, indeed, be targeted and reversed at the basic cellular-biological level."

To find out more Google: "prnewswire telomeres HBOT." Before I read this report, I believed that buying a hyperbaric chamber for the home was simply too expensive; however, if allows me to live five or ten years longer, I may take the plunge.

TA-65 SUPPLEMENT

A biotech company called T.A. Sciences have invented a supplement called TA-65 that they state can lengthen telomeres. Their website states that they have completed a randomized, double-blind, placebo-controlled study with the following results:

TA-65 is a dietary supplement based on an improved formulation of a small molecule telomerase activator that was discovered in a systematic screening of natural product extracts from traditional Chinese medicines. This study summarizes the findings on telomere length (TL) changes from a randomized, double blind, placebo-controlled study of TA-65 over a 1 year period. The study was conducted on 97 relatively healthy cytomegalovirus-positive subjects aged 53 to 87 years old. Subjects taking the low dose of TA-65 (250 U) significantly increased TL over the 12 months period, as compared with the placebo group (530 ± 180 bp; p = 0.005), whereas subjects in the placebo group significantly lost TL (290 ± 100 bp; p = 0.01). The high dose of TA-65 (1000 U) showed a trend of improvements in TL compared with that of the placebo group; however, the improvements did not reach statistical significance. TL changes in the low-dose group were similar for both median and 20th percentile TLs. The findings suggest that TA-65 can lengthen telomeres in a statistically and possibly clinically significant manner.

This supplement has been around since 2007 and appears to be very well tolerated, with few to zero side effects to date. I have been taking the supplement for several months without any side effects, though it has had little positive effect on my overall health. I have had my telomere length measured a few months ago and I will get them re-tested shortly to find out for myself whether the supplement works. If it does lengthen my telomeres then we may have a game changer on our hands. The supplement is very expensive, about $600 for 90 capsules, and the recommended dose is one capsule per day, which works out at about $200 per month.

RESVERATROL

I have discussed this important supplement earlier in this book as it provides many benefits of including reducing blood pressure, increasing insulin sensitivity and potentially suppress cancer cells from multiplying. It may also help increase the good HDL cholesterol levels and increase life span.

In a study combining calorie restriction with resveratrol titled, "A Comparative Study of Anti-Aging Properties and Mechanism: Resveratrol and Caloric Restriction," by Juan Li et al., it was found that resveratrol and calorie restriction exhibited similar anti-aging properties in rats. More specifically, they combined inhibited senescence (gradual deterioration of functional characteristics in living organisms) and apoptosis (form of programmed cell death that occurs in multicellular organisms). Furthermore, this combination restored cognitive impairment, oxidative damage and could upregulate telomerase activity (reduce telomerase degradation) and increase expressions of SIRT1 (sirtuin-1 is a protein that is encoded by the SIRT1 gene).

Although this animal model study does not necessarily translate to humans, it does provide an insight as to how we may be able to slow the aging process. As you may be aware, resveratrol is found in red wine, but to get enough to be beneficial would take several bottles of wine a day. Sounds like a fun excuse, but you might die of cirrhosis of the liver before you derive the benefits of resveratrol, so probably best to stick with the supplements.

CHAPTER SUMMARY

- The modern diet, stress, smoking, drug abuse, alcohol abuse, environmental toxins, and physical inactivity are all known to shorten life span.
- Fasting is the only proven way (at least in small mammals) to extend life span. Fasting methods include taking one day off from eating per week, eating one or two meals per day, and intermittent fasting (such as 16/8, that is 16 hours of fasting and eating in an 8-hour window).
- Blue zone areas are places where the average life span is much longer than average. The blue zone diet is mainly vegetarian, low sugar, fresh, locally grown foods, small amounts of alcohol, and the blue zoners stop eating when they're 80% full. Blue zoners move around a lot, live in strong social structures, and get enough sleep.
- Live long enough to live longer by extending your telomeres through using HBOT or supplements.

Chapter 22

PUTTING IT ALL TOGETHER

"If you're reading this, congratulations, you're alive. If that's not something to smile about, then I don't know what is."

Chad Sugg

That was quite a marathon of information, so how to make sense of it all?

First of all, make sure your family and friends are aware of your condition. Make sure you communicate effectively exactly how you feel and what is going on in your life. Breakdown in communication is, generally speaking, the major reason relationships break down.

Let's briefly break down the potential causes of chronic fatigue:

- Chronic response to a prior retrovirus, enterovirus, or Lyme.
- Long COVID.
- Possible reaction to a vaccination.
- A chronic pathogen colonization in your mouth, lungs, or any area that is exposed to air.
- A mechanical problem with your spine or the base of the skull.
- A foreign body causing chronic autoimmune such as mercury fillings or silicone implants.
- Gulf War syndrome.
- Mast cell activation syndrome.
- A traumatic event that has not been resolved.
- Dysregulation of the CRFR2 neuroreceptor.
- A combination of any of the above.

Unless you've got long COVID, you may never know the real cause of your fatigue. The truth is you do not need to know the source in order to recover, save for checking whether you have a mechanical problem with your spine. Unless you have long COVID, you must have this checked out. **Remember, over 80% of patients with chronic fatigue have a spine issue whether they know it or not.**

Chronic fatigue lingers due to a variety of factors that cause chronic inflammation. Oxidative and nitrosative stress coupled with low antioxidant levels also leads to an immune-inflammatory pathology. And this is coupled with the possibility of retroviruses staying active in the gut lining, leading to further inflammation of the brain through the gut-brain connection.

Chronic inflammation coupled with mitochondria dysfunction causes post exertion malaise.

DEPRESSION

Depression makes fatigue worse and fatigue makes depression worse, a negative vicious cycle you must break before you can make full recovery feasible. Bite the bullet and get antidepressants from your doctor if you need them. If you feel you don't need them or are suffering from mild depression (just low occasionally), then try the following supplements: St. John's wort, SAM-e, 5-HTP, gamma-aminobutyric acid (GABA), magnesium, folic acid, and B_{12}.

Keep up to date on the progress of psychedelic drugs for depression. By the time you read this, there may be some exciting new drugs on the market that you or your doctor may not know about.

If your depression is mild, introduce the happy foods to replace the high sugar and carbs you may have in your diet, which include, Brazil nuts, fatty fish, eggs, pumpkin seeds, dark chocolate, turmeric, chamomile tea, quality plain yogurt, green tea, and kombucha.

Don't be a sucker and watch cable news all the time it will feed your depression. Watch comedy on TV instead of the news, news apps, social media, horror movies or anything else that might increase stress.

Be wary of negative relationships in your life. Try to make a clean break if you know a relationship cannot be mended.

So you have stabilized your mood and now have motivation to kick on and get better. Your next step is say goodbye to your primary care or general practitioner physician and say hello to a functional physician or naturopath. Google: "FUNCTIONAL DOCTOR NEAR ME." DO IT NOW!

Ask your new doctor to help you get the widest blood test possible; remember, what you don't know can kill you. The blood test will show up any deficiencies, which you may be able to bolster through supplements and/or medications, a great start on the road to recovery. Don't forget to get a poop test to cover as much of the bacteria in your microbiome as possible. Make sure your microbiome is in balance, with plenty of good bacteria to ensure your immune system stays healthy.

SLEEP

Your next step is to concentrate on getting a solid night's sleep every night. Recovery from fatigue is extremely difficult if you're only getting 2 hours of sleep at night.

Sleep strategies include:

- Consistent bed time and wake time.
- Make sure it's very dark at night so use black out blinds or curtains and make sure there are no electronics emitting light.
- Use blue light blocking glasses at night when watching TV or using a computer. Read for an hour or two before bed to tire your eyes and calm your system.
- Wear ear plugs if you are sensitive to sounds. Make sure bed is comfortable and room temperature is optimal before going to bed.

- Don't drink caffeine after midday. Don't drink a lot of fluid an hour before bedtime to save having to go to the bathroom in the night. Avoid taking naps in the daytime if at all possible.
- Check out the latest electronic devices that may help you including Cove (feel cove.com), Bedjed (bedjet.com), Dream on (dreamon.co), Restore (hatch.co).
- If you snore, try breathe right strips, mouth tape, head straps, nasal dilators, magnetic nose strips, nose vents, anti-snore electronic rings or mandibular devices.
- Listen to your partners breathing rhythm and try to match it. If that doesn't work, record yourself breathing while asleep and play it back at night to help your brain get in sync with your sleep breathing pattern.
- Try the tap-tap method. Sit up in bed, close your eyes and gently tap your hands alternately on each thigh at 1-second intervals. Slow this down over 5 to 10 minutes to about 3 seconds between taps. This form of tactile entrainment can work for many.
- Avoid anxiety keeping you awake by writing down all the issues that you think will keep you awake. This should lighten the load and help you sleep.
- Try natural herbal supplements before you try sleep aids, antidepressants and sedatives. The list of herbal supplements includes multivitamins, tryptophan, melatonin, valerian root, hops, passionflower, magnesium, chamomile and ginseng. Try different combinations that best suit you.
- If herbal supplements definitely don't work for you, then try over the counter sleep aids next, such as ZzzQuil, Bendryl, and Unisom (but get generic versions).
- Harder hitting medications include antidepressants such as tricyclic antidepressants and trazodone (nortriptyline and amitriptyline), but come with side effects.
- Sedatives include Ambien, Lunesta, Silenor, Restoril and Rozerem and also come with some side effects.

- Take the time to get a sleep study. They can find out if you have sleep apnea or narcolepsy.

FIX YOUR NERVOUS SYSTEM

Now you have a great doctor, have got depression under control and can sleep through the night, or at least get 7 hours, then you can concentrate on fixing your autonomic nervous system, reducing inflammation and reversing your mitochondria dysfunction.

The autonomic nervous system is proven to be overactive with most chronic fatigue sufferers causing a major energy drain. The best way to calm the sympathetic nervous system is to stimulate the vagus nerve known as increasing vagal tone. It is probable that the vagus nerve is being compressed by a misaligned vertebra. Fixing the upper spine is paramount. A chiropractor or orthopedic practitioner should be consulted first. Get an X-ray and eliminate this possibility as soon as you can. The use of a cervical collar or inversion table may be short-term fixes, but consult your doctor first.

Ways to stimulate the vagus nerve include:

Deep slow breathing, meditation, yoga, tai chi, humming or singing, massages, acupuncture, aromatherapy, cold therapy, more sunlight, more laughing and smiling, listening to calming music, and listening to binaural beats. Electronic devices that help stimulate the vagus nerve include Muse, Xen, Alpha Stim, and grounding mats.

HYDROGEN PEROXIDE, GLUTATHIONE AND VITAMIN D

Next is to start using the therapies I have expounded throughout this book, the three key therapies are hydrogen peroxide nebulization, glutathione nebulization, and high-dose vitamin D. The most important being hydrogen peroxide therapy. HP therapy is the most effective way to ward off all potential pathogens and will provide you with sustained energy. This is my daily routine:

- I only nebulize HP for best results. I don't drink it, even though there are many people who do. Nebulizing is both safer (much smaller quantities) and more effective.

- I only use 3% food grade HP and dilute from 3% to 2% using a saline solution. I use 2-3 ml HP in a nebulizer. Treatment takes about ten minutes for 2 ml and about 15 minutes for 3 ml.

- HP therapy could change your life, save your life, and extend your life.

Next very important therapy is to nebulize glutathione, which is an amino acid that is present in the body's cells. It is a vital antioxidant that destroys free radicals and reduces oxidative stress. Free radicals cause inflammation, especially in the brain of chronic fatigue patients.

Glutathione levels drop as we get older so it is very important to boost our levels in order to protect ourselves from the pollutants, chemicals and toxins. Long COVID and ME patients have lower amounts of glutathione in brain matter than healthy subjects of the same age. Glutathione is the key substance to abate mitochondria dysfunction and to help generate ATP. Glutathione also promotes natural killer cell function, absolutely vital for a healthy immune system.

A study in 2020 concluded that glutathione inhibits viral replication and that glutathione deficiency is associated with a more severe manifestation of COVID. Ask your functional medicine doctor to prescribe you a form of reduced glutathione that you can nebulize and use 2 ml in a nebulizer 3 to 4 times per week.

Next important therapy is oral high dose vitamin D, which is not actually a vitamin, but a hormone that is produced from direct sunlight and some foods. The body uses vitamin D as a hormone to perform endocrine and autocrine functions. Vitamin D is a known immunomodulator, which is a substance that modifies the adaptive immune response. This adaptive side has a long-term memory and prevents pathogens infecting us more than once. Vitamin D can help defend against pathogens by adjusting the immune response to respond more effectively. A recent study aimed to investigate the impact of vitamin D in reducing inflammatory markers of COVID 19 showed a significant reduction in ALL measured inflammatory markers. Vitamin D is an extremely useful tool in reducing inflammation and incredibly important for battling chronic fatigue. Those deficient in vitamin D are 3.4 times more likely to die of COVID. I took 30,000 IUs per day for the first 2 weeks of therapy, then dropped it down to 20,000 IUs per day.

If you use the three therapies above combined, you may never get a cold or flu ever again, virtually eliminate the risk of COVID and will have more energy than you thought possible.

OTHER IMPORTANT THERAPIES

There are other innovative therapies your doctor has probably never even thought about that can boost energy, if you use them often enough. I use Pulsed electrical magnetic field therapy (PEMF) mat, which I put on my desk chair and leave on all day. PEMF therapy works by emitting very low electromagnetic fields that stimulates the electrons in cells, which helps to increase ATP production and increases cellular pH to help make the cells more alkaline and improves oxygen uptake and improves circulation.

Other benefits of PEMF include: decreased pain, increased micro-circulation within minutes, enhanced uptake of nutrients, reduction of stress in the body, improved sleep patterns, faster healing of soft tissue, reduced inflammation and swelling, acceleration of nerve regeneration, faster functional recovery, enhanced capillary formation, increased cellular energy levels, improved ability to rejuvenate cells, improved immune response.

The other device which is extremely useful in the pursuit of energy production is the use of red light and near-infrared light. The red light delivers energy to cells by applying different ranges of visible and invisible wavelengths of light that penetrate the skin.

Positive effects include: anti-aging, pain relief, fat reduction, clearer thinking, wound healing, reduced anxiety and depression, increased testosterone, increased muscle mass, increased bone density and potentially reduced addiction to substances. It also reduces inflammation and increases mitochondria function. To use red light therapy effectively, don't wear clothes, makeup or sunscreen. Use it in 10–20-minute sessions at least 5 times per week. Always wear light blocking goggles.

If you have the financial means and can spare the time, the hyperbaric oxygen therapy is an excellent therapy to help beat chronic fatigue. HBOT is the medical use of oxygen in a pressured environment, which allows oxygen to dissolve and saturate blood plasma. HBOT reduces inflammation and reduces proinflammatory cytokine release. It also reduces inflammation in swollen and inflamed tissues. HBOT significantly reduces pain, reduces fatigue and increases quality of life for both ME/CFS patients according to a 2013 study and reduces fibromyalgia symptoms according to a 2019 study (see HBOT chapter for further information). Furthermore, HBOT helps to destroy the *Borrelia* bacteria that causes Lyme disease. A 1998 study showed that over 84% of Lyme patients had significantly improved symptoms.

It has been postulated that CFS/ME patients suffer from a condition called endocannabinoids deficiency, that is low production of this lipid based neurotransmitter that bind to cannabinoid receptors. This deficiency causes an overabundance of metabolic enzymes, so the endocannabidiol cannot bind to a receptor.

It is worth trying CBD oil to see what effects it will have on your fatigue and sleep pattern. Do not confuse CBD with cannabis, which may take away your motivation to beat fatigue and may make you crave junk food, which is disastrous for beating fatigue issues. CBD oil is available in most states, so Google: "CBD oil for sale." If you do take cannabis, take it immediately before bed and it will help you sleep.

OTHER INNOVATIVE THERAPIES

The lighting process is a seminar-based learning program that helps you recognize when you are suffering from fatigue and use specific tools to feel better. For some people it has proved to be a total cure for fatigue.

Ketamine therapy is a game changer for many! I urge you to learn more, be brave and give it a try. I did and I'm so happy I tried it.

Interactive apps/websites that provide cognitive support and advice may include Curable (curablehealth.com) and Mymee (mymee.com).

The distasteful but effective fecal microbiota transplant therapy (somebody else's poop inserted into your colon) may be a cure for irritable bowel syndrome in those with ME/CFS.

Ozone therapy can help to kill viruses and bacterial infections. A 2018 study showed that ozone therapy increased energy in 70% of ME/CFS patients.

Vibration therapy through use of stand on vibration machines can improve circulation reduce joint pain, increase bone mass, increase muscle mass, reduce stress, and increase metabolism. It can reduce the symptoms of fibromyalgia.

Acupuncture combined with moxibustion may be energizing to some.

Halotherapy is the act of inhaling salty air. The benefits include: reduces mucus, prevents respiratory infections, reduces inflammation, reduces effects of allergies, reduces asthmatic symptoms and reduces effects of bronchitis. The inhalation of negative ions increases serotonin, increases oxygen flow to the brain which increases mental sharpness and energy. Negative ions are generated in large quantities near moving water.

The New York Center for Innovative Medicine offers a very wide range of therapies that are worth exploring (nycim.com).

ANTI-INFLAMMATORY DIET

First step in reducing inflammation is to cut out as much sugar in your diet as you possibly can, including empty carbs, pasta, potatoes, rice and all treats and sugary drinks. I know….boo hoo. Reducing sugar should eliminate *Candida* overgrowth, a fungus that grows in the gut and thrives on sugary foods. *Candida* exacerbates fatigue issues for COVID and ME patients. Keep a food journal to track your progress as it creates awareness of how much you eat, what you eat, and how often you eat.

Eat organic foods only to help eliminate ingestion of pesticides, fungicides and insecticides on fruit and vegetables and eliminate ingestion of hormones and antibiotics in animal products. (Remember that glutathione is vital for combatting these annoying but inevitable additions to our food supply.) Organic foods have denser nutrients, antioxidants more vitamins, minerals, micronutrients and enzymes than non-organic. Try to avoid genetically modified foods, while probably safe, there is no evidence that they actually are.

The ketogenic diet is an excellent life style change, as it reduces reliance on using sugar for energy, which is not metabolized properly and converts energy production from sugar to fats.

A simpler and easier to follow diet is to eat anything that grows on a bush, tree or grows out of the ground (BTG diet). Take it easy with meat and dairy.

The Boyce superfood breakfast is very filling and very nutritious. Mix small amount oatmeal, ground flax seeds, chia seeds, shaved coconut, cacao powder, cacao nibs (if you like chocolate taste), your favorite nuts, then add your favorite berries. Top it all off with almond milk (or cashew milk or oat milk) and enjoy.

FASTING IS NOT TRENDY IT'S ENERGIZING

If you're having an energy crash, try not to eat for 24 hours and see how you feel. Fasting is a good way to reduce proinflammatory cells called monocytes.

Intermittent fasting is important for both COVID and fatigue patients. Fasting for 16 hours and eating within an 8-hour window is easy to stick to and allows your body to rest and conserve energy, while helping to regulate blood sugar and reduce insulin resistance. Intermittent fasting helps to reduce triglycerides, stabilize blood pressure, reduces inflammation, increases muscle growth and may increase life span.

Is the source of your water actually clean? You do not need to be dealing with unknown toxins. Buy a TDS water tester if you think your water is not pure. A great investment is a filtration system, even if it's a simple Brita filter.

VITAL SUPPLEMENTS AND MEDICATIONS

Add D ribose powder to your water. It is an essential component of adenosine triphosphate (ATP), the power source for all cells. A study of 257 people with CFS showed that D ribose supplements of 5 g, three times per day over 3 weeks resulted in an average boost of energy in 61% of subjects involved.

Also add L-carnitine powder to your water. It helps to convert food into cellular energy and reverse mitochondria dysfunction. In a study on 90 CFS patients 59% of acetyl l carnitine group and 63% of the propionyl l carnitine group showed considerable improvements in energy.

Also add electrolytes to your water (powder or tablet), to provide proper hydration, this in combination with 5g of D ribose and 500 mg of acetyl-L-carnitine (or propionyl-L-carnitine) will kickstart your day.

Low magnesium levels indicate potential mitochondria dysfunction. Take magnesium (400 mg) everyday but take the more easily absorbed versions including glycinate, malate, and L-theonate magnesium.

The next important supplement is CoQ10, which is stored in the mitochondria of the cells and helps to produce energy. They also protect cells from oxidative stress, bacteria and viruses. Take 400 mg each day, the ubiquinol form is the most absorbable.

Perhaps the most important of all the supplements is the combination of both NMN and NAD supplements, which work to help to speed up the process of building back ATP thus reducing fatigue times. Combining NMN with NAD increases cell metabolism. Studies show that combining these with CoQ10 increases energy levels.

Krill oil may be the cleanest and most effective way to take omega-3 oil. Take 2,000 mg of omega-3 oil soft gels to help reduce inflammation.

Take a good quality multivitamin every day. Make sure you do some research to find a good quality one.

Phosphatidylserine is a supplement that is particularly useful if you suffer from brain fog. It can also reduce muscle soreness if you do have the energy to work out.

Resveratrol provides a multitude of positive health benefits and animal studies have shown that resveratrol reduces inflammation in the hippocampus part of the brain.

Mitopure is a supplement made by Timeline Nutrition and provides a digestible form of urolithin A, which helps in optimizing mitochondria functioning.

Super B vitamin complex is essential for cellular energy, blood cell formation and protein metabolism. A past study showed ME/CFS patients are low in B vitamins.

PHARMACEUTICAL MEDICATIONS

Pharmaceutical medications in development for chronic fatigue include CT38 by Cortene Inc (corteneinc.com), Ampligen by AIM Immunotech (aimimmuno.com), Valcyte (Valganciclovir) by Genentech (gene.com). Check their respective websites for updates on developments.

Low dose naltrexone is available now (gentleldn.com) and can reduce inflammation in the brain.

Acute COVID medications include remdesivir and soon to be FDA cleared, Molnupiravir (Merck and Ridgeback) and Paxlovid (Pfizer). Ivermectin (Merck) is in trials for COVID, as is anakinra (made by Swedish Orphan Biovitrum). These drugs may be useful for long COVID in due course.

Long COVID drugs under development include LYT100 - Deupirfenidone for reduced inflammation in the lungs. Also, Zofin by Organicell (organicell.com) and Virologix by CytoDyn (cytodyn.com). Again, check their respective websites for updates.

HOW TO EXERCISE

Exercise is extremely challenging if you have chronic fatigue. But doing nothing is going to reduce your life span and increase the probabilities of further chronic illnesses. Exercise with oxygen therapy (EWOT) will allow you to get back on the road to physical recovery. The therapy entails undertaking gentle exercise while breathing pure oxygen through an oxygen generator hooked up to a large bag. You can walk, run, bike or lift light weights while breathing the oxygen.

When you use EWOT, oxygen is increased to all the cells in your body increasing ATP production. Websites where you can buy EWOT systems include: ewot.com, live02.com, hypermaxoxygen.com, promoife.com.

If you find EWOT is not for you, you can try ultralight weight training, which entails lifting very light weights with multiple reps, but without building up lactic acid. It allows you to build muscle slowly, without the risk of crashing, but patience is required.

Take it very easy with any aerobic exercise, so only do about half as much as you think you can and this should reduce the risk of crashing the next day.

EMERGENCY PLAN DAY

When you absolutely have to be somewhere, right in the middle of a major energy crash try this:

Don't eat anything the day before. On the day, drink a cup of coffee take one Adderall, Dexedrine, Ritalin or modafinil. Sit up in bed and try 5 minutes of deep breathing through your nose. Add 5 g of d-ribose powder and 500 mg of acetyl-L-carnitine powder and a packet or sachet of electrolyte powder to a flask of water. 10 minutes of nebulizing 2 to 3 ml of 2% food grade hydrogen peroxide. Rinse out nebulizer and nebulize 2 ml of reduced glutathione. Take a cold shower. More deep breathing. Wear an ice cap for as long as you can stand. Follow this protocol to the letter and you will be just fine.

MOTIVATION AND POSITIVE THINKING

If fatigue is making it hard for you to get motivated, then try the following:

Before you go to bed each night, write down all the good things that happen to you each day, forget the bad.

A smile can change your mood, even a fake smile, as your brain will make serotonin based on the movement of your face muscles. Always laugh easily, don't hold back, even at the silly things in life. If you have a rather stiff personality, let loose as much as you can. There are no downsides to this.

Forgetting to take supplements, medications or not bothering to do therapy is OK and not worth beating yourself up over. Just be sure to get back on the horse the very next day.

Make doing your therapies a habit by creating a trigger (visual cue), motivation (write it on post-it notes) and give yourself a reward (breakfast). Remember your outcomes in life are a lagging measure of your habits.

Positive affirmations can help you make positive changes and assist you in making sure you do the therapies and take the necessary supplements etc.

Positive thoughts lead to positive actions and negative thoughts leads to negative actions. The frequency of positive or negative thoughts creates the sum of the quality of your life.

(This last sentence may be the most profound thing I've ever uttered. Maybe worth writing down and putting on your fridge!)

STRATEGIES FOR A LONGER LIFE

Chronic illness is a known life shortener. You can counteract this issue by using longevity techniques to live to 90 and beyond. The Western diet, stress, smoking, drug abuse, alcohol abuse, environmental toxins, and physical inactivity are all going to shorten your life, in addition to your chronic illness, so deal with them in the best possible way you can.

Try intermittent fasting to provide energy and to extend your life. The 16/8 lifestyle change is easier to follow than you think—that is 16 hours fasting and only eating in an 8-hour window (say, 10 am to 6 pm).

If you really don't know where to start with a diet lifestyle change you can try the blue zone foods. Blue zone areas are places where the average life span is much longer than average. The blue zone diet is mainly vegetarian, fresh locally grown foods, small amount of alcohol and very little sugar. They stop eating when they're 80% full. Blue zoners move around a lot, live in strong social structures, and get enough sleep. (Google: "Blue zone diet books" for recipe ideas.)

Learn about extending the length of your telomeres. These are the caps at the end of your chromosomes that shorten as we age. We can arrest this trend and potentially reverse it through a combination of supplements and hyperbaric oxygen therapy.

THIS IS HOW I EFFECTIVE MANAGE MY CHRONIC FATIGUE AND REMAINS MY CONSISTENT ROUTINE

Daily Morning:

- 1 cup of coffee first thing.
- If I feel tired in the morning, I take one half modafinil (50 ml).

If I feel completely exhausted and I have a commitment I really must keep, I take one modafinil (100 ml).

- Take a regular warm shower, switching to cold for two minutes.
- One scoop of electrolyte powder, 5g of D ribose powder, 1g of acetyl L Carnitine powder and a sachet of Mitopure powder (mitopure.com) added to 40oz flask of water with ice.
- I take 20,000 IUs vitamin D (30,000 IUs for first two weeks of recovery), one super B complex supplement and one CoQ10 (400mg). I take both NMN and NAD supplements. Also liposomal vitamin C (1,000 mg).
- Wear cervical collar for 3 or 4 minutes, if you feel it helps you.
- 5 minutes nebulizing 2 ml of 2% to 3% food grade hydrogen peroxide.

Daily Evening:

- I nebulize 2 ml reduced glutathione.
- I take 2,000 mcg sermorelin.
- Herbal sleep concoction includes: magnesium (500 mg), valerian root, hops, sleepy sleep. If happen to wake up in the middle of the night, I have a Unisom melt tablet (diphenhydramine) on my bedside table that I stick under my tongue, as it absorbs into the system faster than swallowing.
- If any of the herbal sleep remedies just won't work for you, the next best solution are antihistamines refashioned into sleep meds such as Unisom and Zzquil.

3 x PER WEEK THERAPIES

- I lie down on top of a PEMF mat with two red light units either side for 30 minutes. I also use an Alpha Stim unit with ear clip electrodes at the same time.
- If I'm feeling up to it, I undertake a short walk on the treadmill

while wearing an oxygen mask hooked up to an EWOT oxygen bag (exercise with oxygen therapy) followed by a short ultra-light weight training session.

1 x PER WEEK THERAPIES

- Self-administered B_{12} shot (8ml). Your functional medicine doctor or naturopath will prescribe you the shots based on your blood work. Top tip - the B_{12} shot comes with a big scary needle! Mine measures one and a half inches long. You may find it psychologically difficult to inject yourself with this behemoth, so instead buy a large pack of diabetes syringes from Amazon or your local pharmacy. They usually come in superfine gauge with a capacity of 1ml. Fill four of these syringes with the B_{12} and inject into four separate areas in your gluteus maximus, you won't feel a thing.

- If you're male, your doctor may prescribe you testosterone shots if your t-levels are a little low. This comes in a high gauge needle due to the low viscosity of the serum. Again, this may be psychologically tough to self-administer, especially if you're allergic to pain. You can transfer the serum to a diabetes syringe, but you will have to use some force to get the serum into your bloodstream.

- Hyperbaric oxygen therapy (HBOT). If you are willing, able and have the time and means, then find your nearest HBOT therapy treatment clinic. Please reread the HBOT chapter to refresh your memory as to how important and therapeutic HBOT is to cure fatigue. HBOT also increases telomere length, which may add years on to your life span.

MAKE THE ROUTINE HABITUAL

In order to make something a habit, there needs to be a trigger. As stated earlier, the trigger should be tied to something you do every day, such as cleaning your teeth, making your coffee, taking a shower, or going to the toilet.

To add the various powders to your water, put your water bottle next to your coffee machine, put your powders next to your coffee (even if you keep your coffee in the fridge). When you make your coffee, you would be hard pressed to forget your electrolyte, D ribose, acetyl L carnitine mix, which will power start your day.

Put your nebulizer on top of the toilet cistern, so when you go you will know that you need to use it. The nebulizer that is, not the toilet. Remember to give yourself a reward for complying with your routine, such as eating breakfast only after using your nebulizer and taking your supplements.

I WISH YOU HEALTH AND HAPPINESS

I have thrown a lot of information at you in this book. It may seem a little overwhelming a first, but take each therapy one step at a time. Take your time to research each therapy that you believe is most pertinent to your situation, whether that is buying and reading books, watching YouTube videos or searching the infinite pages of information on the internet. Some determination and fortitude on your part is required to gain good health again. Do not fret or despair, reread this book as many times necessary to remind you of what you need to do. Remember to take charge of your health, do not leave it to others to care for you or your doctors to magically fix you, they can't. It is up to you and only you to help yourself get better. I believe in the power of the human spirit to change things for the better. I believe in you, you can do this, and remember the immortal words of Yoda, "do or do not, there is no try."

A DDENDUM

Further resources to help recovery

"When I was 5 years old, my mother always told me that happiness was the key to life. When I went to school, they asked me what I wanted to be when I grew up. I wrote down 'happy'. They told me I didn't understand the assignment, and I told them they didn't understand life."

John Lennon

Building upon your education on how to beat ME and long COVID is vital for your long-term health and wellbeing. I've categorized the books into ME/CFS/long COVID knowledge and therapeutic knowledge. I've also provided brief information of some salient websites that provide essential information to further your recovery. I have also referred to some movies that have been produced on the subject; however, I have not reviewed them a la Rotten Tomatoes style, as each film provides something different for the viewer and I don't want to impress my views. So, without further ado:

ME/CFS KNOWLEDGE

While I believe I have covered most, if not all of the potential triggers, you should make sure you have a very good grasp of all the potential causes in order to help you best find treatment. Unfortunately, most books do not focus on how to recover from ME/CFS (that is the primary motive for my research and writing this book), but they are good at explaining the potential causes and triggers. I am reticent to critically review the books, as that is not my remit here. Instead I have paraphrased the marketing blurb for each book. Here is a brief breakdown of the ones I have read and recommend:

***CFS Unraveled - Get Well by Treating the Cause Not Just the Symptoms of CFS, Fibromyalgia, POTS and Related Syndromes* by Dan Neuffer.**

You get sick and all you want is to get your health back. But so many of us that experience ME/CFS, Fibromyalgia, POTS and other variations of this syndrome can't even get their illness acknowledged as real, let alone treated effectively. With countless books having been written about treating the dysfunction and symptoms of this syndrome, you have to ask yourself: Why haven't they worked for you? Why do some approaches and treatments seem to work for some individuals and not others? Why do some people get the illness in such different ways? Why do people experience so many different symptoms? Is a full and lasting recovery even possible? CFS unraveled answers these important questions by delving deeper into the pathogenesis of the illness that connects the different symptoms and dysfunctions that you experience. This comprehensive understanding allows you to tailor a path to recovery to fix every system and symptom that you are experiencing.

***The Healer Within - My Recovery from Chronic Lyme, CFS and Autoimmune Disease* by Holly Chameli**

After nearly a decade of struggling with chronic Lyme, CFS and autoimmune disease, Holly Chameli found her way back to health using food as her medicine. In, The Healer Within, Holly shares how she healed her body when doctors could not. The mystery illness hijacked her life, rendered her bedridden for two years, and disabled for the better part of a decade. Doctors were stumped. She sought the help from all sorts of practitioners - from top medical doctors at the Cleveland Clinic to holistic and traditional Chinese medicine practitioners. Holly's symptoms ranged from chronic, bone-crushing fatigue to joint pain, insomnia and body tremors. She was eventually diagnosed with Lyme disease, but doctors offered little help aside for prescription medications that made her feel worse.

In desperation, she turned to natural remedies for relief. While bedridden and disabled, she researched alternative treatments using her body as a virtual science experiment. Recovery took time and patience, but she did it and so can you.

Diagnosis and Treatment of CFS and ME - It's Mitochondria, not Hypochondria by **Dr. Sarah Myhill**

One of the most common problems leading people to the doctor's office is fatigue. Dr. Sarah Myhill, a veteran clinical physician with over thirty years' experience treating patients, has spent years studying the relationship between chronic fatigue and mitochondria malfunction. In this book, Dr. Myhill examines the essential role our mitochondria play in the production and management of energy at the cellular level and why it is key to understanding and overcoming CFS and the inflammation that often accompanies it. She explains the importance of healthy mitochondria, how we can assess how well they are functioning, what we can do to keep them healthy and how to restore them if problems arise.

She reviews the new research and clinical findings on this debilitating disease—one that is too often dismissed by medical professionals as all in the head—and includes insights as why ME/CFS is the most poorly treated condition in Western medicine. She explains the role of the gut, the causes of inflammation including allergy, autoimmunity, Lyme disease and other chronic infections; how to reprogram the immune system. Her approach offers those suffering from ME/CFS a comprehensive and much needed roadmap to recovery.

CHRONIC - The Hidden Cause of the Autoimmune Pandemic and How to Get Healthy Again - by **Steven Philips, MD, and Dana Parish with Kristin Loberg.**

In this eye-opening book, Steven Philips, MD, and his former patient, singer songwriter Dana Parish, reveal striking evidence that a broad range of microbes, including the Lyme bacterium, cause a variety of recurrent conditions and autoimmune diseases. Chronic explores the science behind common infections that are difficult to diagnose and

316

treat, debunks widely held beliefs by doctors and patients alike, and provides solutions that empower sufferers to reclaim their lives. Dr. Phillips was already an internationally renowned physician specializing in complex chronic diseases when he became a patient himself. after nearly dying from his own mystery illness, he experienced firsthand the medical community's ignorance about the pathogens that underlie a deep spectrum of serious conditions - from fibromyalgia, lupus, multiple sclerosis, CFS, and rheumatoid arthritis to depression, anxiety and neurodegenerative disorders. Parish, too, watched her health spiral after 12 top doctors missed an underlying infection that caused heart failure and other sudden debilitating physical and psychiatric symptoms. Now, they've come together with a mission: to change the current model of simply treating symptoms - often with dangerous, lifelong drugs - and shift the focus to finding and curing root causes of chronic diseases that affect millions around the world.

LONG COVID KNOWLEDGE BOOKS

As I write this it is still relatively early days for understanding long COVID and its long-term effects. Notwithstanding, there are already a few publications that have tackled the subject, albeit short and sweet.

Long Haul COVID - A Survivors Guide - Transform Your Pain and Find Your Way Forward **by Dr. Joseph J. Trunzo and Julie Luongo**

This book is an invaluable and easily accessible guide to helping individuals cope and thrive with the challenging impact of long Haul COVID. It is also useful to any of us dealing with the impact of living through pandemic and to individuals who have other health conditions. Dr. Trunzo presents a clear description of the scientifically supported approach called Acceptance and Commitment Therapy (ACT) including instructions and exercises to help apply this approach to coping with long haul COVID. The book is easy to read and implement and can have the powerful effect of allowing readers to pursue a fulfilling life even in the face of long haul COVID. The actors deliver on their promise to transform your pain and find your way forward, so that we can make meaning and purpose amid our COVID challenges and craft a life that keeps us connected to the things that deeply matter to us.

Beating Long Haulers: World's Top Physicians Explain Brain Fog, Fatigue and Other Symptoms of PASC (Long COVID) and Why Patients Should Have Hope by Michael Bowker

The book contains numerous interviews with top physicians and clinical directors worldwide. They share their views about the huge increase in COVID long haul cases and why millions of patients should have hope. The book recounts emotional stories of patients battling long COVID and the unexpected effect it is having on children around the world.

Coping with Long COVID and Other Long-Term Health Conditions: Practical and Psychological Strategies for Self Help by Sheila Granger and Dr. Sue Peacock

This is an incredibly important and useful book for anyone struggling with long COVID symptoms. From both a patient and clinician's perspective, it offers a full range of evidence-based symptom management principles and ideas, taken from up to date research and knowledge from integrative science and clinical practice. The book is engaging and interactive from the outset, leaving you feeling what you have learned can be usefully applied in a very real and practical way.

THERAPEUTIC KNOWLEDGE BOOKS

I have thrown a lot at information regarding therapies at you in this book, including red light therapy, pulsating electromagnetic field therapy, hyperbaric chamber therapy, hydrogen peroxide therapy, exercise with oxygen therapy, and an array of other therapies aimed to get you over the finish line to enjoying great health once again. Learning more about the therapies that help you the most is vital. So here are some books that I hope you will find helpful.

Rapid Virus Recovery - No Need to Live in Fear! **by Thomas E. Levy MD, JD (hydrogen peroxide therapy via nebulization)**

It's normal and appropriate to fear an infection that can take your life, especially when you believe that you cannot avoid getting it or that you cannot cure it once you have it. The COVID pandemic now has most of the world petrified.

As it turns out, the healthy immune system can kill ANY pathogens that it encounters. The number of potential infections that get repelled on a daily basis is enormous. But sometimes even a strong immune system needs a little help to keep the body well.

It turns out that there are many remedies that directly use and stimulate the body's natural ability to kill pathogens. Particularly for COVID and other acutely contracted respiratory viruses, the treatments can be incredibly quick as well as effective. In fact, when applied properly, the infection always loses.

Furthermore, the primary treatment discussed in this book is easy to take and literally cost only pennies. There are no toxic side effects, and it is readily available to anyone. Loads of legitimate science proves that the amazing information presented herein is not too good to be true. Let's all put COVID in the rearview mirror forever.

The One Minute Cure - The Secret to Healing Virtually All Diseases **by Madison Cavanaugh (hydrogen peroxide therapy)**

As far back as 170 years ago a simple therapy has been used in the South Asian continent to successfully cure a wide variety of diseases. This 'cure all' healed everything, from minor health conditions like colds and flu, all the way to life threatening, incurable and even terminal diseases.

In 1960s, this therapy was rediscovered and turned into a one-minute cure for healing virtually all diseases, and has since been hailed by many as the world's greatest healing miracle of all time.

The book reveals the remarkable, scientifically proven therapy which creates an environment within the body where diseases cannot thrive. The book reveals how HP therapy not only kills diseased cells but also simultaneously revitalizes and rejuvenates healthy cells, thereby creating vibrant energy and wellbeing. It also reveals how this safe, inexpensive and powerful therapy has been administered by an estimated 15,000 European doctors, naturopaths and homeopaths to more than 10 million patients in the past 70 years to successfully treat over 50 different diseases. The book also shows how anyone can self-administer this little known therapy at home, easily and painlessly at a cost of less than 2 cents per day.

The Glutathione Revolution, Fight Disease, Slow Aging and Increase Energy with the Master Antioxidant by Nayan Patel, Pharm D

We have long known that glutathione (GSH) plays an integral role in detoxing, our systems and helping to prevent disease. But by we I mean the medical establishment; unfortunately, few people have ever heard of glutathione. So, I'm grateful that in this book pharmacist and researcher Nayan Patel is not only bringing glutathione to wider attention, he is also helping us understand how it works, where the GSH research has been - and where it's heading - and, most important, how we can get more of it.

The body has a remarkable ability to ward off disease and heal itself, and it does so with the help of the most important antioxidant you've never heard of: glutathione (GSH) the "master antioxidant." This indispensable molecule, which we make ourselves, holds the key to immunity, vitality and lifelong health, helping to flush out toxins, fight DNA damaging free radicals, and rebuild other essential antioxidants like vitamin C and E. It's been linked to longevity in centenarians and it protects against diseases like cancer, diabetes and Alzheimer's. It plays a role in lesser ailments too: low glutathione levels could be the culprit behind your fatigue, aches, and pains.

At the forefront of the latest GSH research, Dr. Nayan Patel shares all the information you need to boost your glutathione levels, revitalize your body and transform your life with this naturally occurring super antioxidant. In The Glutathione Revolution, he addresses the most important questions about GSH: What exactly is glutathione? What happens when your GSH levels are low? What diseases does GSH ward off? How can you naturally increase the amount of GSH your cells produce? What foods should you eat - and not eat? What are the safest and most effective GSH supplements?

With a wealth of practical information and three easy, accessible action plans that you can tailor to your own life and health concerns, you too can harness the power of glutathione.

The Optimal Dose - Restore Your Health With the Power of Vitamin D3 by Judson Somerville, MD

Are you, a loved one or a friend still suffering from a health issue after you have exhausted traditional healthcare options? Do you constantly feel fatigued or feel something is wrong, but can't figure out why? Do you wake up multiple times at night, have sleep apnea or restless leg syndrome? Are you overweight and always hungry and wonder why?

You might be surprised to learn that all these problems may be the result of a deficiency of one substance that has been misunderstood since its discovery in 1939. That substance is vitamin D3.

While it is called vitamin, D3 is really a hormone. It was first used to treat a childhood bone disease called rickets. Nearly all the research on the benefits of vitamin D3 has been done at doses that are 80 times lower than the optimal doses described in this book. This ground breaking book is your opportunity to regain your health quickly, safely and easily.

In The Optimal Dose, *Dr. Somerville reveals how vitamin D3 saved has own life when all else failed and explains how this essential vitamin is key to finding answers to your own health questions and challenges.*

The Oxygen Revolution (Third Edition), *Hyperbaric Oxygen Therapy: Breakthrough Gene Therapy for Traumatic Brain Injury and Other Disorders* **by Paul G Harch, MD, and Virginia McCullough**

Hyperbaric oxygen therapy (HBOT) is based on a simple idea - that oxygen can be used therapeutically for a wide range of conditions where tissues have been damaged by oxygen deprivation.

Inspiring and informative, The Oxygen Revolution, is the comprehensive, definitive guide to the miracle hyperbaric oxygen therapy, HBOT directly affects the body at the genetic level, affecting over 8,000 individual genes - those responsible for healing, growth and anti-inflammation.

Dr. Paul Harch's research and clinical practice has shown that this noninvasive and painless treatment can help those suffering from brain injury or such diseases as: Stroke, Alzheimer's, Parkinson's, multiple sclerosis, autism, cerebral palsy and emergency situations requiring resuscitation such as cardiac arrest, carbon monoxide poisoning or near drowning.

For those affected by these seemingly hopeless diseases, there is finally hope in a proven solution: HBOT.

PEMF - The 5th Element of Health - Learn Why Pulsed Electromagnetic Field (PEMF) Therapy Supercharges Your Health Like Nothing Else! **by Bryant A. Meyers**

You probably know that food, water, sunlight and oxygen are required for life, but there is a 5th element of health that is equally vital and often overlooked: The earth's magnetic field and its corresponding PEMFs (pulsed electromagnetic fields). The two main components of earth's PEMFs, the Schumann and Geomagnetic frequencies are so essential that NASA and the Russian space program equip their spacecraft with devices that replicate these frequencies. These frequencies are absolutely necessary for the human body's circadian rhythms, energy productions and even keeping the body free from pain. But there is a big problem on planet earth right now, rather, a twofold problem, as to why we are no longer getting these life-nurturing energies of the earth. In this book we explore the current problem and how the new science of PEMF therapy (a branch of energy medicine), based on modern quantum field theory, is the solution to this problem, with the many benefits listed below:

- *Eliminate pain and inflammation naturally*
- *Get deep, rejuvenating sleep*
- *Increase your energy and vitality*
- *Feel younger, stronger and more flexible*
- *Keep your bones strong and healthy*
- *Help your body with healing and revelation*
- *Improve circulation and heart health*
- *Plus many more benefits.*

Red Light Therapy - Miracle Medicine by Mark Sloan

If you could pack photons of red light into a pill bottle and sell it, you would have a billion-dollar blockbuster drug. Are you ready to discover the healing miracle of red-light therapy?

The 6x international #1 bestselling book Red Light Therapy: Miracle Medicine *brings you everything you've ever wanted to know about near-infra-red and red-light therapy in one concise, simple and complete guide.*

Backed by evidence from over 50,000 scientific and clinical studies, red light therapy can help you melt fat, heal acne, reduce pain, eliminate anxiety and depression, reverse hair loss, boost brain function, detoxify the body, enhance athletic performance, increase strength, muscle gains and speed healing of all injuries and diseases. Red light therapy is the safest and most effective medicine ever discovered.

Vagus Nerve and Polyvagal Theory Exposed by Sharon Copeland

Very few people are aware of the importance of the vagus nerve. Did you know it is directly responsible for not only your physical, but psychological well-being as well.

As the longest nerve in the body - beginning in the brain stem - it connects to almost all organs. From proper gut work to managing stress, the vagus nerve plays an indispensable role in human overall health.

Many studies have found that the vagus nerve works in favor of the parasympathetic nervous system. As such, it is the calming aspect of our nervous system. Just by optimizing the work of your vagus nerve, you can significantly improve your well-being. If you are willing invest in your health, you should be intrigued to know more about this nerve and how it is related to polyvagal theory. You're probably asking yourself: What is the vagus nerve? What is polyvagal theory? What makes it crucial for your health? How does it affect your mental health? How can you improve its function?

This book offers answers. Aside from explaining the scientific background of the vagus nerve, the author also makes sure to lay it all out plain and simple so everyone can grasp the idea. Moreover, you'll get introduced to the third type of nervous system, as suggested by the polyvagal theory. Even if this is the first time you're hearing about it, it has majorly affected your social engagement.

OTHER BOOKS TO CHECK OUT

Recovery from CFS – 50 Personal Stories by Alexandra Barton

Living with ME: The Chronic, Post-Viral Fatigue Syndrome by Dr. Charles Shepard

The Great Thyroid Scandal by Dr. Barry Peatfield

From Fatigued to Fantastic by Dr. Jacob Teitelbaum

The Long Awaited Cure by Dr. David Mickel

I Cured Chronic Fatigue Syndrome, You Can Too by Jeremy Carew Reid

Beat Fatigue Handbook by Erica White

Recovering from ME by Dr. William Collinge

Adrenal Fatigue: The 21ˢᵗ Century Stress Syndrome by James L Wilson

Chronic Fatigue Syndrome: The Facts by Frankie Campling and Michael Sharpe

Reverse Therapy by John Eaton

WEBSITES

MEpedia (me-pedia.com)

MEpedia is an excellent resource for searching everything you need to know about chronic fatigue, its causes, triggers, therapies and medications. MEpedia is constructed through contributions from the patient community via crowdsourcing knowledge. It has many main topics which to explore, including: what is ME?, nervous system, cardiovascular system, digestive system, energy metabolism, endocrine system, immune system, pathogens, treatments, history, and people.

SOLVE ME (SOLVECFS.ORG)

The Solve ME/CFS Initiative (Solve M.E.) is a non-profit organization that serves as a catalyst for critical research into diagnostics, treatments, and cures for ME/CFS, Long COVID and other post-infection diseases. Our work with the scientific, medical, and pharmaceutical communities, advocacy with government agencies, and alliances with patient groups around the world is laying the foundation for breakthroughs that can improve the lives of millions who suffer from various "long haul" diseases.

Founded in 1987 and incorporated in North Carolina in 1990 as The Chronic Fatigue and Immune Dysfunction Syndrome (CFIDS) Association of America, Solve M.E. relocated to Los Angeles, CA and officially changed name in 2014.

FED UP WITH FATIGUE - FEDUPWITHFATIGUE.COM

A useful and informative website referencing the latest research on drug development for chronic fatigue and fibromyalgia. The website states:

This is my attempt to weed through the thousands of medical studies and claims out there and find out what really works when it comes to reducing the symptoms of fibromyalgia and chronic Lyme. As I continue on this journey, I hope that what I learn and share here at fedupwithfatigue.com can be helpful in your healing too.

CHRONIC FATIGUE INITIATIVE - CFINITIATIVE.COM

This website is aimed at educating the medical community about chronic fatigue, by offering research grants and through collaboration. If you know anyone in the medical community who is interested in researching CFS, then please direct them to this site. They state:

Chronic Fatigue Initiative has mounted the first scientifically-rigorous and statistically-significant wide-scale research into the underlying infectious, immunological and toxicological causes of chronic fatigue syndrome ("CFS"), which had previously attracted little to no resources for basic research. As the causes of the illness are deciphered, CFI's goal is to disseminate its findings in order to equip the broader research community to work on mechanisms of the disease as well as diagnostics, treatment and prevention. CFI, which is located in New York City, was created and funded by the Hutchins Family Foundation.

By simultaneously seeking the causes and treatment of CFS and leading research to understand the breadth of the affected population, CFI aims to build awareness, reduce social stigma connected to the disease, and ultimately improve patient lives in a comprehensive way.

CFI believes that as more policy makers and industry experts grasp the full scale of CFS, they will more likely respond in kind and increase efforts to promote research surrounding the disease.

326

OTHER WEBSITES TO CHECK OUT

ME Association - meassociation.org.uk

Phoenix Research – phoenixrising.me

International Association for CFS and ME - iacfsme.org

Health Rising (Finding answers for ME/CFS and Long COVID)

www.healthrising.org

www.cfids-me.org

www.me-cfs-treatment.com

www.endfatigue.com

www.afme.co.uk

www.afme.org.uk

www.meassociation.org.uk

www.chronicfatigue-hel.com

www.drmyhill.co.uk

www.forme-cfs.co.uk

www.supportme.co.uk

www.reverse-therapy.com

www.cfs-survivors.org

FACEBOOK GROUPS

ME/CFS Positivity - https://www.facebook.com/groups/187153394962510/

#MEAction Living with ME Support Group - https://www.facebook.com/groups/211058135999671/

ME/CFS Diet - Keto/Paleo/Gut Health - https://www.facebook.com/groups/333728640426460/

The Optimum Health Clinic - ME, CFS and Fibromyalgia Recovery Group - https://www.facebook.com/groups/160418514474580/

TED TALKS

TED talks are awesome, and if you're a bit of geek like me (sorry, I meant to say cool, awesome person who is keen to learn new stuff), there is so much amazing information to soak up. There are several TED talks that cover long COVID and chronic fatigue. Just Google: "TED talk CFS" or "TED talk long COVID."

LONG COVID WEBSITES

covidlonghaulers.com
combatcovid.hhs.gov

MOVIES

UNREST (2017) - NETFLIX

If you do enough research on ME/CFS, then you will come across the story of Jennifer Brea who, like so many before her, was dismally let down by the medical community. She was brave enough not to give up and set up her own film production company to create *Unrest*, currently showing on Netflix. While her story is very familiar to CFS sufferers, it is still difficult to watch without getting both upset and angry, but her bravery and tenacity is a real motivator for those who suffer from this hellish affliction. After a long spell wasting time with many doctors and being told it was all in her head (thanks, medical community), she was finally diagnosed with cranial cervical instability and tethered core syndrome. After being treated for these ailments, she has resumed a near normal life again. Thank you, Jennifer, you are an inspiration.

FORGOTTON PLAGUE (2015) - AMAZON PRIME

This is about the health journey of a journalist called Ryan Prior who was diagnosed with ME/CFS in 2006. His life was ruined by the disease and movie reflects his travails as he sought help and remedies. He effectively makes a strong argument through interviewing many influential people identifying the reasons for the complete failure of the healthcare industry in tackling ME. These failures include severe lack of government funding for research on the disease, healthcare professionals' refusal to admit the condition even exists, and failure of the healthcare industry to try new or non-mainstream healing practices. The movie does a good job of raising awareness for those who have little knowledge about the affliction and provides knowledge of scientific data with a solid narrative story.

Other movies on the subject include:

- *What about ME?* - 2016 US
- *Funny, You Don't Look Sick* - 1995 US
- *I Remember ME* - 2000 US
- *Voices From the Shadows* - 2000 UK
- *Gulf War Syndrome: Killing Our Own* -2007 US
- *Invisible Illness - Stories of Chronic Fatigue Syndrome* - 2015 US
- *The Last Great Medical Cover Up* - 2015 UK
- *Fibro and the New Me* - 2018 US
- *This is ME* - 2019 US
- *Left Out* - 2020 Norway
- *Hope to Our Hands: The Hidden Story of ME/CFS in Japan* - 2020 Japan
- *Dialogues for a Neglected Illness: Patients' Account of Symptoms* - 2020 UK
- *Living with Chronic Fatigue Syndrome* - 2021 Germany

No doubt you will gain some interesting insights and valuable tidbits of knowledge; however, I recommend you don't watch any of these back-to-back. They're all pretty heavy to watch. At least watch a random episode of *Friends, The Simpsons,* or *Ted Lasso* in between!

About the Author

Jason Boyce, BSc (Hons) MRICS, was educated at Oxford Brookes University, Oxford, England, and worked as a commercial real estate consultant in London. Jason and his family moved to New Jersey, in 2003 to work as an equities trader. Jason now lives in Rancho Santa Fe, San Diego, California with his two children, Amelia and Arabella and his wife, Sarah.

Jason was diagnosed with myalgic encephalomyelitis (ME) in 2008 and suffered crushing fatigue and joint pain. Disillusioned by the medical community's lack of knowledge on how to fight this disease, Jason fought back by intensely learning about the disease and how to beat it by using a wide array of medications and therapies. Jason used his own body to experiment on and slowly found a winning combination of medications and therapies to help him live a normal life. Jason took early retirement to work on his health and decided to share everything he learnt in order to help as many people as possible.

His research is encapsulated in his first book, *Chronic Fatigue Gone! A Recovery Plan for COVID Long Haul, ME, Lyme and Fibromyalgia (and for anybody who wants more energy)*. The book is a comprehensive review of all the potential medications and therapies available and for the first time provides a clear pathway for beating chronic fatigue for COVID long haulers, Lyme disease, myalgic encephalomyelitis, fibromyalgia, and other long-term chronic conditions.

Index

Made in the USA
Las Vegas, NV
30 April 2022